70

# BUDGETARY CONTROL
# AND STANDARD COSTS

# BUDGETARY CONTROL
# AND STANDARD COSTS

BY

## J. A. SCOTT

PITMAN PUBLISHING

*Fifth edition* 1962
*Reprinted with minor amendments* 1963
*Reprinted* 1966
*Sixth edition* 1970

SIR ISAAC PITMAN AND SONS LTD.
Pitman House, Parker Street, Kingsway, London, WC2B 5PB
P.O. Box 6038, Portal Street, Nairobi, Kenya

SIR ISAAC PITMAN (AUST.) PTY. LTD.
Pitman House, Bouverie Street, Carlton, Victoria 3053, Australia

PITMAN PUBLISHING COMPANY S.A. LTD.
P.O. Box 9898, Johannesburg, S. Africa

PITMAN PUBLISHING CORPORATION
6 East 43rd Street, New York, N.Y. 10017, U.S.A.

SIR ISAAC PITMAN (CANADA) LTD.
Pitman House, 381–383 Church Street, Toronto, 3, Canada

THE COPP CLARK PUBLISHING COMPANY
517 Wellington Street, Toronto, 2B, Canada

ISBN: 0 273 31471 8

MADE IN GREAT BRITAIN AT THE PITMAN PRESS, BATH
G0—(B.849)

# PREFACE
## TO SIXTH EDITION

THE opportunity has been taken in this edition to re-examine some fundamental principles and there is extended reference to the use of mathematical techniques some of which, with the aid of computers, are now finding practical application in unravelling some of the more intractable complexities in certain industries.

The revised text also reflects the increasing interest in assessing the effect of potential changes in environment, for once management has established an adequate information flow covering the realities of current conditions, with this as a base, it can pay closer attention to such matters and the steps required to meet such changes.

Administrative techniques are a means to an end and not an end in themselves, and if they are to be fully effective, their purposes and concepts must be widely understood by those who are in a position to utilize them to advantage. It is hoped that this edition will continue to furnish a guide to the practical application of such principles.

J. A. S.

# PREFACE
## TO FIRST EDITION

IT is hoped that this book will bridge a gap that has too long been left unspanned between modern Cost Accounting systems and Budgetary Control methods.

Modern methods of management control rely very largely on data produced by the costing system and on the technique of budgetary control to maintain both sales and production efficiency; costing and budgetary control in any advanced business organization are now so inextricably bound together that they can hardly be logically treated separately. Supplementary to these two are reports and graphs, etc., which might be termed Business Statistics.

These three subjects form the instrument of modern management.

Indisputably, the primary function of accounting should be to assist the management in the efficient conduct of the business.

What is the efficient conduct of a business?

Perhaps under the present social system, it is to protect the investment of the shareholders and to ensure for them an adequate return on their capital risk—in other words, to make profit. But it should never be forgotten that a business thrives through rendering useful service to the community. Management also has a definite responsibility for the welfare and happiness of its employees.

The protection of shareholders' interests involves an elaborate body of Company Law and the function of professional accountants and auditors. Nevertheless, this function of guiding the management must always remain the fundamental principle of accounting, even if it serves only to show how much a man owes and how much is due to him, what he has on hand, and what profit he has made.

Unfortunately, for too many businesses the accounting system furnishes only this very meagre information, and for guidance purposes its value may be negligible.

This book deals with accounting for management purposes. It is assumed that the reader is already familiar with some of the standard textbooks on the various aspects of financial and cost accounting, and the existence of some form of monthly or four-weekly accounts is also assumed.

Two basic principles which are accepted right through the book may be stated here—

(1) The principle of exceptions is taken as a governing factor in building up the accounting system. All normal and standard results are not unduly stressed, but all abnormal and excess costs are clearly set out and brought to the notice of the management.

(2) The principle that variations in performance should be clearly stated in terms of cost and all causes for profit or loss should as far as possible be shown up in terms of £ s. d.

In detail, reference has been made to manufacturing businesses, and illustrations have been principally drawn from the engineering trade. But it is hoped that the terminology and references are sufficiently general to enable the principles set out to be easily followed and applied by anyone, no matter in what line of business.

In order to get a clear idea of the method in which the subject has been treated the reader is advised to study the list of Contents before delving into the book. To avoid interrupting the development of the principal theme, details of usual accounting mechanism and procedure have been relegated to an Appendix, which, it is hoped, will be found useful for reference.

The writer is indebted to all the authors on accountancy and management practice who have led the field and on whom he has liberally drawn.

J. A. S.

# CONTENTS

ix

x                            CONTENTS

# PART IV
## ADVANCED BUDGETING

CHAP.                                                    PAGE

XVII.   ADVANCED BUDGETING  .     .      .     . 154
XVIII.  FINDING THE BEST BUDGET    .      .     . 174

# PART V
## FINANCIAL CONTROL

XIX.  FINANCIAL CONTROL, GRAPHS, AND STATIS-
TICS .     .     .     .     .     .     . 194

# PART VI
## ACTION

XX.  ACTION      .      .     .     .     .     . 203

# PART VII
## LONG RANGE PLANNING AND DECISION PROBLEMS

XXI.  CAPITAL BUDGETING AND PROJECT
EVALUATION    .      .      .      . 223
XXII.  MATHEMATICS AND MANAGEMENT    .     . 257

# APPENDIXES

APPENDIX I—COSTING METHODS   .     . 294
APPENDIX II—MONTHLY ACCOUNTS    . 307
APPENDIX III—THE FIXING OF STANDARD
TIMES AND RATES   .     .     . 310

BIBLIOGRAPHY    .     .     .     .     . 319
INDEX .     .     .     .     .     . 321

# CHAPTER I

# INTRODUCTORY

BUDGETARY Control and Standard Costs can be said to form part of a modern management information system but their functions are rather wider since they embody forecasting, planning, initiating and control. These management functions have existed from time immemorial and their quantitative aspects are expressed in terms of numbers, weights, values, units, times and target dates appropriate to the business. Management thinking has often been farsighted, planning and operations have often been well co-ordinated but too often all have fallen short of what is potentially attainable.

Budgetary control is more than an administrative technique which aims to ensure that these functions are in fact carried out in a well organized and co-ordinated fashion. It also aims at strengthening communications and participation and can thus be said to form a manner of business administration.

Standard costs are narrower and more detailed in scope in the fact that they aim to ensure firstly that standards of performance are in fact established in some detail and secondly that machinery is established which will enable performance to be measured against standard.

Both include the particular feature that the final consolidated data is expressed in the common denominator of money terms. The final summary budget thus becomes a model, simulating how the organization is expected to function.

All human activities are basically undertaken for human welfare—even if purely personal—i.e. for the provision of food, clothing, warmth, shelter, health, entertainment,

defence, status, power, knowledge, comfort or satisfaction
—these are the basic objectives. In order to provide these
in adequate quantities, society has long been specialized,
and to obtain a share of what is being produced and
distributed by other specialists one has to be in a position
to offer other required specialized services in exchange. In
this process, society has accumulated many durable assets
which one generation passes on for the benefit of the next.

In a society believing in the value of retaining a
reasonable measure of freedom of choice in life's neces-
sities, luxuries and activities, and recognizing competitive
effort as a way of effectively meeting these needs,
industrial profit becomes one of several means for
achieving several ends, and plays a vital role in ensuring
that accumulations of productive resources are built up
and maintained in those sectors where they are most
wanted to meet these requirements. Its existence makes
retention of funds feasible for this purpose and enables
new funds for development to be attracted from many
sources. Seen in a customer, it gives suppliers confidence
in continued off-take and assurance when granting trade
credit. Seen in a supplier, it gives confidence that supplies
will not dry up at source. Seen in an employer, it gives
faith in continuity of work and the possibility of better
conditions.

In pursuit of its objectives, all businesses operate within
a system of *constraints*, moral, social, political and
economic, some self-imposed and some stemming from
environmental pressures. It has some choice as to the
*parameters* within which it will choose to operate—
e.g. metal working and not leather working, manufacture
but not retail distribution, etc.

Squeezed through between strong forces and normally
only attainable when consumer's requirements are being
effectively met, the existence of profit constitutes evidence

that the organization is effectively geared to meet society's wants but its attainment demands foresight and the planned utilization of resources and information to assist in making the appropriate management decisions at the appropriate time.

Profit can thus rightly be regarded as an end in itself even if against a wider background it may be considered as a means to an end and Budgetary Control and Standard Costs are an aid towards achieving this end.

Non-profit-making organizations to which finance is directed from the public purse however require an almost identical system if they are to operate efficiently and ensure that their input factors are compatible with their output benefits.

Whilst reference may be made to the system, this must not be interpreted in a narrow routine sense. A good system must include something in the nature of a radar scanner which will pause at some point, and undertake a fresh study in depth of a particular sector.

The term Control appears in the title. In modern large-scale industry control is a team job, similarly responsibility tends to be shared, and while different persons may have primary responsibility for certain sectors of a business, this must often be read to mean that although they are in the best position to influence many of the activities in these sectors, they will rarely be entirely free from influences arising from decisions in other sectors. Budgeting tries to ensure that the activities of one sector will enhance and support those of others. It deals with the micro-economics of the firm. Adaptability is a major ingredient of efficiency, for sooner or later most products meet long-term changes and come up against the inexorable effects of the law of supply and demand.

Budgets or Standards of the type described in some detail in this book should ideally take their place and serve their purpose within a long range view of the objectives of the business, its line of product development and market strategy, and the line of development of its organization structure and the timing of such developments within some long range plan, whether or not placed on paper in outline or detail.

The advent of computers and the work of systems analysts may open up vistas as yet faintly seen, and a rather different form of budgeting in the form of business-game-like studies modelled on the firm in relationship to its environment of customers and competitors, may come to form a preface to the budgeting of the future.

This book concentrates on basic principles, in the belief that armed with these, the working details can be modified, adapted or elaborated to suit the requirements of individual organizations. Whilst it is believed that most of the text may be useful to managers who do not possess knowledge of accountancy, it is assumed that most readers are already acquainted with some standard text book, covering the basic aspects of financial and cost accounting, though some outline details of the latter are given in an Appendix. The existence of some form of monthly or periodic interim accounts is also assumed.

The object of Budgetary Control and Standard Costing is to enable management to conduct business in the most efficient manner. In order to do this it must show where and to what extent profits or losses are being made. It should also show what potential profits might be made, and why they are not being realized. The system should supply the answer to the "Whys" and "Hows" of management.

Let us, then, first set out "what management wants to know." (Managers sometimes have to be educated before "what management should know" and "what management wants to know" coincide.)

Persons requiring information may be classified broadly as—

(*a*) Those who want to know in order to guide the broad policy of the business.

(*b*) Those who control sections of the business.

(*c*) Those who carry out the day-to-day details of the business.

Information provided will be suitably analysed or summarized according to the use to which it is to be put. Details of information required will vary from one type and size of organization to another, but the following comprehensive list will help to indicate the type of data which it is sought to provide by the methods indicated in this book.

All information supplied should show "what is" as compared with "what should be," or, in other words, "actual" as compared with "budget" or "standard." This is undoubtedly the most useful form in which information can be given to the management.

### (*a*) Persons who want to know in order to guide the broad policy of the business.

DIRECTORS

Orders received and trend thereof
Output and trend
Net profits and trend
Details of capital expenditure and commitments
Liquid capital position
Total financial position.

### (*b*) Persons who control sections of the business.

SALES MANAGER

Sales analysed by product
Sales analysed by area

Sales analysed by agent or traveller
Sales analysed by consumer class
Profit on sales by product and other analysis
Orders on hand suitably analysed
Work in progress suitably analysed
Cost of Sales Departments
Cost of agents or travellers
Cost of publicity and advertising.

## WORKS MANAGER

Trend of orders received suitably analysed
Orders on hand suitably analysed
Output analysed by product
Output analysed by department
Work in progress suitably analysed
Stocks and trend analysed by classes
Manufacturing profit analysed by product and for departments

Comparative costs of products $\begin{cases} \text{labour} \\ \text{material} \\ \text{overheads} \end{cases}$

Comparative costs of departments $\begin{cases} \text{labour} \\ \text{material} \\ \text{overheads} \end{cases}$

Idle facilities and cost thereof
Scrap and other excess and abnormal costs
Under-recovered and over-recovered (or absorbed) costs
Departmental efficiency
Service costs
Shortages.

## DEPARTMENT MANAGERS

Similar details as for the Works Manager, but relating to their own departments only.

More detailed figures will be given as to details of expenses.

Scrap and other excess costs
Idle facilities
Machine loading
Details of job costs
Comparisons of estimates and job costs
Efficiency of individual workmen.

### Chief Accountant

The Chief Accountant will probably want to see summaries, at least, of all the figures supplied. In addition he will require details of—

Debtors and time outstanding
Creditors
Cash in bank and on hand
All receipts and payments
Liquid capital position
Total financial position.

### (c) Persons who carry out the day-to-day details of the business.

### Foremen

Output of department
Details of expenses incurred
Efficiency of workmen
Scrap and excess costs
Idle time.

### Work Study Officers

Time variations.

### Planners

Orders on hand
Work in progress

Scrap
Department and machine loading.

## ESTIMATORS

Comparison of job costs with estimates
Orders on hand
Price trends.

## BUYERS AND STOREKEEPERS

Stocks on hand suitably analysed
Work in progress suitably analysed
Orders on hand suitably analysed
Materials costs suitably analysed
Purchases analysed by class
Price trends
Profit or loss on stocks
Effects of buying policy.

## WORKMEN

Bonus earnings
Individual scrap
Output of group.

Such are the types of factual information. Another type of information will be in the form of estimates (based on factual information) of the effects of alternative decisions. This is dealt with in the chapters dealing with Advanced Budgeting.

Information is not obtained because it is "interesting," but because it is useful. If on reading through this list you see "figures which would never be used" in your business—eliminate them. An active business should have no time to collect figures which merely "might be interesting." The only information to be collected should be information which will be used to contribute to the more efficient conduct of the business.

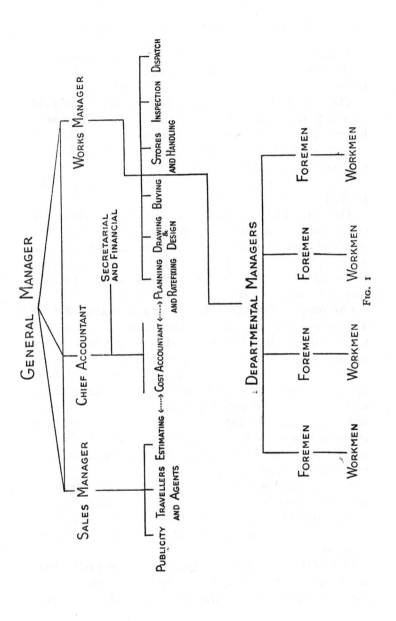

FIG. I

Primary accounting may outline the "front elevation" of the business structure but even to reveal its shape one needs to have side and back elevations and plan.

The value to be obtained from such information should be carefully considered against the cost of obtaining it before figures are abstracted. It should be seen that the issuing of figures which are only temporarily useful does not become part of the regular routine.

Persons may, of course, have to be taught how to make profitable use of certain figures.

The principal advantage of standard costing as compared with the older costing methods is that with a standard costing system management can see at once what a process or product is costing compared with what it should be costing, with emphasis placed on all causes why the standard cost has not been attained.

Ordinary costing methods usually give details of what a product has cost after it has been produced, but information as to what it should cost, and why it has cost more than it ought, is often very deficient.

Before standard costs are set up it is necessary to draw up plans and budgets of what costs of performance should be. This in turn brings us to budgetary control technique whereby these plans are co-ordinated, the responsibility for their being carried out is clearly defined, and routine is devised whereby the measure of achievement can be clearly shown.

Management operates through persons and personalities, not through mere figures, and budgetary control systems should be devised to ensure that the facts shown by the figures are interpreted into action by the persons responsible.

One of the advantages of installing a system of budgetary control is that it immediately focuses attention on the staff organization of the company, and ensures that individual responsibilities are clearly defined and that the requisite authority commensurate with the responsibility is delegated. This is recognized as a fundamental requirement of efficient works management, and yet in very many works this particular aspect of organization is anything but satisfactory.

Before any steps are taken to install a budgetary control system it will be advisable for a chart to be drawn up showing the precise responsibility and authority of each executive. This might be somewhat on the lines shown on page 9.

The product, the methods of production, the plant layout, and the line of responsibility vitally affect the form of budgetary control and cost system.

For example, in a factory manufacturing a wide range of products the method of production may be based on machines of similar type grouped together under a specialist foreman; on the other hand, in the same factory it may be decided that it will be more advantageous to split the machine groups into product groups with line production under the control of a manager for each group of products.

The layout of the accounting system will differ considerably in each case. In the latter case complete Departmental Profit and Loss Accounts for each group of products might be made up, whereas in the former instance this might be impossible.

Standard costing is so closely allied to the other aspects of workshop procedure—estimating, planning, ratefixing, and progressing—and to production methods that it is only after a careful study of these procedures, and by going slowly, step by step, that a full system of standard costing can be brought into effective operation.

Standard costing presumes either in whole or in part some form of standard product or standard process or operation. The trend of modern production methods is more and more towards standardization, and few indeed are the works which have not been affected. But even in works which it is considered have hardly been touched by standardization, it will usually be found that processes or operations, or products or components, are sufficiently "standard" to permit of standard cost methods being adopted with their definite advantages.

Standard costing lays the stress on performance rather than on product.

**Standard Costs** might be defined for the purposes of this book as "the normal costs both for individual orders (excluding the cost of faulty work and other excess costs) and for processes and the business as a whole, for normal production efficiency at a normal or planned level of output."

To obtain this standard cost it is necessary to draw up a **long-term budget** showing the estimated details of cost at the normal level of output, particularly as regards overheads.

The short-term budgeted costs (referred to as the **Budget**) are the estimated costs for the immediate future at the estimated output during that period.

The term "progressive budgeting" might be applied to schemes which emphasize control *before* the event by programming and sanctioning through frequently prepared short-term budgets in contradistinction to the term "flexible budgeting" applied to standard costs "flexed" *after* actual output is ascertained to the relative allowable levels.

Standard costs[1] refer more particularly to the costs of individual orders, products, or processes, and are so

---

[1] In one edition of the "Terminology of Cost Accountancy" the Institute of Cost and Works Accountants define a Budget as "A financial and/or quantitative statement, prepared prior to a defined period of time, of

applied. The budget is used more as a plan and measure of efficiency of departments and of the business as a whole.

Budgetary control methods can be effectively used without a system of standard costs, and vice versa. The two are, however, closely bound together, and though they may be utilized independently the author advocates a system whereby the information furnished by both the budgetary control and the standard cost systems is co-ordinated so that it may form one of the most useful tools in the hands of the management.

---

the policy to be pursued during that period for the purpose of achieving a given objective." A standard cost is defined as "A predetermined cost used in standard costing, which is computed in advance of production on the basis of a specification of all factors affecting cost."

CHAPTER II

# BUDGETARY CONTROL

THE term budgetary control is applied to the system of
management control and accounting in which all operations are forecast and so far as possible planned ahead,
and the actual results compared with the forecast and
planned ones.

The plan of operations is the best that can be devised
in the particular circumstances, and reasons and remedies
are immediately sought to correct any adverse tendencies
in the actual results.

For this to form an effective control in the hands of
the management the different figures should as far as
possible be forecast by the persons responsible for their
achievement. All executives should have planned conditions to aim at and improve upon, and the degree to which
this is being attained should be regularly brought to
their notice.

The general advantages of budgeting may be simply
illustrated by comparing two captains sailing down a
wide but shallow river. Both know roughly in what
direction it is flowing and can see its appearance some
distance ahead. But one is provided with a chart and the
other has none. One will be able to steer a centre course
down the main channel, avoiding sandbanks and rocks,
and reach his destination as soon as possible, while the
other will have only his judgment to rely on in avoiding
immediate obstacles as they are encountered, and continually runs the risk of going aground or of long delays
through choosing the wrong channel. The business man
with a carefully prepared budget can be compared to
the captain with the chart.

Budgeting teaches executives to plan ahead, and it is surprising what a real factor this is in achieving business success.

Examples of rocks charted are: overtrading and lack of liquid resources, tying up of excessive capital in fixed assets or stocks, extension of plant in departments where trade might be forecast to fall off, and unnoticed increases in indirect expenses and overheads.

## Advantages

The following have been stated to be the objects and advantages of budgetary control—

(1) To map out the objective and goal aimed at.

(2) To co-ordinate activities and secure co-operation.

(3) To centralize control with delegated responsibility and authority.

(4) To check the progress towards the objective and provide warning of danger.

(5) To show where success or failure in achievement has occurred and where standards have been attained.

(6) To emphasize the corporate objective of the company.

"Budgetary control provides a basis for (a) administration control, (b) direction of sales effort, (c) production planning, (d) control of stocks, (e) price fixing, (f) financial requirements, (g) expense control, (h) production cost control."

The budget co-ordinates sales, manufacturing, and finance, and, as Dunkerley stated,[1] "forces executives to think, and think as a group." Moreover, it enables management to decide policy with some knowledge of the results thereof, provides an objective and measure of success, provides a stimulus and emphasizes collective

[1] Roland Dunkerley, at the Sixth International Congress for Scientific Management.

effort and the profit objective, and, finally, as he so admirably sums up, "substitutes considered intention for opportunism in management."

## Ideal or Attainable?

As stated in Chapter I, the author advocates a system whereby a standard (or long-term) budget is set up showing normal costs for output at normal operation level, in addition to the short-term budget giving the forecast attainable figures for the immediate future. The former is used as the basis for the standard costs. In certain circumstances the two may be combined.

The author feels strongly that the short-term budget should be capable of achievement. This applies to the Production Budget in particular. Undoubtedly this is the most effective method of obtaining efficient control.

If budgeted figures are based only on the "ideal," persons responsible for seeing that they are accomplished may well become discouraged. If these figures are based on the "normal," in times of depression (or boom) little interest will be taken in comparing budget with actual, and a manager accused of never achieving budget figures may well be excused for offering as his only plea, "Well, look at trade conditions."

If, on the other hand, the budget figures are the forecast achievable performance for the current period, arrived at after consultation and discussion with the parties responsible, then any variations must be specifically accounted for. Managers will take a real interest in seeing that budget figures are achieved and that variations are properly accounted for, and, most important, that steps are taken to improve unfavourable results and conditions.

## The Budget Controller or Budget Officer

Some person should be appointed with the specific

duty of administering the budget. Whether this is a whole-time post or not will depend on the size of the organization. As his work will deal with the drafting and co-ordinating of figures, he will usually be a person with accountancy training. In some cases the assistant to the secretary may undertake this work. The more knowledge he has of the technical side of the business, however, the better.

It will be his duty to scrutinize and investigate the figures submitted by the managers, to discuss them, co-ordinate them, and amend them. It may be his responsibility to draft them.

Where a fully organized system of budgetary control is in operation his status should be at least on a level equal to that of the Chief Accountant.

The Chief Accountant or the Cost Accountant may, in fact, act as Budget Officer, aided, perhaps, in the detail work by an assistant.

**Budget Committee**

The Budget Officer will be assisted by the Budget Committee (whether or not graced by this title).

The personnel of the committee will vary with each individual firm, according to its organization, but will generally include—

The General Manager (Chairman)

The Sales Manager

The Works Manager/Production Engineer or Controller

The Accountant/Cost Accountant and/or the Budget Controller

The Departmental Managers.

It will be the duty of the Budget Committee to submit, discuss, and finally approve the budget figures.

The Budget Committee should then meet regularly,

daily, weekly, or at least monthly, depending on its precise functions, for the purpose of discussing and *acting* on the figures submitted. These figures will principally be comparisons between budget and actual figures for the various spheres of the firm's activities.

A separate meeting may be held with each departmental manager.

In addition, other interests may be represented on the Committee or their presence or advice requested, e.g.—

| | |
|---|---|
| Technical Manager | Personnel Officer |
| Chief Draughtsman | Works Superintendents |
| Chief Estimator | Foremen, etc. |

The Budget Committee (under the guidance of the Chairman) should also perform the broader function of training executives in the principles and wider responsibilities of management.

It may be worth while in suitable cases to take members of the Joint Production Committee (if any) into consultation in certain aspects of the Budget programme.

In its widest sense the Budget Committee may well form the management of the concern.

## Preparation of the Budget

Much of the effectiveness of budgetary control depends not on the system itself but on the method by which it is applied.

The Budget Controller should seek the fullest help from the parties responsible for its execution in the preparation of the budget if he is to retain their close co-operation and confidence. An attitude of, "There are our figures, take them or leave them," will achieve no good purpose whatever. Detailed explanations should be given as to how budgeted figures are arrived at, precisely why it is considered they can be attained, and the aims and ideals which are to be striven for.

Budgeted figures must be drawn up and co-ordinated by a competent person co-operating with the management. Badly drafted budgets and standards badly applied will do more harm than good. They will simply "disgust, amuse, or discourage" the individuals expected to live up to them, according to their respective temperaments. As has been stated, the short-term budget figures should be capable of achievement. The psychological factor counts for a great deal here. The interest, appreciation, and co-operation of the departmental managers must be maintained.

Self-congratulation at having achieved a budget and the stimulus to greater efforts provided by an "achievable" budget both help, with the guidance of a wise manager, to direct the best efforts of the staff towards the prosperity of the business.

Praise or blame from the higher executives means a great deal to most men. The wise manager will encourage, advise, or chide as the particular occasion or person merits.

### " Prompt Budgets "

To ensure that budget figures are promptly made up and receive proper consideration before approval, it is necessary to establish a routine setting out specific dates for departmental managers to submit their estimates so that the budget figures may be issued before the period to which they refer has commenced. These estimates may have to be submitted by completing a standard printed form.

### Administration of the Budget

The budget is administered through the Budget Committee. The data on which the Budget Committee bases

its actions are provided in the form of Budget and
Cost Reports, mainly emanating from the Accounting
Department. These will usually be drawn up by the
Budget Controller.

These reports, or a summary thereof, may form the
real agenda for the meetings, though it may be well to
have a more formal meeting at longer intervals with full
agenda and minutes.

Such reports should be furnished to all members of the
Budget Committee, supplemented by special reports in
detail to individual members which are of interest to
themselves in particular and on which they in turn may
have to report to the Committee as a whole.

These reports must be prompt.

It is suggested that a very brief Daily Report be made
out. This will be followed by a more detailed Weekly
Report, and, if monthly accounts are in operation, a full
Monthly Report or series of reports will be submitted.
Such reports will generally be in the form of a comparison
of budget and actual figures, both periodic and cumulative. Details of these reports are given in Chapter XV,
where they are fully considered.

When a budgetary control system is started, it may
be wise to limit its sphere to a very few persons or
departments and then slowly extend the scope of its
operations. At first in practice it may be found that
actual figures may vary considerably from budget figures
in detail, though in total the budget may be attained.
Too much criticism of variations should not be made
till some time has been given for the technique to be
mastered. Cumulative figures may help.

## Accounting for Budgetary Control

Budgetary control is fundamentally planning ahead
with the manifest advantages of planned production. It

has naturally developed along the lines of comparing actual achievements with plan.

Slight modifications may be required in the accounting and costing system to provide analysis by "persons responsible," but as this will normally agree with the departmental divisions it will not usually prove difficult.

Finally, it must never be forgotten that the control and management of a business are achieved through individual persons with the assistance of figures, and not by the figures themselves.

This is one of the fundamentals of budgetary control.

## Budget Period

The distance ahead for which one can reasonably expect to plan will depend to a large degree on the type of business. It will often, however, be found convenient to prepare and approve the short-term budget each quarter in some capital goods industries. In consumer goods industries, longer periods as a basis for planning and control and as targets for endeavour may be quite satisfactory. Where detailed budgets are for periods of less than a year, each submission may be accompanied by a more generalized forecast for the balance of the next twelve months. These figures will be broken down into months. The actual results will be compared with the budget each month-end and discussed with the Budget Committee.

Budgets may have to be revised at shorter periods if conditions change.

## Budget Management

For budgetary control to be fully effective it is essential that the chief executive takes an active part in its operation, co-ordinates the activities of the members of the committee, and ratifies their decisions.

# PART I
## PREPARATION OF THE BUDGET

# CHAPTER III

## THE SALES BUDGET

THE Sales Budget (and by "sales" we here mean "orders received") forms the fundamental basis on which all the other budgets are built up. Every possible step must be taken to ensure that its figures are as accurate as possible. Only at boom periods and in special circumstances, as where firms are booked up with orders for many months ahead, does the importance of an accurate Sales Budget assume smaller significance.

The Sales Manager should be made directly responsible for the Sales Budget, and even if he is not the actual compiler, though this is advisable, he assumes responsibility when he agrees to the figures.

### Preparation of the Sales Budget

In the preparation of the Sales Budget the compiler will require to bear in mind the following factors—

### (1) PAST SALES FIGURES AND TRENDS

The compiler of the Sales Budget should be assisted by graphs recording past sales and the general sales trends. Graphs showing both monthly and seasonal fluctuation in total and by product may be used as well as smoothed curves showing the long-term expansion. But in considering these, the factors affecting the figures, e.g. seasonal fluctuations, growth of market, growth of business, trade cycles, etc., should be borne in mind.

They should be supplemented if possible by detailed records of—

(a) Sales for previous periods analysed by product; [1]
(b) Sales for previous periods analysed by area;
(c) Sales for previous periods analysed by class of consumer;
(d) Sales for previous periods analysed by traveller or agent;
(e) Sales for previous periods analysed by customer.

This record of previous experience will probably form the most reliable guide as to future sales, bearing in mind, of course, the other factors.

## (2) SALESMEN'S ESTIMATES

He should have in his hands estimates of sales by product group for the coming period from each traveller or agent. The danger here is that these estimates will tend to be over-optimistic or too conservative, depending on the traveller's temperament.

## (3) PLANT CAPACITY

Information as to the plant capacity available, and present utilization for different product groups, should be known. One of the primary essentials of profitable business is to ensure proper utilization of plant facilities, and "one of the basic needs of the Sales Budget is to provide economic and balanced production in the factory." Proposed plant extensions will be allowed for.

Preliminary sales figures will almost certainly require to be adjusted in the light of this factor.

[1] *Note.* Throughout the book the term "product" is used to cover either "product" or "product group," for where there are several products having very similar characteristics (e.g. manufacturing process, size, composition, profit margin, etc.) it will usually be found advantageous for accounting, and for management control purposes, to group these together by classes.

## (4) General Trade Prospects

In very many industries the probability of the sales trend going up or down will depend largely on the "general trade prospects." This is especially true in the case of national distributors. In other cases the trade prospects for a particular industry must be considered.

In this connexion valuable information may be gleaned from financial publications such as the *Financial Times*, the *Economist*, and from Government publications such as *The Monthly Digest of Statistics*. Useful notes, too, may be taken from special newspapers and trade supplements, such as those published by *The Times*, *The Guardian*, and the *Glasgow Herald*. Particular trade papers and magazines may also furnish valuable pointers.

## (5) Orders on Hand

In boom periods or where production is a very lengthy process, the value of orders on hand may have considerable weight in determining the value of sales to be budgeted for in a particular period, or what sales "push" is to be made   Eventually, of course, orders received must balance with orders delivered, with the former the vital factor.

## (6) Proposed Expansion or Discontinuance of Products

Notes which have been gathered regarding lines proposed to be pushed or discontinued will be consulted and the steps necessary for any adjustment taken.

The margin of profit on each product and the facilities for manufacture, as well as the visualized potential market, will be the factors influencing this decision. The proposed volume of advertising must also be considered in this connexion.

## (7) Proposed Alterations in Quality and Price

The effect of any such adjustment on the volume as well as on the value of sales must not be forgotten in preparing the Sales Budget. It is often very difficult to determine the precise effect any such alterations may have, and careful market research studies may require to be made before the result can be predicted with any confidence.

The fact, too, that high volume at low price is *not* always the most profitable policy should not be lost sight of. But this brings us into the realm of price-volume study, which is hardly within the scope of this chapter.

## (8) Seasonal Fluctuations

In allowing for seasonal variations, past experience will be the most reliable guide. With the ideal of an even flow of production in view, however, a determined effort should be made to minimize the effect of this if possible. Consideration should first be given to the cause. Is it climatic, or due to holidays, to trade custom, or just to habit, or is it due to the repercussion of these causes on allied industries?

The steps taken to minimize the effect might be special advertising or special concessions or added inducements during the off-season. On the production side the problem might be tackled by the introduction of different supplementary or alternative lines when the demand for the principal product is slack, or by the controlled building up of stocks. But the cost of all such proposals must be set against any benefits expected.

This problem should be settled before the Sales Budget is finally approved.

## (9) Potential Market

A reliable estimate of the potential market for a

company's products is essential to the whole of a company's policy. It determines the capital required, the building of plant, when extensions should be carried out, and what sales force and what advertising should be employed. The estimate may be based on one man's unrecorded knowledge of a particular trade or be the result of carefully undertaken market research.

The factors to be considered here include—

(*a*) *Demand*

     (i) Is the product capital or consumer's goods?
     (ii) Is the product a necessity or a luxury?
     (iii) Is the product old-established and standard or new and novel?
     (iv) Is the product durable or flimsy?
     (v) What breadth of appeal has it—women, children, butchers, bakers, etc.?
     (vi) Change of fashion or style.
     (vii) Quality of the goods.
     (viii) Price of the goods.
     (ix) Volume of replace and upkeep orders.
     (x) Purchasing power of consumers.
     (xi) Technical developments.

(*b*) *Supply*

     (i) Alternatives or substitutes available.
     (ii) Effect and intensity of competition.
     (iii) Monopoly or patent.
     (iv) Variety and permanency of sources of supply.

With regard to purchasing power, available statistics such as number of car registrations, number of telephone subscribers, density of population, percentage unemployed, etc., in each district may be very useful, especially where the business is on a national distribution basis. All this should tell if the sales curves ought to go up and where.

## (10) AVAILABILITY OF MATERIALS AND LABOUR

A controlling factor which sometimes arises in drafting the Sales Budget may be the availability of supplies of materials (or labour). The likelihood of obtaining adequate supplies of materials must be fully investigated before drafting the sales programme. If it is apparent that this factor will limit deliveries the programme will require to be modified accordingly.

## (11) TRADE CYCLE

This appears to be a definitely established phenomenon, but the causes or the cure are not so definitely established. We all see the ups and downs, but the trouble is that no one appears to be able to tell us exactly when we are going to go up or down, or how far we are going to go either way.

Some explanation has been given as to the causes, however, and there are various methods of endeavouring to anticipate the future trend. The ideal for any business would be to find some other business or trade whose fluctuations were almost parallel, but whose variations took place some time ahead of its own. In some cases it is possible to find something to correspond to this.

To-day, political events and Government control of external and internal trade and finance, however, play such a large part in trade conditions that it would appear advisable to place more reliance on a detailed consideration of all the factors affecting the current situation and likely to influence the future than to be guided by any apparent regular cyclical fluctuation.

## (12) FINANCIAL ASPECT

One other factor which must be taken into account here is the financial position.

Sales expansion will usually involve capital outlay.

More credit accounts may be opened or credit extended, new plant may be required, salaries and wages, perhaps, need to be paid which will not show an immediate return. In a company with good credit standing or a plentiful supply of capital this may not assume such importance, but in a small firm or one in which capital is difficult to obtain, Sales Budgets will require to be kept within the bounds of financial capacity.

Very many firms have got into serious difficulties through straining their financial resources, and many have succumbed, not from lack of orders, but from too rapid and uncontrolled expansion.

If any big sales expansion is budgeted for, it must be seen that facilities are available to finance the operations.

Viewed from another angle the sales volume planned should be such as will produce an adequate return on the capital employed. This may be expressed in terms of a percentage dividend on issued capital or better still as a percentage profit on the net worth.  (See Chapter XIX.)

Generally speaking, then, the procedure for preparation of the Sales Budget will be on the following lines.

(*a*) A preliminary budget giving totals for the principal product groups will be made out from reference to previous experience and general trade prospects.

(*b*) Another more detailed budget will be made out based on salesmen's and agents' reports for the coming period.

(*a*) and (*b*) will be compared side by side and each modified in the light of the other after further investigation.

This adjusted budget will then be considered in relationship to plant capacity and balanced production, and with reference to proposed extensions. Items to be pushed or discontinued will next be adjusted.

This revised budget will then again be considered in

the light of trade conditions and of policy and the other factors enumerated.

It may be found worth while to make up the budget again (1) by product, (2) by area, (3) by consumer class, each analysis balancing with the other. This may help to evaluate the principal factors.

The Sales Budget will then be ready for incorporation in the Master Budget ready for submission to and approval by the Budget Committee.

## Standard (or Long-term) Sales Budget

The standard Sales Budget will be the normal budget for a normal year.

The short-term Sales Budget will be the practical level attainable in the immediate future.

The same factors and the same principles govern the preparation of each. In the former more emphasis is placed on full or envisaged plant capacity and on anticipated market development. In the latter, current trade conditions, seasonal fluctuations, and present plant utilization assume full weight, and full details are given.

The former gives the normal level of operations and enables standard costs to be set up and current operating levels to be compared with standard.

## Operation of the Sales Budget

The Sales Budget will usually be put into active operation by the issue of sales quotas to the salesmen or agents. When these differ from the estimates submitted by the salesmen it is wise for explanations to be given as to the reason for the revised figures, either verbally by the Sales Manager in discussion with the salesman, or in writing.

For the achievement of the budget, reliance may simply be placed on the salesman's enthusiasm and integrity, supplemented by the periodic issue of reports comparing

budget with achievement and with letters of encourage-
ment or reproof aided by personal conversation with the
Sales Manager.

Further stimulation may be given in the form of a
special bonus scheme for budgetary achievement. The
type of scheme will depend on the type of salesmen
employed and the type of goods sold.

Sometimes the details of a salesman's quota may have
to be revised in the middle of a period and salesmen urged
to concentrate on a particular line where orders have not
come up to expectation.

The advertising programme may have to be revised
for the same reason or even, contrariwise, because orders
for a particular line are flowing in faster than they can
be handled.

Salesmen's expenses should also come under the
budgetary control system. Salesmen will be notified of
their budgeted allowance and detailed explanations will
be sought for all excesses.

It is interesting to compare a chart of actual and
budgeted sales, alongside a chart drawn up to show
forecast business conditions against actual business conditions, where a reliable index of the latter can be obtained,
e.g. the *Economist* index of business activity for business as
a whole, or, say, car registrations or steel production, for
the relative industries.

Such figures help to indicate the relationship of business
accruing to a particular firm to the level of business
activity of the trade as a whole, and form a supplementary
measure of salesmen's activities.

Although the sales budget forms the normal starting
point, the production budget may take this place where
there is a long order book or assured off-take.

# CHAPTER IV

# THE OUTPUT OR PRODUCTION BUDGET

BEFORE preparing the outline of the general Production Budget it is almost essential to have some data as to the relative incidence of the various cost items, the main headings being, of course, material, labour, and overheads. This should be available from previous records with varying degrees of suitability, analysis, and accuracy.

The basic figures can usually be abstracted from previous Profit and Loss Accounts, adjusted if necessary.

Figures may be taken for the business as a whole, or they may be available departmentally. If possible, they should be analysed somewhat as follows—

|  | Percentages | | |
| --- | --- | --- | --- |
|  | To Output | To Direct Labour | To Total Cost |
| Materials (detail if necessary) . . |  |  |  |
| Direct Labour (detail if necessary) . |  |  |  |
| Directly Variable Charges (Sundry Indirect Supplies, etc.) . . |  |  |  |
| Semi-variable Charges (Indirect Labour and Materials, etc.). . |  |  |  |
| Fixed Charges (Rent, Rates, Depreciation, etc.) . . . . |  |  |  |

This analysis should be made over a wide series of years and at various values of output.

It may prove very useful to plot the figures on a chart showing the experience of cost incidence at varying volumes of output, but allowances will have to be made for changes of conditions and methods.

Even if suitable previous records are not available it will still be advisable to try to make up a graph on these lines for future conditions. Such a graph may not show budget expense details for departments, but it will prove exceedingly useful for checking up budget figures and ensuring that all figures are kept in proper relation to one another and that expense trends are kept in line with output values.

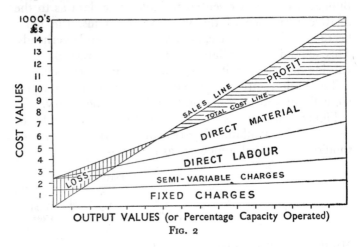

FIG. 2

When the actual Production Budget is being compiled, all its component parts—material, labour, and overheads, by departments and in total—will require to be adjusted and readjusted, one in the light of the other, before the final budget is accepted.

It may also be necessary to distinguish clearly between Sales of Factored Goods and the cost thereof, and Output of Manufactured Goods and their relative costs.

The Production Budget is really governed by the Sales Budget, but the Sales Budget is largely determined by the production capacity and by production costs. Where reliable previous records are available of production capabilities the Sales Budget may fairly well be prepared in advance, subject to modification in the light of the Production Budget, but in other circumstances the two budgets may almost require to be prepared side by side. In any event they are interdependent and must be prepared in co-operation with both the Sales and the Works Departments.

The basis of the Production Budget may vary, according to the type of business. Where the course of production is a matter only of a few hours or days and, say, direct to customer's order (e.g. a jobbing printer), orders received and output will practically coincide, or will do so with a certain regular time lag. In a case of this nature the Output Budget will be based directly on the Sales Budget figures for each period.

Where, however, the course of production is a lengthy business of weeks or months, or the goods are made for stock or to contract (e.g. heavy engineering), although the Output Budget must be co-ordinated with the Sales Budget in the long run, the short-term budget may be based on the records of the Planning Department or its equivalent.

In the case of the engineering trade an efficient system of planning and production control must be in operation to enable accurate figures for output and delivery to be stated.

Successful achievement in fulfilling the Output Budget is in fact largely dependent on the efficient operation of Production Control in its widest sense.

The various systems of planning and progressing scarcely come within the scope of this book; but these entail the study of plant capacities, machine running times and loads, materials scheduling, etc., and involve some system of forms and reports, in order that the work of the various departments may be co-ordinated and also that the date of completion of the product can be accurately forecast. In certain circumstances it may be possible to build up the Production Budget from records of machine loading, the details being calculated from the standard costs per standard hour plus the materials cost.

The responsibility for the Total Production Budget lies with the Works Manager. Departmental Production Budgets will be the responsibility of Departmental Managers.

It should be pointed out that the term "output" is not necessarily synonymous with "deliveries."

Where there is a steady flow of short-cycle production which is delivered immediately it is produced, deliveries and factory output may be taken as one and the same. Where, however, factory production is of the long-cycle type with the building up of work in progress and finished parts spread over two or three months before deliveries are effected, it is necessary to take into account the variation in value of work in progress and finished parts in order to arrive at an "output" figure (see Appendix I).

In such cases both "Deliveries" and "Output" figures should be budgeted for and controlled.

The Departmental Works Managers should prepare their Production Budgets in co-operation with the Budget Controller. It is the Works Managers who should know and understand the plant capabilities, the nature of the orders on hand and the work in progress, and the relative production problems and difficulties. It is they who should be in a position to state the volume of output for each period. (Sometimes, however, this may not quite work out in practice, the higher executives being firmly of the opinion that such and such an output is possible at such and such a time or the Departmental Manager being left to work out his own salvation as best he can.) (See also Chapter XII.)

## Cost of Production Budget

When, after discussion, the volume of output is determined, the cost of procuring this output must be obtained. The production will be split up into material, labour, and plant requirements.

Where a factory is well established, and the production routine regular, most of the information can be fairly easily forecast by reference to previous records. In this case the Budget Controller will have the assistance of the financial and cost records and will be able to guide the Works Manager, or even to go a long way in the preparation of the Production Budget himself.

The system may be for the Budget Controller to prepare a draft of the Production Budget after the Works Manager has submitted figures for the volume of output. This draft will then be discussed in detail with the departmental managers and amended where necessary.

On the other hand, departmental managers may be asked to submit draft Production Budgets giving full details of costs. These budgets will be scrutinized by the Budget Controller with reference to the cost and financial records. He will discuss them with the managers and point out amendments which he thinks necessary.

Where the Budget Controller is sufficiently experienced and has the proper status (see Chapter II), he may even be in a better position to judge what the relative costs should be than the managers themselves, and will have the authority to insist on certain amendments.

The exact procedure by which the Production Budget is built up will vary according to the capabilities of the managers and of the Budget Controller.

The Production Budget should be finally approved by the Budget Committee.

# CHAPTER V

# MATERIALS BUDGET

In drawing up the Production Budget one of the first matters to be considered is materials.

## Stock

The question of stocks is a vital factor in drawing up this budget, and a word had best be said regarding this first of all. In the case of seasonal trades the question usually resolves itself into endeavouring to keep production at as even a level as possible without building up too cumbersome stocks on hand, and in certain cases it may even be possible to tackle different products in different seasons, following the old example of the versatile roasted chestnut and ice-cream vendor.

In most factories the problem of *buffer* stocks between different processes and operations has to be considered, so that delay in one process will not bring all other processes to a standstill.

### Raw Material Stocks

The Buying and Stores Departments have to deal with the problem of maintaining the minimum adequate stocks consistent with efficient uninterrupted production and allowing for contingencies.

Consideration must be given to such questions, too, as available storage facilities and cost of storage, discount on bulk orders, deterioration, capital available, and interest charges thereon.

Every effort should be made to keep the amount of capital locked up in stocks as low as possible.

## FINISHED STOCKS

These should be kept at a certain level, depending on the type of business and the efficient meeting of customers' demands, and certain figures should be budgeted for preparing the Output Budget.

## WORK IN PROGRESS

Although not a question of materials only, we may consider this item here. The necessity for keeping work in progress at the lowest pcssible level is vital in every factory, both from the sales point of view of quick deliveries and the financial point of view of capital locked up, not to mention the usual slowing down of production that accompanies an abnormal amount of work in progress lying on the shop floor. Quick turnover must be aimed at. The ratio of work in progress to output in each department or for each product should be examined, compared, and questioned. Departmental Managers should submit budgets of the future levels of work in progress they expect to maintain.

The value of opening stocks must therefore be considered, and the value to which it is desired to increase or decrease stocks at the end of the budget period must be taken into account, before budgeting for the amount of materials to be purchased. (Similarly the labour required to build up or decrease work in progress or finished parts must be allowed for in the labour budget.)

It will normally be found, even when budgetary control is not in operation, that there is some form of short-term forecast of the requirements kept by the Buying Department, but this is not usually translated into financial terms or correlated to the general policy of the company. It is essentially a matter of anticipating the future requirements of the company.

In total the Materials Budget can be judged to be a certain percentage of the Output Budget as shown by previous records modified in the light of current price trends.

Materials can be divided into direct and indirect. Indirect materials will be dealt with under the heading of works overhead expenses, but their purchasing will be under the control of the Buying Department. Direct materials may be in the form of raw materials, semi-finished goods, or component parts, though the distinction between one and the other is often very slight; for, of course, what is "raw material" to one firm may be regarded as "finished goods" by another.

## Raw Materials

In fixing both the long-term and the short-term budgets for raw materials consideration will be given to the following matters.

The percentage of raw material to total cost of products should be calculated (this will be shown from previous records). A rough total value of raw material required for the budgeted output will thus be obtained and will be reviewed in the light of current price trends.

This figure should be broken down into the raw material required for the different product groups or departments.

For each product group, a summary of the amount of each kind of raw material required for that group to meet the budgeted output will be drawn up.

In the budget statement the budgeted figure for raw material will normally appear under product groups (or departments), but a supplementary summary should be made up combining the requirements of each product group by totals for each type of raw material.

This latter summary should be checked, and if necessary amended, by the Buying Department in the light of their knowledge and experience, having regard to price trends, available sources of supply, etc. The Materials Budget for each product group will then be corrected if necessary to concur with the Buying Department's recommendation.

Consideration must then be given to the amount of stock to be carried. Figures should be got out showing the anticipated raw material stocks to be held at different dates. The rate of consumption of the different items will be ascertained.

The time between order and delivery is an important factor to be taken into consideration.

Having budgeted for the raw material requirements, the Buying Department will then proceed to find the most profitable means of meeting these requirements. Consideration will be given to the matter of making long-term contracts or of building up stocks against regular seasonal price fluctuations or anticipated upward movements. (This latter is not to be recommended except in exceptional circumstances.)

Even the question of taking over or acquiring the sources of supply should be considered.

## Semi-finished Goods or Component Parts

The same procedure and considerations apply to this type of material as to raw material, with the difference, perhaps, that the question of whether these materials should be bought out or manufactured internally will bulk more largely. This can be answered only in the light of accurate comparative cost information and plant capacity.

Reference should here be made to the detailed schedules which will usually be required to be made up by the Planning and Buying Departments in conjunction, in order that certain parts or goods shall arrive on certain specified dates as and when required for the production programme.

Material requirements for the replacement of scrap should not be forgotten.[1]

## Sub-contracting

The volume and cost of any sub-contracting work given to outside firms, to whom "free issues" of materials are made, should not be forgotten and may be included in the Materials Budget.

Planning, buying, and stores should all be linked up by an efficient system of stores records, enabling balances on hand and on order in each section to be easily computed and the rate of consumption to be ascertained.

The Stores Record Cards, held by stores or by production control department, should be designed to provide this information, together with a record of what quantities are reserved or allocated to jobs coming forward.

The system should ensure that goods will be ordered in ample time to allow for delivery before the stock on hand is exhausted.

Most stores requisition systems work on the basis of setting up maximum and minimum balances.

---

[1] Where there is a fairly smooth flow of finished production and the labour force is fairly stable, it may be possible to assume that the labour and works overhead element in the value of work in progress remains a constant. Where this assumption is valid the work of budgeting and of reporting actual results can sometimes be simplified. (Simplification can sometimes also be achieved by basing profit computation on finished production priced at sales value, rather than on deliveries, reserves for reducing finished stock to cost being carried and adjusted for fluctuations in holdings of finished stock.)

# CHAPTER VI

## LABOUR BUDGET

THE next item to be considered in drawing up the Production Budget is labour.

### Direct Labour

Here again rough figures may first be obtained by reference to previous records of the percentage labour cost in the total cost of each product group, or department, and the volume of output budgeted for. This figure may then be got out in some detail for each section under the headings of different classes of labour, e.g. turners, millers, drillers, grinders, fitters, etc., showing, if necessary, numerical strength. (This budget may be submitted by the foreman or departmental manager.) The figures will be adjusted in the light of proposed expansion or technical considerations.

The cost figures will be revised with regard to any changes in rates of pay and totals shown in the budget statement for each product, section, or department.

A supplementary summary should be made up giving total requirements for each class of labour. This will enable the Personnel Department to carry out schemes of training and transfer and to locate sources of suitable labour so that every effort may be made to avoid difficulties arising in production through lack of suitable men.

It may also be found possible to compute labour requirements by reference to calculations of total productive man-hours required to give the budgeted output of each product.

Indirect labour will be considered under overhead charges.

Labour required for any capital extensions, etc., should not be forgotten.

## Overtime

The question of overtime must often be taken into consideration in preparing the Direct Labour Budget. Regular or continuous overtime is to be condemned, and where such is the case, and cannot be remedied by shift work or the engagement of additional employees, the question of extension of plant must be seriously considered, having regard, of course, to trade prospects.

Where trade is seasonal, overtime may require to be worked at a certain time of the year, but in this case the building up of stocks should be considered. Some periods of overtime appear almost inevitable, even in the best-regulated factories, owing to urgent orders, the incidence of holidays, or through unexpected breakdowns.

This overtime from whatever cause should be anticipated as far as possible and budgeted for. It may all be included in direct labour, but it is considered that the best method is to treat the extra allowance (e.g. the quarter in the case of payment of time and a quarter) as overhead expense. On the other hand where double day-shifts or three shifts are the standard conditions shift premiums may most conveniently be included in direct labour. (The effect of shifts and shift premiums on output and costs is best shown by the "break-even chart" type of analysis.)

# CHAPTER VII

# WORKS OVERHEAD EXPENSES BUDGET

WHEN a system of budgetary control is first installed it is often started from this angle, for it is felt that here is something which can be controlled and something which can usually be fairly simply budgeted for in the light of past experience. Admittedly, even budgetary control of expenses only may prove an invaluable tool in the hands of the management, but it must be regarded in the light of the general production policy of the company, and not applied from a narrow, niggardly, cheeseparing point of view.

## Indirect Labour

The budgeted figure for this item will usually be drafted in the light of previous experience at various volumes of production, but all cost figures should be interpreted in the form of numerical strength, and a big "why" constantly asked. Where expansion is planned, estimates by technical men should be obtained. In the case of members of staff, summaries should be prepared showing salaries and all proposed increases. Items to be considered would be, for example—

| | | |
|---|---|---|
| Labourers | Inspectors | Works' clerks |
| Storekeepers | Tool-setters | Millwrights and |
| Truckers | Foremen | repair men. |
| Cranemen | Ratefixers | |
| Packers | Progress men | |

Foremen and works superintendents may be consulted with regard to indirect labour, and direct information sought as to what is considered the necessary cost at different volumes of output. At what point will an additional labourer or storekeeper be required, and why, etc.?

Indirect labour cost should bear some normal ratio to direct labour cost.

## Indirect Supplies

Here again previous experience at various volumes of production will form the basis of the budget, but economies and the elimination of waste must constantly be sought. Items included, and to be considered, might be such as—

> Oils and grease
> Waste
> Types of small tools, etc.

On the buying side economies may be found by the elimination of haphazard purchasing of such items. An eye must be kept, too, on the balance of stocks held.

Foremen and storekeepers may again be consulted as to the cost of these items, or may even be asked to submit detailed estimates. Reasons for variations from best performances should be explained.

## Works Service Departments

Costs shown under this heading are those of departments not directly productive but serving other departments (to which the costs of the service departments will ultimately be allocated), e.g.—

Heating (cost of coal, furnacemen, boiler repairs, etc.)
Lighting (cost of electricians, supplies, repairs, etc.)
Power
Works maintenance
Inspection
Internal transport
Stores
Receiving and dispatch
Tool room (if treated as a works service).

Previous experience and best performances would again be called on in preparing the budget, but the management should be continually on the watch for improved methods.

## Repairs and Maintenance

It is often advisable to show this as a special item by itself, as it may sometimes amount to very formidable figures.

Repairs and maintenance should never be carried out in a haphazard fashion but should form part of a regular routine of inspection, testing, and overhauling. In spite of this, exceptional breakdowns will still occur, and it might here be mentioned that the author recommends the carrying of a Suspense Account for this item, a regular proportion of which will be charged as actual costs each period. To this account will be charged all exceptional repair items. A close watch must be kept on the balance of the account to see if the regular periodic charge requires to be increased.

Some scheme should be drafted in co-operation with the Maintenance Department to ensure that all repairs and overhauls are as far as possible anticipated and budgeted for, and preferably spread over evenly throughout the year.

## Fixed Charges

These can usually be forecast very accurately from previous statements and current intimations, and will cover such items as Rent, Rates, Insurance, Depreciation, and perhaps some of the items which might be shown in some firms as part of the Service Department costs.

These costs will, of course, be allocated on some such basis as recorded figures for floor space. Depreciation will be allocated on capital value in each department, properly recorded in a well-kept plant register.

## Scrap, Idle Time, etc.

No reference has been made to the cost of scrap, waste, or of idle time in the foregoing budget for overhead expenses. The treatment of this item depends on the cost system. It may be lost in the total cost of materials, direct labour, and overheads, and treated as part of the cost of a particular order or job. But it is urged that wherever possible the cost of scrap, idle time, and other such excess costs be shown separately and budgeted for, and the reader is referred to the detailed consideration of this matter in the Costing Section.

## Departmental Analysis

Budgeted Works Overhead Expenses will as far as possible be analysed under departments (see Fig. 16A, Chapter XV), and data setting out the budgeted figures, and later, the actual figures, will be circulated to the responsible managers.

A clear distinction should be made between expenses which are considered to be controllable within the department and those which are mainly the responsibility of the general management.

## Fixed and Variable Expenses

Some distinction should be made between expenses which tend to vary with changes in volume (stores consumption, power, etc.) and those which tend to persist at fixed levels. The content of each embodied in product costs should be roughly assessable to enable the effect of volume changes in the output of particular products to be readily forecast.

# CHAPTER VIII

# ADMINISTRATION EXPENSES BUDGET

THERE should be little difficulty in budgeting the figures for administration, which will cover the expenses of all the central offices and of management salaries. The real difficulty lies in the subsequent fair allocation of the cost, and on this point readers are referred to the Appendix on Costing Methods.

Under this heading will appear the salaries and sundry expenses of such departments as—

| | |
|---|---|
| Accountancy | Research |
| Costing | Training |
| Typing | Buying and Stores Control |
| Filing | Drawing and Design, etc. |
| Planning | |

Lists of anticipated changes in salary should be provided and office managers consulted.

## Selling Expenses

The proportion of these expenses may vary enormously depending on the type of business. A general control is usually made by determining that these should form a certain percentage of the total value of sales. Items to be included would be—

Sales Manager's salary
Central Sales Office
Travellers' salaries and expenses
Agents' salaries and expenses
Agents' offices
Advertising and publicity.

Distribution expenses would cover carriage outwards,

packing (which might be included in cost of manufacture, etc.), and road transport.

Considerable space might be devoted to the consideration of the relationship between selling expenses as advertising, etc., and sales, but much depends on individual circumstances and policies. Advertising expenditure may be budgeted for in the form of a block grant to be spread over all products throughout the year, or special allocations may be made against specific products for development, etc. But no matter in what manner this is fixed, haphazard advertising should be avoided at all costs, as it can be most wasteful.

Travellers' and agents' expenses may or may not be budgeted in detail for certain areas.

Once determined, budgeted selling expense figures should be closely controlled.

# CHAPTER IX

# FINANCIAL OR CASH BUDGET

WHILE the Sales and Production Budgets are still under consideration, a tentative budget of the working capital required and available at different periods should be drawn up. If the financial resources of the company are adequate for the proposed programme, detailed consideration of this point may be left till the Production Budget is approved. If, however, this is not the case, either the Sales and Production Budgets may require to be revised to come into line with the company's financial position, or their adoption cannot be approved till arrangements have been made to provide the necessary capital.

This latter may involve negotiating for special bank loans or for the issue of shares or debentures. Assuming, however, that the financial resources of the company are adequate for normal operation, the building up of a Cash Budget still forms an important part in co-ordinating the efficient working of the company.

When the Production Budget is finally approved it will provide figures for the orders delivered period by period.

Previous experience (which should be tabulated) will show the average lag between deliveries and payment, and a budget for cash receipts may be drafted accordingly. These figures, in conjunction with the balance outstanding at the beginning, will enable a figure for debtors outstanding to be made up.

The Materials Budget prepared as part of the Production Budget will give material requirements, and the Buying Department should supply figures as to the amounts which, and the dates on which, they propose to purchase to meet these requirements. This, after allowing for the balance due at the beginning of each budget period and the usual terms of settlement, will enable a figure for creditors to be set up together with dates when their claims will have to be met.

The Labour Budget will show the amounts to be paid in wages.

Works Expenses Budget will show the amounts required for these items.

Administration Expenses Budget will give figures for salaries and other office expenses, etc.

The dates on which such items as rent, rates, or insurance have to be paid must be determined.

Distribution of profit must not be forgotten, nor capital receipts or interest, dividends or rents, and payment of Taxation must be allowed for. From the final budgeted Profit and Loss Account the cash required to meet the estimated dividends can be calculated.

Proposed Capital Expenditure will also have to be carefully budgeted for.

Project Costing and Asset Replacement Analysis is almost a specialized subject. Regularly reviewed long-term planning is essential. Product demand trends have to be studied and the future timing of replacements scheduled, if hasty and ill-considered decisions are to be avoided and work is to be put in hand in accordance with well thought out priorities.

From the figures abstracted from these budget statements, a statement of estimated receipts and expenditure for each period will be made up, and a balance of cash on hand or in bank brought forward.

When this statement has been prepared, it will be found at what point liquid resources are likely to be strained, and temporary loans can be advantageously arranged to meet such situations in advance.

This all tends to promote production and sales efficiency.

The advantages of intelligent anticipation of financial requirements, as against the dangers of haphazard trading with its associated periods of financial strain and anxiety, and perhaps even restricted selling and interrupted production, are self-evident.

The advisability of preparing a Cash Budget may be even more imperative in some trades than in others, e.g. in trades where there are wide seasonal fluctuations or where long contracts are undertaken. Where cash requirements are anticipated beforehand, arrangements to meet them can be much more easily and advantageously made than when these arise unexpectedly and have to be hurriedly negotiated.

Where a Cash Budget can be produced, the negotiation of a bank loan can be much more easily carried through. But, apart altogether from loans, the intelligent consideration of future cash requirements should enable most potential financial strains and crises to be avoided altogether.

# CHAPTER X

# BUDGETED PROFIT AND LOSS ACCOUNT AND BALANCE SHEET

WHENEVER the Sales and Production Budgets are prepared it will be possible to draw up the budgeted Manufacturing and Profit and Loss Account. The summarized totals for the whole concern may, in certain circumstances, be supplemented by Departmental Profit and Loss Accounts, or they may have been built up from these. The Manufacturing and Profit and Loss Account will be prepared primarily on the lines of Fig. 27a, Appendix I, but it may also be compiled in the form of Fig. 27b (or Fig. 18, Chapter XV).

In some cases budgets may, in fact, be prepared by partially working back from the finally desired form of the Profit and Loss Account.

In conjunction with the Plant (and Extensions) Budget and the Financial Budget, the projected Balance Sheet can now be drawn up. This should be scrutinized and analysed for any adverse tendencies as indicated in Chapter XIX before the different budgets are finally approved.

Fundamentally, however, it boils down to not allowing the firm to slip into or towards a position where it is going to have great difficulty in meeting its current obligations, whether to suppliers, loan holders, or others.

Apart from the effect of continued trading at a loss to an extent amounting to a cash drain, this position can arise with expansion of stocks, debtors and plant, at a scale which ties up funds in excess of retained profits and provisions, where other (long-term) funds have not been or cannot be obtained to bridge the gap.

Actual and potential lenders are generally happy if they are satisfied that the prospects and maintainable good management appear to indicate that existing (or proposed) loans (after covering interest) will be repaid when due out of unspent retained earnings, or that at that time the prospects and standing of the firm would be such that old loans could be repaid out of readily granted new borrowing or permanent funds, if necessary from new sources.

It may be found necessary to modify certain of the other budgets if an unsatisfactory balance-sheet position is disclosed. After they have been readjusted, the approved budgeted balance sheet can be made up. This is the climax of the budgeting procedure.

Very many firms adopting budgetary control methods may not reach this glorious end, and yet derive most of the benefits of budgetary control. It must not be thought that for budgetary control to be effective it must be adopted *in toto*. In fact, where it is only being developed this might be positively unwise or misleading. Budgetary control technique in each individual firm should be developed bit by bit; but finally it will form a fundamental part of the entire field of industrial management.

Budgetary control in some form is regarded as essential for any efficient business, even if it exists only in its very simplest form of a forecast of anticipated orders receivable and of output in total, with an estimate of the relative total group costs for material, labour, and overheads permissible in order for a profit to be shown.

### Checking and Reporting on the Budget

The final seal of approval will usually be given to the budget at some form of management meeting. For this purpose it will usually be accompanied by some form of report or covering note pointing to salient features and giving summary comparisons with previous years.

A final check should be made that there have been no fundamental oversights such as inadequate allowances for goods returned, rejects, claims, obsolescent stocks, or replacements under guarantee, and that the relationship of one item to another shows a consistency in proportion (e.g. routine maintenance materials often show a fairly stable relationship to maintenance labour).

Tests should be made on the sensitivity of the budgeted results to limited changes in price, volume and costs, for one is always forecasting under varying degrees of uncertainty. Such potential effects can receive comment in the report and may be illustrated in graphic form.

The covering report may also give opportunity for up-to-the-minute comment on the validity of the budgeted invoiced sales as seen against the latest known trends if such things as stocks of goods in the pipeline between producer and end user, estimated share of the market and activities of competitors are known. Opinion may also be expressed as to whether or not the financial backing is robust enough to be able to withstand shocks. Thus in effect, the report should present an overall picture of the latest developments and indicate the direction in which the company is moving.

It should be remembered of course that in public companies, where budgets may form a background to cautious public forecasts, one may have to be conscious of the effect of such on share prices which are influenced by future prospects and which may in turn indirectly affect the ability to raise funds.

In due course actual results will be compared with budget—usually giving both period and cumulative comparisons for key figures.

## Experimental Budgets

A basic approach to budgeting has been outlined which can be elaborated or simplified according to circumstances and environment, but even before reference is made to certain more complex aspects—marginal costs, budgeting from standard costs, limiting factors and the like, it should be pointed out that in the course of compiling the finally approved budget, earlier versions may have been compiled, and the opportunity should be seized in the process (and at other times) of compiling experimental budgets illustrating the potential effects of changes in its component parts, and particularly changes in the product mix. Even rough calculations working from sales values less materials costs can often uncover hidden potentials and be extremely valuable to management in formulating longer term plans.

Ideally, short-term budgets should form stepping stones towards longer term goals.

It is well to remember that not a few otherwise able men have contrived to move remarkably quickly from point A to point C as below, but having come by this cost route have been defeated by any attempt to get to a viable point B, let alone a modified A, if selling price falls, say, to £0·200 per unit.

|  | A | Per Unit | C | Per Unit |
|---|---|---|---|---|
| Units | 50,000 | | 90,000 | |
|  | £ | £ | £ | £ |
| Income | 13,000 | 0·260 | 22,950 | 0·255 |
| Costs | 9,750 | 0·195 | 19,350 | 0·215 |
| Profit | 3,250 | | 3,600 | |

All Management Accountants will be well advised to compile a model of where the firm will stand, given movements of plus or minus 15 per cent in volume and/or price from the budget level.

3—(B.849)

Obtaining the benefits of organized budgeting entails accepting the rough with the smooth. It is not for adoption by top executives, who, whilst accepting the maxim that the most successful generals are those who are more often right than wrong, do not possess the fortitude to see on occasion, laid plain in black and white, the sometimes unpalatable fact that their endorsed expectations have emerged as being well removed from what has actually come to pass.

# PART II
# STANDARD COSTS

# CHAPTER XI

## WHY STANDARD COSTS?

STANDARD (Total) Costs were originally devised to contribute towards improving manufacturing and commercial performance and to acknowledge the following fundamental requirements and ideas.

(1) That, where practicable, the study, recording and establishment of attainable standards of performance in different sectors of a business, is in itself an important management principle in the interests of efficiency.

(2) That knowledge of deviations from such standards should be available to those who can influence improvements.

(3) That such information should be available promptly and that, therefore, it should be extracted at the point of origin.

(4) That it should be available as far as possible classified by reason.

(5) That, where practical, the favourable or unfavourable effects of such deviations or "variances" should also be expressed in monetary terms.

(6) That if standard performance could be accepted as "normal", one should operate on the "principle of exceptions" by concentrating one's reporting techniques on deviations from the "normal".

(7) That such a basis offers scope for simplification of certain recording techniques.

(8) That, apart from providing measurement of

detailed operations at processes, or of the usage of materials, the general principle might be applied in one form or another, in whole or in part, to the measurement of performance of the business as a whole and to its commercial aspects, as an aid towards affecting improvements.

(9) That, when appropriately applied to product costs, the concept of "Standards" offers (a) a sound basis for assessing desirable selling prices in relation to resources effectively required and applied in their creation, and in relation to the position as it might be viewed by competitors and potential competitors, and (b) a sound guide for the selection of such products in the product range, for which markets were worth cultivating with a view to the long-term development of the most profitable product mix in relation to the demand and prices obtainable in the open market.

(10) That, as developed for product costs, they provide a sound cost basis for the valuation of work in progress and finished stocks necessary for the measurement of achievement and the true and fair allocation of profits to appropriate time periods.

(11) That the principles could also be applied to product income and the reporting of variances from "standard" prices.

(12) That there was need for clear recognition of the concept that anything which could be referred to as "the total cost of a product" (a) could only exist under a specified set of conditions, and (b) that these conditions could only relate to the resources effectively utilized in product creation.

Thus the cost of running a factory under conditions of fluctuating volume fell into two clear parts, (i) the cost of resources effectively utilized in creating the products, and (ii) the cost of carrying under-utilized facilities (where some of the resources were not being effectively utilized to create products).

The second part is not considered part of the standard cost of the products, but is shown as an Adverse Volume Variance from the specified standard conditions. Note that Favourable Volume Variances can arise where there is an exceptionally high resource utilization.

This represented a vital new distinction, the omission of which had bedevilled the use of so-called actual job costs when any attempt was made to utilize them for measuring the effectiveness of performance. The earlier methods of actual job costs, though they served many useful purposes, had tended to fall short of what was felt to be desirable under many of the above headings, and their common method of attack on inefficiencies based on belated post-mortems after all the information has been consolidated, failed to meet many management requirements.

The flow of information under a full standard cost system is illustrated in the diagrams at the end of this chapter. (See Figs. 3 and 4, pp. 76–77.)

Information related to the past is required as a basis for estimating the future. It was recognized that the form in which information was collected must be such that it can also be used to help to serve another management need; that of being able to readily assess the effects and probable effects of change, i.e. change in the business as a whole or in its segments, change in volume, in method, in capacity, in product mix, in batch size and level of stockholding. This requires a subtle subdivision of the elements into those classes which are likely to be most susceptible to different types of change so that they can be grouped and re-grouped according to requirements. The nature of the information on what is to be regarded as a "standard" will also differ with different situations.

Standard costs have much in common with budgets,

but whilst budgeting is more concerned with an overall co-ordinated plan, standards are more concerned with internal detail.

The ideal is perhaps an operating climate in which men, skilled in their own jobs and functions, study, develop, set and try to maintain their own high standards of performance and seek to find how the performance of their machines can be improved. Occasional approaches to this may be found, but this is not only an imperfect world, it is also a highly specialized one, and one in which many different functions have to be co-ordinated.

The translation of principles into practice not unexpectedly raises problems, and the practical usefulness of the information must outweigh the cost of its collection. There will be areas where extra efforts to obtain precision will add little to the value of the information which can be obtained by careful sampling or by approximation. Efforts to set up well considered standards will be more valuable in the case of repetitive operations or processes which may continue for years, than those which have an ephemeral life. Carefully established standard product and component costs will have more significance for standardized products and components than for those which are in a state of change and modification, for which a best estimate, if obtainable, may require to be adapted as a "standard".

It must not be imagined that this is a concept which must be taken on an all or nothing basis, there may thus be standards for established products, components and processes, but not for those in the process of development; standards of materials usage for such products, but not standards for materials price; standards for labour utilization but not for wage rates, etc., dependent on the degree of fruitful corrective action which can be brought into play when there are deviations.

Provided the system is so designed that one can give the relationship (a ratio or percentage) of the variance from standard to the respective standard (standard plus variance from standard equalling actual), one may have a valid and useful hybrid system containing a mixture of elements for which standards have been established, and those for which they have not.

If one is to obtain a full appreciation of "why standard costs" one must go deeper and ask why the need for analytical costs of any sort, and for this one must look further back into the developments in management accountancy.

## The Evolution of Costing

In the early days of the industrial revolution the major items of cost were materials and manual labour, both of which could be closely identified with particular products. The increased use of power and the growth in scale of operation in turn led to the need for specialized supervisory staff and service departments. The spread of automation led to the embodiment of the work of engineers and others in the cost of machine tools and plant, taking the place formally held by direct operative labour, and a greater portion of the cost becoming less closely and directly identifiable with particular products.

In this situation, the need for detailed cost information emerged most clearly in those multi-product industries, where it was seen that the various products demanded for their production the use of a significantly different share of a firm's resources, where some passed through a different sequence of operations, demanded a different share of space, required more costly machines, or more machine time, or needed more supervision and backing up services than others.

As originally conceived, this need was related to two main problems (1) that of determining target product prices, and (2) that of providing guidance on product selection. There was dissatisfaction with the crudeness and apparent unreliability of cost estimates of complex products, seen in the light of failure of actual results to come near to expectations, and there were associated problems of stock valuation where there were multiple components and sub-assemblies in varying stages of completion and wide fluctuations in the size of stock-holdings.

It is worth while outlining the conditions where, though cost control remained of dominant interest, these other particular problems were not so acutely felt. This might apply to firms whose products were mostly of the same general type passing through the same sequence of processes or where they did not, at least no great differences were apparent in the amount of resources attached to different processes; where there was a steady flow of deliveries of small items with a relatively short production cycle coming off from the manufacturing process, and the ratio of stocks of finished goods to turnover was relatively low and not normally subject to wide fluctuations; where fixed overheads formed a relatively low proportion of total costs; where selling prices were determined centrally for the "season" after a close study of the market, and of the prices being asked by a few large, known and possibly dominant competitors, and there was a trade tradition of maintaining stable prices over relatively long periods; where firms were in the refining industries, and there was a significant element of "Joint Products"[1] extracted from

[1] With joint product industries there may not be a rational basis for splitting the common base cost of raw materials, or the common processing cost of the early stages of its separation into components, other than in proportion to the selling price obtainable, e.g. is the cost of coal to a gas works, the cost of coke or the cost of gas?

a common base; where effective management was highly centralized and ample time was available for assessing the effects of different price/order acceptance/rejection decisions.

Today it is firms where there is a significant combination of the majority of the above conditions who may find a basically marginal costing (or standard marginal costing) approach with fixed cost attachments, adequate for their requirements, and in certain cases, may be attracted to profit reporting on a marginal basis of stock valuation, where the circumstances are such that this might be accepted as "true and fair" and is unlikely to be misleading. This is discussed more fully later.

It is with industries with the characteristics of those in the former category, however, that some of the illustrations in this book are mainly concerned.

The need for analytical (total) cost information was based on the concept that in the long run, prices (related to volume) obtainable for particular products must more than cover the cost of resources necessary for their production, and that business required appropriate information if it was to move steadily towards the state where income would more than cover costs.

Costing sought to tackle on the broadest front, the classic economic problem of optimizing the utilization of resources by trying to ensure that scarce resources were allocated to achieving economic ends, i.e. to those whose consumer demand in relation to supply as indicated by price was strong.

A secondary need concerned the appropriate time at which profits should be reported in relation to "achievement" within the "tyranny of the financial year." Since this will be affected by the value placed on finished and partly finished goods carried into subsequent periods, and the value which could be attached to them, as signifying the worth of the businesss, the problem was most significant in industries where such stocks were subject to wide fluctuations. The theory generally adopted was, that products acquire costs as they pass through the factory by the application of all factors effectively applied in their production.

Standard costing emphasized this *effectively*, standard product costs thus being built up from a basis related to the "normal" use of capacity effectively employed.

## Standard Costs Related to Accounting Principles

The four corner-stones of what are regarded as generally accepted accounting principles are

(1) *Consistency of treatment* as between periods, and as to classification of items—any change in the basis on which figures are thus calculated thus call for a publicly reported explanation.

(2) *Continuity.* In placing values on items it is assumed that a business will continue unless there is definite evidence to the contrary. This introduced the concept of making provision for maintaining capital intact before distributing gains.

(3) *Conservativism.* Experience of the effects of booms and slumps has led to recognition of the dangers of what may be optimistic valuations and has led to the adoption of "cost or realizable value whichever is the less" applied to published stock valuations, a tendency to apply the practice of "historicity" and a reluctance to report profits unless they are actually realized.

(4) *Matching of costs against resultant benefits.* Costs not matched by benefits in any one financial year may thus be held in suspense and treated as an asset, with a value carried forward into subsequent years, when benefits in subsequent years are reasonably certain.

A fifth principle could be added; that of "economic practicability."

These principles must be taken together, for they modify and qualify each other, and are subject to the overriding principle that accounts should be "true and fair"—fair, and not misleading to interested parties.

Conceptually routine accounting thus operates within a stressed framework, and designers of enduring structures as modified for particular environments but built to these principles must give close attention to balancing the inherent and foreseeable stresses.

The application of the above principles has been subjected to several challenges, the most severe of which arises from general inflation. The general public may be acclimatizing themselves to think in terms of dual standards—original cost and replacement cost. Institutional bodies are, however, reluctant to accept a double standard of measurement or of stewardship, other than terms of money contracts, or of information presented in two ways. (This problem remains unsolved.)

The rather complex effects of the relationship between the volume of production and the volume of despatches, inherent in the application of the principles, has therefore led, on the one hand, to suggestions that all production going into stock should be held in stock at selling price, and on the other that it should be held at "variable" cost, thus giving reported profit trends clearly related to production levels in the one case and to despatch levels on the other.

It must be appreciated that even with a proper sense of proportion and balanced judgement, there will still be an element of approximation in reported figures. This will be most obvious when one thinks of the provision for depreciation charged before arriving at profits, or included in the cost of particular products, and in the case of plant and machinery, the carry forward balance, treated as an asset whose effective working life and number of product items served, can only be an estimate.

Standard costs appropriately applied will be found to satisfy these principles.

## Standard Marginal Costs

The term "marginal costs" is sometimes used by accountants to apply to costs which tend to vary proportionately with changes in volume, though economists have applied this term to the increase in costs which arise with the addition of one more unit of output, which, though suited to theoretical analysis, is impractical to apply, for the real incremental position is usually in a state of flux as orders move in and out. The terms "direct costs," "variable costs" and "differential costs" with slight differences in shades of meaning, are often used almost interchangeably with the term "marginal."

For everyday use, costs which tend to persist in the short run are often given the term of "fixed."

In the long run and for major changes in volume and major changes in the proportions of different products in the same total volume, all costs are in some degree variable or can be made to vary in relation to volume. At one extreme, a supplementary new factory will involve extra heat, light, rates and naturally, management, at the other, idle space can be sold or let. As certain products grow and others shrink, space allotted will be altered, additional machines added and idle machines scrapped. For a greater degree of precision and clarification one would really have to refer to costs as being variable "short term," "medium term," "long term" and "very long term." Thus with "very short term," the only costs likely to change with volume change may be raw materials used, packing materials and power costs.

For practical use, costs can, however, be sub-divided into the two loose categories of "variable" and "fixed," and in this sense it would appear that variable may be considered to apply to those which change or would be changed in close relation to volume by the end of say three months, and within say changes of volume of up to fifteen per cent from the normal starting point.

Provided this classification is not used unmodified for calculations of effects outside these limits, this sub-division can serve many useful purposes related to rapid calculations of the probable or actual effects of change.

Systems have been advocated of collecting, analysing and presenting management information primarily in marginal form with or without analysed fixed costs attachments. Under this concept the difference between the sales value of products and their variable or marginal cost is considered to provide a "marginal contribution" towards a general pool of fixed overheads, the surplus over this representing profits.

The circumstances in industry where this can be readily accepted as the one and only form of necessary product cost and income information would appear to be limited.

The concept of standards and variances from standards as outlined here would then be concentrated on the variable costs. Fixed costs would be watched by comparison with budgets.

The circumstances where modified versions of this as a basic approach may be applicable have already been indicated.

It may also be possible to apply some of the mechanics of information collection without accepting the principles, by absorbing the fixed costs on a supporting statistical basis without building them into all the individual transferred details of the recording system.

In out-and-out extreme form, a theory is put forward that certain costs are "period" or "stand-by" costs, and should not enter into the cost value of inventories carried forward into subsequent periods. This tends to conflict with some of the principles outlined earlier, except where the effects are not material.

The effect of applying this, where such periods costs form a significant portion of the total, is that where the physical volume of finished stocks and work in progress are rising, reported profits in the period will be less than those which would be reported under more generally accepted accounting principles, and that the converse will occur where they are falling.

Similarly, where such period costs form a significant portion of costs, the value placed on stocks may be regarded as ultra-conservative.

The remoteness of some costs from the current individual products has sometimes been used in support of the marginal approach.

These lie mainly in the area of the "costs of continuity" and are in the nature of an insurance that customers will have made available to them their next year's requirements, and suppliers their next year's outlets.

In theory, possibly, all such costs should be capitalized each year and the amortization selectively charged in the following year(s) to the products which have matured; but much the same effect will generally be achieved in practice, by thinking, as it were, of such current costs as being back-dated into preceding years. Though design work on current products can be made a direct charge, there will always be a quota of design and research work on successors, personnel will be in training, and the Chairman may be developing contacts for next year's supplies, next year's finance, and working on the requirements for next year's organization.

Unless steps are undertaken over the years to collect adequate information as to the product groups which can rationally be viewed as requiring and benefiting from such activities, in order to establish a standard quota of such resources for standard cost purposes, there can rightly be a charge of arbitrary allocation rather than an acceptance of this as a reasonable standard approximation.

The valuable uses of variable costs, as such, for assessing the probable effects of short-term changes must not, however, be confused with a system of financial profit reporting geared to marginal costs.

## Product Costs and Product Prices

Although the concept of standard total cost as originally conceived was primarily concerned with providing management with a better technique for monitoring factory performance, when considered in relation to marginal costs, the focal point where differences have arisen has been the relationship between product costs and product prices, and the usefulness or necessity of information in certain forms, particularly in the type of industries with which we are mainly concerned.

In the long run, it can be agreed that prices are determined by the laws of supply and demand. In a perfect market, costs only affect price by their effect on supply, as a particular range of manufactured goods will usually be withdrawn when the market price falls below out-of-pocket costs, the supply having been contracted in favour of other goods as it approaches this stage and not being restored until scarcity of supply in relation to demand once again raises prices.

In the short run, in imperfect markets, where the prices of competitors or the potential prices competitors may be prepared to quote are imperfectly known, notions of cost by a firm and by its competitors can in practice have quite a direct bearing on price.

Costs, as it were, form a base line on top of which price structure is erected.

Standard total product costs have the virtue of forming a *normal* base line. Out of pocket marginal product costs may be regarded as a short-term base line in extremis. (Refinements of this are discussed later.)

In this context, the main virtue of "Standard Total Product Costs" based on normal use of capacity in multi-product industries, where snap decisions are often called for, probably lies in the fact that it provides the best possible first approximation to the probable normal base line as seen by one's competitors operating around the same scale with a different product mix, or even as single product producers. Each will recognize a mutual reluctance to let prices fall below this base in conditions of profitable demand. This may in fact in some cases be virtually the only available point of reference for sales staff in competitive tendering.

Built up from this base will be a complex price tier acknowledging a price/volume/available capacity relationship, and aimed at setting target prices capable of giving satisfactory return on capital employed.

In efficiently run companies, it is clearly recognized that there is no question of a flat rate uplift from standard total product costs in arriving at target price, but that prices bear relation to demand, and to demand of one's own products *vis-à-vis* that of competitors. Products will also carry an imputed worth not related to product cost and not entirely related to the product itself, but acquired by virtue of a firm's reputation for supplying reliable products in the past, or for giving good service, or from tangible or intangible ideas associated with the product, such as its appearance of complexity or style, or its exclusiveness or prestige value as conveyed by advertising.

Unfortunately many holding quite responsible positions, still translate any reference to the cost of the product as the cost in all circumstances, and such qualifying adjectives as marginal, total or standard are lost sight of as representing unimportant academic refinements.

One may also meet up with legitimate methods of pricing according to "what the traffic will bear," paralleled with allocations of expenditure on the same basis. Though it may not be so labelled, one is then talking of pricing not costing, and one may be talking of camouflage, not of arriving at the most economic utilization of resources.

From the experience of many, it would seem to be the natural instinct for the majority of persons directly or indirectly in contact with the movement of goods to think firstly of volume and secondly of price. Where there are no established price lists and where, by the nature of the industry, authority for price determination has to be delegated, so that snap decisions have to be quickly made by individual salesmen as to the acceptance or rejection of orders at proffered prices, and even when this condition exists at the centre, there is a strong body of opinion that where cost information has to be widely given to supply a base line, standard costs rather than marginal costs are best suited for normal purposes.

Ideally all efficiently run companies will have the total situation and all emerging trends under constant supervision and control. In the absence of this ideal situation however, problems are encountered, an example of which is as follows. Work is initially accepted at a cut price for some product which provides some marginal contribution to fill up a temporarily under-utilized capacity, thus giving profit improvement in the first stage. Repeat orders at this price follow the apparent initial success, and the relative ease of obtaining orders at this price progressively erode those at the former price for this product. Efforts to sell other products may be neglected because of the relative ease of maintaining volume at the cut price, and some of the capacity best suited for other products may be used less effectively to produce added volume of the cut price one. Other profitable products may be progressively displaced and contacts with their markets lost. A decline in profit may start to emerge even though capacity is now fully employed. Even greater volume may be suggested as the cure, until it is discovered that the income from the added volume will not cover the total costs of plant, space and supervision expansion now suggested. In offering sprats to catch mackerel one can readily become a popular purveyor of sprats!

Management is faced with the perennial tasks of ensuring that current actions do not prejudice the attainment of potential long-term gains, and of trying at the same time to obtain the best short-term advantages in current conditions.

In this context in multi-product factories, total standard product costs aim to give guidance on the first half of this problem, controlled marginal product costs can also be relevant to the second half.

Standard total product costs (with marginal cost attachments), in relation to the price/volume problem thus aim firstly to assess the cost of producing individual products under the specified standard conditions, and secondly and equally, to provide a "first shot" approximate indication of what a product would cost if one worked or priced oneself into a market to reach a point where that product, probably at the expense of other products, comes to form a much greater or major portion of the total product output. When used for the latter purpose they thus assume that in the long run, product for product, all attributed product costs tend to be variable and that resource requirements shift with changes in product proportions.

In this longer term context, there is also an assumption that there is freedom to change the proportions of the product mix within the total scale of production, and in this sense, costs may be regarded as unrestricted product costs. In the short run, this freedom to change can be temporarily curtailed because of processing and other restrictions which may have to be removed to clear bottlenecks before the pattern can be economically re-balanced.

The incidence of such restrictions (which are dealt with later) will also apply to the use of marginal costs in this context.

## Compromises

Ideally, cost, income and capital data are required in different groupings for different purposes, not all of which are entirely compatible or required concurrently. As far as possible, one should attempt to build up the various sub-analyses at the time of compiling the budgets or standards, rather than attempt to drag them through the entire accounting systems with every routine collection of data. Most accountants have felt obliged to arrive at compromise solutions, bearing in mind frequency of demand, the time available for collation and interpretation by the users and naturally, the training and ability of the latter.

The tendency has been towards taking a long-term view, while presuming a continuation of the current pattern of activity. One may find benefits from having a flexible general purpose tool, rather than a highly geared but rigid special purpose one, and short cuts are permissible when their implications are fully realized.

It will be seen that the accountant has plenty of scope for his ingenuity in catering for these requirements.

## Standard Costing Methods

Where little or nothing exists in the way of standards of reference, the prompt pinpointing of variations in performance by reason or source becomes almost impossible.

A standard costing system endeavours to remedy this situation, and in so doing its object is to ensure that steps will be taken to eliminate the faults and wastes, and increase efficiency in performance.

It is much more important to know what a product should cost and the excess over this cost, than what it has cost.

Under a standard costing system, the cost of a particular order (if required) will appear as the cost of that order under normal operating conditions (variations in cost due to variations in volume of output being shown elsewhere) allowing for production difficulties intrinsic to that order, but excluding abnormal costs (scrap, tool troubles, etc.) due to general production difficulties. (These are accumulated separately and written off in the Profit and Loss Account or shown as excess costs of particular departments or product groups.)

In other cases, it may be more appropriate to obtain the standard cost of operating a particular process, and to produce regular statements of the variations between standard and actual costs of carrying out that process or operation. (Each individual job being valued at standard cost only.)

Standards may be introduced initially for one process only or for one product group, or for some component, leaving other products or processes to be dealt with later.

When cost control is mentioned, it is control of costs per unit of output that is vital, and because increased volume will generally reduce unit costs through the wider spread of overheads (increased productivity from the established facilities) cost control will be effected by maximizing output and minimizing outlay.

Similarly, while the budgeting aspect of budgetary control may be considered in terms of forecasting and planning, the control aspect must be looked on as operating at two points, control by programming and sanctioning, and control by checking achievement.

## Cost Accounting Data Flow

The following figures show the flow of data between accounts within a standard costing system.

Figure 4 gives a quantified variant of Fig. 3. In Fig. 3 transaction data originates in the Control Account on the right-hand side and after moving between accounts ends up in the Trading Account or in the closing stocks.

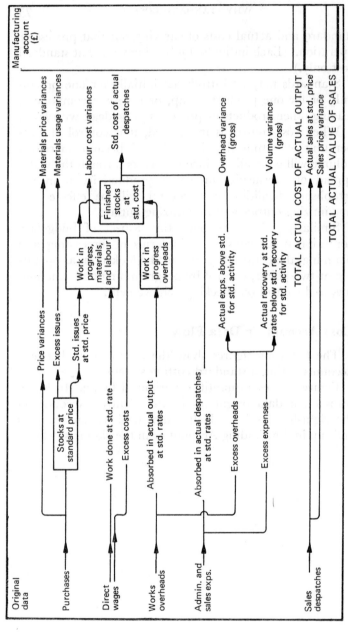

Fig. 3. Chart of one form of Standard Costing Procedure

| Item | Trading Account (Costs) | Raw Material Stocks | Work in Process | Finished Stocks | Process I | Process II | Admin. Expenses | Control Account | Control Account narrative |
|---|---|---|---|---|---|---|---|---|---|
| Opening Stocks | | +500 | +200 | +300 | | | | +1,000 | Opening Stocks |
| Sales Product A / Sales Product B | 2,000 / 900  −2,900 | | | | | | | −2,900 | Invoiced Sales |
| Material Price Variance | +50 | +1,950 | | | | | | +2,000 | Materials Purchased |
| Materials Usage Variance | +50 | −1,300 | +1,250 | | | | | | (Materials Issued) |
| Wages Rate Variance | +25 | | | | | | | +400 | Wages Earned |
| Labour Efficiency Variance | +45 | | +330 | | +225 | +150 | | | (Absorbed by Production) |
| Unabsorbed Overheads | +30 | | +270 | | +210 | +90 | | +300 | Works Expenses and Depreciation (Absorbed by Production) |
| Variances from Standard Cost | +200 | | −2,000 | +2,000 | −200 −25 +210 −190 −20 | −130 −20 +90 −80 −10 | | | (Work Completed) |
| Office Administration Expenses | | | | | | | +100 | +100 | Office Administration Expenses |
| Standard Cost of Sales A | +1,880  +1,300 | | | −1,260 | | | −40 | | |
| Standard Cost of Sales B | +580 | | | −540 | | | −40 | | |
| Works Profit | −820 | | | | | | | | |
| Unabsorbed Administration Expenses | +20 | | | | | | −20 | | |
| Net Profit / Net Profit Transferred | −800 / +800 | +1,150 | +50 | +500 | | | | +800  1,700 | Closing Stocks |

FIG. 4. Matrix of Cost Accounts

Debits + Credits —

# CHAPTER XII

# NORMAL COSTS AND NORMAL LEVEL OF OUTPUT

STANDARD costs might be set up on a basis of (a) best attainable performance, (b) ideal—no allowances for inefficiency, (c) expected actual for the immediate future, or (d) estimated "normal."

Method (d) is advocated for general purposes because it provides the most practically useful figures. Methods (a) and (b) can of necessity only be used as yardsticks against which performance may be measured. Sometimes, however, it may best suit management's purposes to base one or more of the various cost elements on basis (a) or (b). Method (c) has the defects of the orthodox cost system.

It is now necessary to decide what is "normal."

## Normal Level of Output

The normal level of output will presumably be the average level of a series of periods, good, normal, and bad, which it is hoped will be attained. In the case of an established factory past experience should supply some guide, after making allowances for any changes in the reigning conditions, present market prospects, and developed plant capabilities. Where the factory is newly established the standard will be based on the output which it is estimated will be obtained when the factory has got into full production.

How far ahead should one look in building up standard costs? It is suggested that from one to three years would form a suitable basis for consideration.

In determining this standard output much more weight

will be given to the question of normal factory capacity than is done in preparing the short-term budget. Most efficient and economical output will, of course, be obtained when the factory is working as closely as possible to normal capacity, i.e. the capacity it was intended for. Sales efforts will be continuously directed towards this end, though naturally production capacity is also being continually adjusted to meet sales demand.

The normal level must be an attainable level in a normal year, and the following factors must not be forgotten in deciding it.

(a) The normal operating level for the whole factory will usually be below the sum of the production levels for each individual department. Production capacity must be modified in the light of the producing and consuming capacities of previous and subsequent processes and departments (unless there is an external market for the products of this particular department).

(b) Maximum production capacity must be modified to allow for normal interruption and disturbances of production, breakdowns, and mishaps.

(c) Productive capacity must be modified in the light of capacity to sell. In this mechanized age, it is recognized that in most industries maximum productive capacity is considerably above normal selling capacity.

The reader is here referred to the chapters on the preparation of the Sales and Production Budgets. The procedure adopted in drawing up the budget for standard costs will follow almost similar lines as for the ordinary budgets. It is simply a long-term budget.

In the case where a business is working steadily at what is considered normal capacity, then the budget and the standard cost figures may coincide, but it will usually be found that some abnormal figures may be included in the budget forecast, e.g. special repairs, which will require to be eliminated before the budget can be said to represent "standard."

It is suggested that standard costs (for overhead absorption purposes) might be based on a broad three-year forecast of output and costs. This will be roughly sub-divided into yearly figures. The budgets themselves should be drawn up, say, every three months and sub-divided into budgeted figures for each month. Monthly revisions of budgets may be required in certain circumstances.

Standard costs should normally be adjusted, say, once a year in the light of current events and tendencies.

Under the proposed system costs are to be absorbed at the standard rate, and in the properly analysed Profit and Loss Account over- or under-absorbed costs will represent the profit or loss due to variations from "normal" or "standard."

If the "normal" operating level is set too high—e.g. near maximum productive capacity—it will result in a heavy loss on unabsorbed costs, normally appearing in the accounts, which will be of no practical value. The standard cost of individual orders in such a case would also be misleading. The reverse would be the case where the standard was set too low. (It may, however, be advisable to keep memorandum figures of cost rates at maximum production capacity in order to be able to judge the advisability of accepting orders or fillers in sufficient quantity to cut losses, and also for the purpose of showing the cost of excess capacity.)

Common sense is the real criterion by which any standards should be judged, and in setting up standards for any factory the question must be regarded from every possible angle and then the common-sense point of view adopted. No rigid rule can be laid down as to what is the best basis, and the particular circumstances of each individual business must be given full weight.

## Normal Costs

Having determined the standard output, it will be necessary to proceed to draw up relative costs. The procedure will follow practically the same lines as for drawing up the short-term Production Budget (see Chapter IV). At the standard or normal level of output, however, a certain standard or normal profit margin is to be expected. When setting up the standard costs this normal margin of profit should be planned for.

The method adopted may be to build up the costs necessary to give the required output, and see what margin of profit is left, then to find out if certain costs can be modified and adjusted to provide the required margin of profit; or the problem may be tackled from the other end, and the desired margin of profit be deducted from the sales value to give the total cost. This total cost will then be analysed into its components and these investigated to determine whether they can be attained and the required margin of profit ensured.

The margin of profit should not be an ideally optimistic figure, but one capable of actual achievement under normal conditions.

In determining what should be the future standard or normal margin of profit, much the same considerations apply as in determining future sales. What are the trade prospects? Is the market an expanding or a contracting one? Is competition severe? Are substitutes available? What are the normal profits in the trade? What is the condition of the plant and equipment, and how does it compare with that of competitors? What is the ratio of profit to capital employed? How does quality compare with that of competitors?

These standard or normal costs will be made out for the business as a whole and for departments. They need not be set out in anything like the detail that is shown in the short-term budget, however, as naturally anything like the precise make-up of the costs cannot be forecast so far ahead.

For the purpose of establishing standard overhead-cost recovery rates, it will be the normal cost of overheads at the standard output which will be most important.

Standard overhead will be analysed or allocated to departments and production centres in accordance with the usual cost accounting principles, for the purpose of setting up of standard cost rates. This is one of the most important principles in the standard cost system, namely, that *the overhead recovery rates are based on the standard (or normal) level of production* (see Appendix I).

In all cases where standard costing is to be employed it will be necessary to draw up a schedule showing the relative proportion of the various costs at the standard level of output.

## Safeguarding Profit Margins under Standard Cost System

Where standard costs are used, the percentage of unabsorbed costs to total costs should always be calculated, and should be made known to all persons responsible for estimating, Sales Managers, etc. Normally profit margins should be obtained (and must be obtained in the

| STANDARD AND ACTUAL PROFIT MARGIN | £ |
|---|---|
| Selling price . . . . . . . | 60 |
| Standard cost . . . . . . . | 50 |
| Current percentage unabsorbed cost (10 per cent) . | 5 |
| Actual cost . . . . . . . | £55 |
| Actual profit . . . . . . . | £5 |
| Standard profit . . . . . . . | £10 |

long run (if one is to stay in business) which will more than cover any such adverse variances (see table, p. 82).

Sometimes it may be sufficient if those responsible for pricing realize that part of the difference between standard cost and selling price will not be realized because of adverse variances.

Usually it will be worth while to establish standard or target selling prices, or alternatively standard "mark ups" on the various elements of cost (perhaps differing for different product types), from which deviations in actual prices can be measured. Such prices may be set in various ways, e.g. prices set by the "price leading" firm in the trade, trade association recommended minimum prices, targets carefully related to costs and rates of production, or based on market research.

Apart from recording deviations from such normal or target selling prices in the form of Sales Price Variances (as part of the analytical accounting system explaining profit changes after deliveries are made) such variances from target price can (a) be useful in helping to decide whether or not certain orders should be accepted, (b) form part of the reporting system on orders received, and (c) become the key factor in arriving at revised short-term profit forecasts based on orders received or on hand, when allied with current levels of production.

### Conclusion

To sum up then, the standard budget will be drafted as far as possible to give practical figures showing how production can be most efficiently and economically carried out at the standard level of output. Moreover, a condition should be aimed at where it will be possible to set a normal standard level of output at which the largest margin of profit can be maintained with the available capital and production facilities. Except in the cases where performances better than standard can be recorded, every effort will be made to bring actual results more into line with standard, and in this process Sales and Production Departments will strive to render it practicable to draw up *attainable* short-term budgets which will steadily approach more and more towards the desired standard, whilst an attempt should be made to bring standards nearer to ideal.

CHAPTER XIII

# INTERNAL STANDARDS

PROCEEDING from consideration of the long-term or
standard budget, we come to the question of internal
standards, and by this we mean detailed standards of
operating efficiency within the factory, applying to
particular processes, jobs, or operations.

Where a system of standard costing is most fully
developed, detailed standards will be set up for material
usage, quality, and price, for labour rates and operating
efficiency, and for the incidence of overhead.

The fullest advantage of detailed standards can be
taken in factories working on a mass-production basis,
where fixed predetermined selling prices are the rule.

In the case of a firm making a wide range of products
to customers' special requirements, and where the price
can be adjusted in each individual case, the advantages
of fixing detailed standards for material and labour are
not so marked, but a standard overhead rate is advisable.
But even where products are widely varied, processes and
operations are often relatively standard, and it is hoped
to demonstrate how standard costing methods can be
advantageously applied in these cases also.

A general picture of the variations between standard
and actual costs will, of course, be shown on comparing
the actual with the budgeted figures, and in certain cases
(especially in process costing) if the budget is sufficiently
detailed it partakes of the nature of an internal standard.
Where, however, a closer analysis and investigation of
variation are required, it is necessary to utilize a proper
standard cost system.

Standards of efficiency will be set up in detail for

material and labour. Thereafter the figures which matter will be the variations from standard, and a routine must be devised whereby it is possible to show the degree to which standard has been attained, and to analyse and clearly state the variations from standard.

## The Planning Department

The adoption of internal standards of efficiency pre-supposes the existence of some person or body of persons capable of authoritatively setting up such standards. In an up-to-date factory this will devolve on the Planning Department, by whatever name it is actually called.

As stated, such standards may be set for materials usage, price, or quality, or for production times and rates. This may involve the issuing of standard schedules of materials to be used on particular jobs or processes, and the compiling of lists of standard material prices. Standard times will be set for particular operations and standard allowances determined for waste, scrap, and other excess costs. The setting of standard operating times is the function of what, in the engineering trade, is called the Ratefixing Department, and the issuing of standard material schedules might fall to the Drawing Office.

These two may be considered as subdivisions of the planning function. Accordingly it is the Planning Department which will issue instructions as to how work is to be carried out, and the sequence of operations, and set up standards for performance.

Where planning is not fully developed standard costs may be initiated for certain regular lines by working from previously recorded actual costs; averages for material and labour can be worked out excluding abnormal items, and overheads can be adjusted to the standard rate. Carefully compiled estimates can also be used as standards.

## Standard Cost Cards

Where operations and products are sufficiently standardized, standard cost cards are usually drawn up for each product, assembly, or operation. These, as we have seen, may be in the form of a standard bill of material together with a standard labour card showing standard or allowed times for performing each operation. A summary standard cost card may be made up therefrom, giving standard cost of material, standard labour time extended at standard rates, together with standard rate of overhead, giving the total standard cost of the job.

It may take the form of a schedule. Provision should preferably be made for showing an approximate split of costs between their "fixed" and "variable" elements (required for purposes of rapid assessment of the effects of changes in production pattern).

Care must be taken to see that these cards are kept continually up to date in the light of new methods, materials, and processes. Provision of extra columns for recording alterations may be made, and in some cases a periodic revision of all standards may be carried out. The revision of operation standards may be the direct responsibility of the Production Control or Planning Department, but the Cost Accountant is well advised to keep a check on this matter. He may have a difficult enough task in providing adequate explanation of variations from standard without having the additional liability of suffering from out-of-date standards.

Standard Assembly Schedules with standard prices may also be prepared and used as stores requisitions or a complete set of pre-prepared requisitions covering each job may be issued to the shops.

Other matters which require careful watching are the routines for recording waste, scrap, extra or unplanned operations, etc. Unless a tight grip is kept on these, works sources of cost information may become very unreliable.

## Estimating, Planning, Work Study, and Costing

If the most effective use is to be made of the cost figures it is essential that the closest possible co-operation exists between the Estimating, Planning, Work Study (or Ratefixing) and Costing Departments. Where a firm is on mass production at a fixed price, of course, the question of estimating will assume smaller proportions.

The Planning Department must endeavour to plan for the job to be done within the estimated cost, and the Cost Department supplies figures which both guide and check the Estimating and the Planning Department's work.

As only a proportion of estimates submitted are likely to become definite orders, estimates must be approximate only for economical working of that department. Various "short-cut" methods may be adopted in preparing the estimates, especially where there is considerable previous experience of similar work or where market prices largely govern possible profit margins.

When an estimate becomes an order, the Planning Department will plan the work in detail. Steps should be taken to see that the detailed plan, which becomes the standard cost, is kept within, or falls below, the estimated cost. A regular routine of notifying the Estimating Department of faulty estimating should be set up.

The Cost Department supplies figures showing variations between planned (or standard) and actual costs. Here again a regular routine should be devised for notifying both the Estimating and the Planning Department of, at least, exceptional variations between actual and planned estimated costs. Where orders are estimated for, variations in cost may be recorded for each individual order; on the other hand, where production is being carried out to a predetermined plan, variations may only be recorded by operation or process and notification given to the Planning Department accordingly.

It will be best if the forms used by the Estimating Department, the Planning Department, and the Cost Department are so drawn up that direct comparison of the principal cost elements can be made in each case, and in certain circumstances it may even be possible to utilize a set of multiple carbon-copy forms for this purpose.

Job Cards and Route Cards issued from the Planning Department should have standard or allowed times or standard prices inserted before issue.

From the actual cost figures, the Estimating and the Planning Departments must accumulate that knowledge which will enable them to draw up future estimates and future plans which will fall into line with attainable actual costs.

The Planning Department in its widest sense may be taken to include the Ratefixing Department, the Drawing Office, the Buying Office, the Stores, and even the works layout, or its scope may be limited to determining operation sequences and times. Where highly organized central planning is adopted, however, the department should have the highest authority and standing, and be staffed with the best brains in the firm. If its instructions can ever be regarded with ridicule or scorn, its whole purpose is largely defeated.

Such a Planning Department will set up standards of efficiency for all productive activities and lay the foundation for all standard costs.

Once reliable planned or standard costs have been set up it may be possible to reduce the compiling of cost information merely to a record of total variations from the planned costs. The planned or standard cost sheet for each job then becomes the only job cost record, variations being recorded by reasons and class only.

## MATERIAL STANDARDS

On the materials side, standards may be set for (1) the quality or price of material to be used, and (2) the quantity of material to be used for a particular process, job, or operation.

### Purchased Material Price Standards (Direct Materials)

Price standards may be desired for the purpose of (a) checking and guiding the Buying Department's activities, or of determining the effect of price variation of the different classes of material on costs and production; (b) checking the difference between standard, or estimated, and actual prices in individual jobs.

In case (a) the usual method of procedure will be to prepare a complete schedule or set of index cards for all types and sizes of purchased materials and fix standard prices. Invoices received are then extended in the Purchases Day Book, or its equivalent, at standard and at actual prices. (It may not be necessary to extend every invoice to standard, as it may be possible to sort and total a series of invoices by quantity or weight, and only have one extension at standard. Or where materials are contracted for in bulk, contract price may be standard.) The fact of having a standard price is also, of course, a most effective check on the invoice price.

The difference between standard and actual will be debited in total from the Day Book to a Materials Price Variance Account (if possible by Material Classes). Stocks, Job Costs and Work in Progress Accounts will then normally be carried at standard.

Alternatively, Goods Received Notes can be priced at standard from prices noted on the Stock Record Cards. The quantities would be checked with the Invoices. The difference between Goods Inwards Sheets priced at standard and Invoices at actual, would be posted by group totals to Variance Account.

This procedure is relatively simple when there are comparatively few varieties of materials purchased, e.g. manufacture of dry batteries or bicycles.

In other cases it may be necessary to work on composite figures, non-standard material being dealt with at actual cost throughout.

Materials should be classified into groups having similar characteristics so that it is possible to state the ratio of actual to standard price for each group.

Where there are standard prices the time spent in pricing stores issues will be greatly reduced, for the need to calculate latest average prices is entirely eliminated.

The effect is also, that, if stock record cards maintained by the stores are duplicated by Stores Ledger Cards kept (in value) by the accounting section, the latter cards and the associated volume of work can be eliminated. Requisitions will be priced from the standard price appearing on the stock record cards or from the standard costs cards or price schedule. The financial or cost accounts for stores should then be maintained by total control accounts only divided by stores, e.g. Castings Store, Raw Materials Store, Finished Parts Store, and perhaps sub-divided by material classes. A periodic cross check of the control totals will be made by listing the stores record card balances and extending at standard prices. A perpetual inventory check, under the auspices of the accounting staff, should also be carried out, confined not only to the audit of the stores record card balances with the physical stock, but covering also the general accuracy and treatment of all stores documents.[1]

In case (b), the procedure will, of necessity, be different. The value of materials purchased in this case may be kept at actual only, or as for (a).

Standard schedules of materials for each job will be made out and extended at standard price. When the parts are actually requisitioned, the requisition slip, after being checked with the standard list for quantity, will be extended at actual price, and the total of these requisitions listed to give the variation between standard and actual price for a particular job. (Alternative methods are to price the requisition at standard and actual, or to enter the actual value beside the standard on the standard materials list.)

The cumulative effect of price variations should be shown up in total for each product group.

Materials price variations may be further analysed by cause, e.g. (a) Change in market price, (b) Increase in quantity purchased, (c) Emergency purchase in smaller quantity, (d) Supplies not available from contract or at agreed price, etc.

Indirect materials may be dealt with at actual prices.

## Material Quantity Standards

It will be desirable to set up standards for materials usage for either (a) departments or processes as a whole, and/or for (b) individual jobs or operations.

Requirement (a) may be capable of being met within the budgetary control system, depending on the type of production, or it may be possible to set up technical standards for the actual level of output, based on experience or chemical formula, and to evaluate the cost of variations therefrom. Or, again, the only record taken

---

[1] In some cases it may be more suitable to hold raw materials stocks at actual cost and to extract the variation between standard and actual at the time they are issued to work in progress (see Example, Chapter XVI).

may be that relating to all waste, scrap, replacements, and other excess costs. Standards may, however, include a percentage allowance for normal wastage.

Where details of variations from standard are required for each job or operation, recourse will have to be had, again, to the issue of detailed standard material lists for each job. All quantities required over and above standard will be specially recorded (less allowances for any returns). In this case all totals for materials usage variance should be collected for each product group.

In certain trades it may possibly be considered that the information available by separating price variations from quantity variations cannot be put to any profitable use. When interested parties arrive at a decision that this is so, the material variation figure may be combined (as it will be when comparing budget and actual). A combined material variation figure may be obtained by similar methods to those referred to.

Stock depreciation or write-down should be clearly shown as a separate item on the Profit and Loss Account.

## Substitution of Material

Where a substantial variation from standard may arise from the substitution of other materials than those planned, it may be advisable to show a special variation account.

This information may be recorded by using special "Substitution Materials Requisitions," which will show the cost of standard materials at standard rates and the value of the substituted material at its standard rate. The difference in cost will be debited to Materials Substituted Variance Account.

## LABOUR STANDARDS

Labour standards may be set for (1) grade of labour to be used, i.e. wages rates; (2) the standard time for each process, job, or operation; and (3) the operations to be performed.

## Standard Wages Rates

The effect of wages rates may be desired either (*a*) in totals for departments or product groups, or (*b*) for individual jobs or operations.

In case (*a*) this may often be simply obtained, by taking the actual time extended at actual rates by departments as per the pay-roll, and then extending the actual time at the standard rate. The difference will give the labour rate variation by departments. It may be possible to sort the workmen's time cards into product groups and obtain a similar calculation.

If such variations are required for individual jobs as in case (*b*), it will be necessary to stipulate on the standard cost card the grade of labour to be employed and the rate. If any other than a standard rated man is employed, it will be necessary to extend his time at standard and actual rate and tabulate the difference in cost (the same applies to machine rates). A list of standard rates for each operation should be made up.

## Standard Operation Times

In all cases where premium bonus wage payment or piecework payment systems are in operation it may be said that there is some form of labour time standards, though they may not be recognized as such, or may not form a fundamental part of the cost system. Time standards may, of course, be in operation too, even where payment is on a salary basis. In the engineering industry there is a highly developed ratefixing system.

Taking for the present these labour time standards to apply to set standard operating times, the method will usually be for the Ratefixing Department to study the operation to be performed, employing where possible analytical work study techniques.

If the operation has been performed in the past, the ratefixer will be able to refer to the previously recorded time. Where there is no need to separate the wage rate element the labour variance can be obtained by setting the actual payment made against the standard or allowed time extended by a computed standard rate (set to give nil variance at standard efficiency).

The allowed time will be recorded on the standard cost card or entered on the workman's operation ticket, and against this his actual time for the operation will be booked.

It should be remembered that under a premium bonus system "standard time" should in theory represent the time a workman of average ability, working at normal speed, should take to do the job. "Allowed time" is the time set which should enable an operator of average ability to earn a certain percentage bonus, above time rates, excluding National Bonus, and is peculiar to British Engineering Wage Agreements (i.e. bonus is calculated on the base rate). A statistical measure of efficiency for a man or department can usually be made by calculating the percentage of bonus paid.

The labour efficiency variance for individual jobs, or for departments or products, can then be calculated by taking the difference between the total actual time, extended at standard rate, and the total standard time extended at standard rate.

If the allowed times are set to enable a workman of average ability to earn an abnormally high bonus for policy reasons, then the allowed time will require to be reduced by the abnormal bonus margin before the extension is made. Alternatively, the allowed time may be used, the standard rate being appropriately adjusted.

(See Appendix III.) The calculation may not be as simple as this; it depends on the bonus scheme employed, and in some cases it may even be necessary to take simply an average figure.

Allowance will also require to be made for cases where the time taken has exceeded the time allowed.

One basis for this calculation will be that in the case of a saving over standard, the increase in the labour rate per hour for the time saved will be set off against the saving in overhead at the overhead rate per hour for the time saved. Where time taken exceeds standard there is a loss in overheads for such time, at the overhead rate per hour, less any reduction in the labour rate.

This variation between standard and actual times should not normally be charged against individual orders, as it will usually be purely fortuitous, depending on the particular man chosen to do the job, though it may be possible and desirable to analyse it under major product groups. It is probably best written off direct to the standard Profit and Loss Account or shown as an overhead of the department concerned.

In general, the actual cost of doing a job or operation will be calculated on the workman's job card. Alongside this will be inserted the standard price for the job. The difference between standard and actual can be tabulated and transferred in total or by department to Labour Variance Account. Alternatively, it may be found possible to price job cards at standard price only and transfer the difference between that section of the payroll for direct labour, and such job costs for the week at standard, to Variance Account. This latter method will, however, render detailed analysis difficult.

The standard rate for calculating the variation may be for labour only, or it may be by separate or inclusive rates for labour and overhead. One may apply a single rate for a whole department, or separate calculations may be required for sub-divided groups of men or machines.

Abstracts of these tabulations of workmen's bonus earnings should be available for foremen or superintendents in order that they may watch individual efficiencies, and as far as possible explanations should be found for unsatisfactory conditions.

## Costing by Standard Hours (Allowed Times)

When work is produced on piecework, the total of piecework prices paid is a primary measure of output, and overheads may be recovered as a percentage thereon. Overheads (and labour) may, however, be recovered at separate specific standard rates per unit produced at each process particularly where output is fairly homogeneous. (Where operatives are paid day rates some form of standard pricing of output or of firstly applying standard hourly values thereto must be found if variances between actual and recovered costs are to be established.)

Where allowed or standard times are set, the total of *allowed or standard hours for (good) work completed, in each department, in effect becomes the primary measure of activity and output.* When standard overhead rates are then applied to these standard hours produced, recoveries on actual activity (standard hours produced) at standard rates can be compared with such recoveries at the calculated standard activity to produce a volume variance. In some industries recorded machine running hours for good work (at standardized speeds) may be suited to overhead recovery, used in turn as activity measure derived from "Standard Machine Hours Produced."

## Composite Recovery Rates

In certain circumstances it may be possible to employ

a composite recovery rate for a whole series of operations
on different machines. This will be possible only where
the relative proportion of time on each of the machines
in the series remains almost constant for the particular
type of job. The use of such a composite rate may
considerably simplify costing and estimating calculations,
but it must be treated with extreme care and regularly
checked to ensure that there has been no change in
conditions. Any idle or excess times will be calculated
at the individual machine rates, and not at the
composite rate.

**Piecework**

Under a piecework system the method will require to
be modified. A piecework rate sets up a standard labour
cost per unit of output. The labour cost per unit of
output remains the same, no matter what is the speed of
production, but the overhead cost (which may amount
to even more than the direct labour cost) per unit of output will vary according to the number of units produced.
The total cost per unit can remain stable only if the rate
of production on which the piecework prices were
originally set can be maintained (and the overhead also
remains steady). For the effective control of piecework,
therefore, some constant check must be kept on the rate
of production.

Where persons are performing the same piecework
operation continuously week after week, a sufficiently
effective check can be made by comparing their actual
earnings with the standard, and totals for departments
may be similarly obtained.

For example, a piecework price of £0.20 per unit is set
on the basis that a normally efficient worker can produce
50 units per week. The direct comparison between
standard and actual labour cost for a department or group

producing such units is provided by comparing the actual earnings with a standard set at the rate of £20 per person. Variations in number produced on rate of production can be deduced directly from the pay-roll.

Even where the piecework produced comprises some variety of different units, a rough comparison can still be made between standard and actual labour cost by a similar comparison.

Where production, however, though still on a piecework basis, is much more complex, and a workman's earnings are made up of piecework prices for a wide variety of units, along with perhaps some time on a weekly rate basis, it will usually be found necessary to record the workman's time in detail, giving number in each particular batch of units completed, together with the time taken for that batch.

The standard time per unit on which the piecework rate is based must be stated, and an extension made for standard and actual cost, i.e. the piecework system is best on a "time" basis if a thoroughly satisfactory analysis of detailed variations from standard is to be found.

## EXCESS COSTS

### Supplementary Time

Another cause of variation from standard allowed operating times may be what we might call supplementary times. These will arise because of the necessity, under a premium bonus scheme, of allowing a man a reasonable time on which to earn bonus on each operation. Sometimes, owing to external circumstances, such as extra-hard material, over which he has no control, the standard allowed time may be insufficient for that particular job, and it may be necessary to make a temporary allowance over and above the standard time to cover such abnormal circumstances.

This time can be entered on a special card, marked for cause if necessary, and analysed by reasons, in order that steps may be taken to minimize such causes.

An example of analysis is given in Fig. 7 on page 122.

### Rectification Time

Many cases will arise where "extra operations" are required in order to correct faults or errors arising in previous processes, departments, or operations. Such extra operations will not appear on the standard cost card and should be specially authorized and specially marked as "rectification time" (as distinct from replace operations). Probably the simplest method of separating them is to enter them on a specially coloured card. These should if possible be analysed by departments responsible, or by reason (see also "Analysis of Scrap," pages 124 and 125).

In this group also may have to be included operations which are found to be essential but which have been omitted in drawing up the standard cost. It should be seen that where this is the case steps are taken to have the standard cost card corrected. Such cases should be rare where there is an efficient Planning Department and once the standard cost system is in full operation.

(An example of analysis by reason is shown in Fig. 8 on page 123.)

### Replacement Operations and Scrap

Where the faults in particular articles are so bad that they cannot be rectified, the articles must be treated as scrap. The authority to scrap goods should be exercised through the Inspection Department.

Where the goods are of a particular type (as in the case of manufacture against customers' orders) they will usually require to be replaced. In this case, the cost of replacing scrapped articles is the true cost of scrap, and should be separately recorded (i.e. the cost of labour, materials, and overhead up to the point in production at which the original article was scrapped, less the scrap value of the original article).

Where, on the other hand, say, some single special product is being steadily produced, no case of special replacement may arise, and the true cost of scrap will be most easily found by calculating the cost expended on the scrapped article up to the point at which it was scrapped.

Both methods may be used side by side.

The recording of scrap should be in the hands of the Inspection Department, and one method of doing this is for the inspectors to issue scrap notes giving full details of scrap (date, number scrapped, reason, and point in production or operation at which scrapped, etc.), or there may be inspection sheets stating number passed and number rejected, or the information may be taken from route cards. Copies of these will be sent to the Cost Department.

Goods returned by customers may also require to be considered here.

Where replacement costs need not be calculated, the cost of scrap can be found up to the point of scrapping from the standard cost card or from recorded costs.

Where replaces are required, the scrap note may act as an authorization for a replace works order to be made out against which replacement costs will be recorded, or the scrap note itself may be the authority for carrying out replace operations, which will be specially recorded as such.

The question of correct allocation of the cost of scrap may raise some difficult problems. (1) It may be treated as part of the cost of the particular job on which it occurred. (2) It may be separated and treated as an excess cost of the product group in which it occurred.

(3) It may be charged to the department in which it was scrapped. (4) It may be charged to some prior department whose error or fault was really to blame for the subsequent scrapping.

Is it fair that one department should bear the cost of another department's error? Few cost systems are designed to eliminate this entirely, and in some cases it may not be thought worth while to do so, scrap being regarded as part of the cost incidental to manufacture in that department. The author considers, however, that wherever practicable, and where the cost of scrap can be ascertained with reasonable accuracy, the method of charging scrap to the departments responsible is the most logical and effective, and the only method which will ensure active steps being taken to eliminate every possible source of fault. Where this step is taken, various counter-checks will have to be devised to prevent the errors of one department being passed off as those of another.

No matter which method is followed, the total accumulative cost of scrap should never be lost, and scrap should be classified and analysed by reasons, where incurred, persons or departments responsible, etc., in order that really effective steps may be taken to eliminate this source of loss.

In certain circumstances where scrap is inherent to particular jobs, the method of charging scrap against the cost of these jobs may be retained. In general, however, the practice here advocated, of charging excess costs against the overheads of the department concerned, will be found to be the most effective method from a management control point of view. It will be realized that this has the ultimate effect of spreading excess costs over all work done rather than against certain particular unfortunate orders (unless this cost is written off direct to Profit and Loss Account).

If cost transfers are to be made, an analysis will be required by the department where the cost of replacement was incurred and the department to which it has to be charged. An example of the analysis of engineering scrap by reasons is given in Figs. 9A and B on pages 124 and 125.

## Idle Time

Idle time may well be considered here. It may appear either in the form of idle men or idle machines. It may appear as an obvious cost in the form of special wage payments made for waiting time, or in the less obvious, but more insidious, form of the cost of standing charges not fully utilized.

The cost of idle time can be extracted either in the form of direct recordings of all stoppages by men and/or machines, or rather more indirectly, from variances between the absorbed labour and overhead costs calculated at standard rates on the actual output as compared with the corresponding absorption at standard activity. (Both methods may be used side by side, but the former should supply more detailed analyses by reasons.) In this context there are certain advantages to be gained from setting standard activity near to maximum capacity if the significance of the cost effects of idle facilities are to be shown to their full extent in routine reports. (Some of the disadvantages of setting standard activity at a high level, referred to elsewhere, can be minimized in advanced forms of budgeting, where in short-term budgets, one budgets for a variance from standard.)

Where standard costs are set on activity higher than "normal," standard product costs should have a percentage supplement for "normal excess cost."

## Manufactured Components, Sub-assemblies and Finished Parts

Once standard prices have been established for

materials, labour and overheads, and excess costs have been abstracted separately, the debits to individual works orders (if required) and to Work in Progress Accounts (in total) can be made at standard prices.

When work in progress is transferred from the shop floor to stores, the transfer will be made at standard cost, and when manufactured components are issued from stores the requisitions will be priced at standard cost, (obtained from the standard cost cards or previously entered on the stock record cards).

As an alternative half-measure, suitable in certain instances, the standard prices may originate at this stage, debits to component jobs being accumulated at actual cost, and the difference between standard and actual being written off to variation account before the parts are transferred to stores. (See Method I, p. 108.) This alternative effects considerable advantages in the keeping of stores records (see p. 91) but renders analysis of variations difficult.

The financial or cost accounts, first for Work in Progress, then for Component and Finished Stocks, should be kept by control accounts in total only, and the first method caters for this. The control accounts are debited with labour, materials, and overheads at standard cost, and credited with the total transfers or requisitions at standard.

In certain circumstances simplified accounts may be operated by treating all goods as Work in Progress (perhaps in product groups) until they are sold. If this is done, however, financial control of stores is liable to be defective.

CHAPTER XIV

# ACCOUNTING METHODS FOR STANDARD COSTS

THERE are several possible methods of accounting for standard costs. The principal difference between them lies in the allocation and the treatment of the cost of variations, and in the method of arriving at the value of work in progress.

The Profit and Loss Account will be drawn up to show profit on sales after deducting the standard cost of production less the variations from the standard cost of production.

|   |   | £ | £ |
|---|---|---|---|
| Sales . . . . . . . . | | | |
| *Less* Cost of Sales (at Standard Cost) . . | | ___ | |
| *Deduct* Variances from Standard . . . | | | |
| (a) Variances in Material Price . . . | | | |
| (b) ,, ,, Material Usage . . . | | | |
| (c) ,, ,, Wages Rates . . . | | | |
| (d) ,, ,, Labour Efficiency . . | | | |
| (e) ,, ,, Excess Costs . . . | | | |
| (f) ,, ,, Volume (of Activity) . . | | | |
| (g) ,, ,, Works Overhead . . | | | |
| (h) ,, ,, Selling and Administration Overhead . . . . . | | ___ | |
| Net Profit after Variances . . . £ | | | ___ |

Such variances may be shown in total, or by departments or cost elements. These variations (where actual does not come up to standard) are computed thus—

(a) Material price—Actual amount purchased (or used) at actual price less actual amount at standard price.

105

(*b*) Material usage—Actual amount used at standard price less standard amount specified at standard price.

(*c*) Wages rate—Actual time taken at actual rate (per pay-roll) less actual time taken at standard rate.

(*d*) Labour efficiency—Actual time taken at standard rate less standard time specified at standard rate.

(*e*) Excess costs—As detailed.

(*f*) Volume of activity—Standard overheads which would be absorbed by standard absorption rates at standard volume of activity less standard overheads absorbed by standard rates at actual volume of activity.

(*g*) and (*h*) Overhead variance—Actual overheads at actual volume of activity, less standard overheads at standard volume of activity.

If the "Labour Efficiency Variances" as computed above are to relate only to the speed of carrying out productive work, labour time not spent on productive work, e.g. waiting time, must be booked separately and recorded as a separate excess. In some trades it will not be worth while extracting the Wage Rate Variance from the Labour Efficiency Variance and the two may be combined as a Labour Cost Variance, i.e. "Unabsorbed Labour."

## Note on Volume and Overhead Variances

The above method of computing "Volume" and "Overhead" Variances (Method B overleaf) is the simplest method for general purpose use. On this basis the volume variance (gross) must not be viewed in isolation, for where there is an adverse volume variance due to activity being below standard, this may be compensated by a favourable overhead variance due to actual overheads falling below standard at standard activity.

More elaborately analysed methods have, however, been mooted.

## To take an example—

| | Standard at Standard Activity | Absorbed by Actual Output at Standard Rates | Actual Cost | Unabsorbed Costs |
|---|---|---|---|---|
| | £ | £ | £ | £ |
| Overheads "Variable". | 800 | 608 | 700 | 92 |
| Overheads "Fixed" . | 1,200 | 912 | 1,200 | 288 |
| | 2,000 | 1,520 | 1,900 | 380 |
| Direct Labour | 3,000 | 2,280 | 2,500 | 220 |
| | £5,000 | £3,800 | £4,400 | £600 |

Allowed Variables for Actual Output    .    .    £648

Alternative versions of Volume and Overhead Variances are—

|  |  | £ | £ | £ |
|---|---|---|---|---|
| (A) | Unabsorbed Overheads . . | 1,900 — | 1,520 = | 380 Excess |

|  |  | £ | £ | £ |
|---|---|---|---|---|
| (B) | Volume Variance (Gross) . | 2,000 — | 1,520 = | 480 Excess |
| | Overhead Variance (Gross) . | 2,000 — | 1,900 = | 100 Gain |
| | | | | £380 Excess |

|  |  | £ | £ | £ |
|---|---|---|---|---|
| (C) | Volume Variance (Net) . . | 1,200 — | 912 = | 288 Excess |
| | Overhead Variance (Net) . | 700 — | 608 = | 92 Excess |
| | | | | £380 Excess |

But there is a "refined" but more complex version—

|  |  | £ |
|---|---|---|
| (D) | Volume Variance (Net) (or "Capacity Variance") . | 288 Excess |
| | Volume Variance    ("Allowed Expenses")    . | 40 Excess |
| | Overhead Variance    —"Variables"    . . | 52 Excess |
| | | £380 Excess |

Finally, if one counts from labour as "Fixed"

|  |  | £ | £ | £ |
|---|---|---|---|---|
| (E) | "All-in" Volume Variance . | 5,000 — | 3,800 — | 1,200 Excess |
| | "All-in" Cost Variance . . | 5,000 — | 4,400 — | 600 Gain |
| | | | | £600 Excess |

Under Method C overheads are divided between fixed and variable, and the degree of volume deviation from standard at full activity is measured in terms of incidence of the so-called fixed overheads only, it being assumed that all other overheads ought to vary in proportion with activity, and if they do not they become an "excess cost" attributable to failure to change cost rather than to volume decline.

Method D introduces a further refinement.

In highly automated "machine controlled" factories, however, all expenses, including labour, tend to become fixed in the short run, and volume to become dominant. Method E may be appropriate in such circumstances.

Method B has much to commend it. It is sensitive to activity fluctuations, and where there is a full order book directs management's attention, say weekly, to the full effects of interferences with production through poor production planning or labour difficulties. It is that generally referred to in the text. (Exceptions are Figs. 16 and 17, where version E is used after extracting certain specified excesses.) Prompt adjustment of expenses to short-term activity fluctuations is easier in theory than in practice and is a longer-term affair. Version C or D, however, may be more appropriate in certain cases. The guiding principle would seem to be to lay emphasis on the aspect which is most likely to lead to appropriate action in the particular circumstances.

## Accounting Methods

Once the standard costs of the products are established the accumulating of costs of individual jobs can be abandoned. Control Accounts only need be maintained, standard costs being used for transfers and cost of sales.

METHOD I. Work in Progress Accounts are debited with actual costs of labour, material, and overheads, and credited with the standard cost of the period's production. Differences are accumulated and written off (credited) as variances from standard. This variation of actual over standard cost may be analysed under causes.

In some set-ups, Work in Progress Accounts can also be regarded as Departmental Operating Accounts.

Under this method the value of finished goods is shown at standard cost, and for balance-sheet purposes may require to be converted to actual by applying the ratio of actual to standard costs for the various elements in the finished cost.

This is easily obtained by taking the ratio of actual to standard for materials, labour, and overhead costs for the period under consideration and can be abstracted from the Departmental Operating Accounts.

METHOD 2. In this case postings to Work in Progress Accounts are made at standard rates in the first place, e.g. materials by standard quantity at standard price; labour and overheads by standard times at standard rates, and the variations between actual and standard in totals for material, labour, and overheads are posted to the Cost Variance Accounts direct, without passing through the Work in Progress Accounts. Variances will be analysed by departments. Transfers to Finished Parts (if required) and credits for Cost of Sales are taken from Stocks and Work in Progress at standard cost (per standard cost cards).

A variant of this method is to interpolate a Departmental or Process Operating Account which does not carry work in process balances. This account is debited perhaps only with process labour (and variable overheads) and credited and cleared with the standard cost of these items in respect of the production actually achieved each week or month, the corresponding debit at standard going to Work in Process Account. Variances are extracted at this point. Materials may be similarly treated or they may go direct to the Work in Process Account, variances being extracted at the point of issue to work in process.

Once again, to convert work in progress and finished goods from standard to actual cost, ratios obtained from the total accounts for materials and labour and overhead would be used.

The difference between standard and actual value of work in progress might be suitably stated on the Balance Sheet as a reserve, though in most cases the "standard" valuation may well be accepted for Balance Sheet purposes.

## Excess Costs

METHOD 3. From the brief description of Methods 1 and 2 we have seen how variations from standard are usually shown as a separate entry in the Profit and Loss Account, departmental or otherwise, but they might also be shown in cost statements as (a) charged to the particular job, (b) charged separately to the product group, (c) treated as part of the overhead of the responsible departments.

In certain cases a very effective simplified system of control based on standard costs, in conjunction with the budgetary control system, can be set up by simply carefully recording and analysing all excess costs.

Where fully detailed standards are considered unnecessary, or a matured organization capable of setting up standards is not available, or as a preliminary step towards the establishment of fully detailed standards, this method will prove very effective and will enable steps to be immediately taken to eliminate any adverse factors. It is specially useful in the type of work where there is a quoted price (and the subsequent cost of the job is not made a basis of fixing its price, though it may be the basis of future estimates) and where the only standard is the estimated cost and subsequent detailed planning.

By excess costs is meant all replacement, rectification, and similar costs as referred to in the previous chapter.

For the method to be put into operation some form of standard cost or planning sheet should still be available, together with a bill of material.

The simplest way is probably to book all such excess costs on cards or slips of a distinctive colour or mark. Material requisitioned over and above that stated on the bill of materials will be specially marked. Operations carried out over and above those specified on the planning sheet will be entered on special cards. In the case of scrap, it may be necessary to issue a special planning sheet stating replace operations.

Some form of internal check will be necessary to ensure that these provisions are carried out. The storekeeper will check all requisitions with the standard bill of materials.

Works clerks may check operations booked against the planning sheets, or foremen or inspectors may issue special notes authorizing extra or replace operations. (A foreman will naturally be keen to note extra operations incurred owing to errors in other departments, but not so interested in recording errors in his own; for this reason any such procedure will be better under the control of the Inspection Department.)

The cards for all these excess costs will be separated, sorted, and tabulated.

Under this system such excess costs will not normally be charged against individual orders (though they may be noted against them in memorandum form), but totalled and charged either direct to Profit and Loss Accounts or against the departments concerned, or the relative product group.

Although under this method there may be no material price standards or quantity standards used, save in the form of bills of material and the total material budgeted for, and even no standard labour rates (though this is usually advisable, and may sometimes be incorporated, with the machine rate), yet a standard overhead absorption rate is strongly advocated.

Analysis of variations is then provided in total by comparing the long-term standard budget with the short-term budget and with the actual costs together with the details of excess costs. (In certain circumstances the long-term budget may be omitted.)

After some experience, budgeted allowances will be made for excess costs. (See also Chapter XV, "Budget and Cost Reports.")

## Process Cost Standards

In process costing it is usually possible to state the cost figure in terms of cost per unit of output. This common unit may be tons, pounds, gallons, 1,000 items (as bricks), etc.

One of the main points to watch in process statements is to see that like is compared with like. Variations in sizes, mixtures or formulas may result in costs which are not truly comparable. Where the units flowing through a process differ in nature, e.g. coarse to fine, different standard processing costs are often set for each product by dividing the weekly costs at each process by the different rates of production for each product at such process. Sometimes no split in the actual labour cost between products at each process is necessary, control being effected by extending quantities of each product actually produced by standard cost, and comparing this total with the total actual labour cost at that process. Careful records of changes in material content may, however, be necessary. Job costing side by side with, and supplementary to, process costing may be found necessary in certain circumstances.

## Losses due to Sales Fluctuations

It will be appreciated that standard costs are designed to show first of all production losses, e.g. losses due to price of materials, losses due to excess scrap material, losses due to high cost of labour, and losses due to labour inefficiencies.

But losses, or lack of profits, are not caused by production costs alone, but by fluctuations in orders received and consequent sales. These losses or non-attainment of profits cannot be shown on any form of Profit and Loss Account stating only past experience or history, e.g. showing only variances from the standard cost of actual production. They can be evaluated only by a comparison of actual figures with short- and long-term budgeted figures. Their effect is apparent as an absence of the profit margin on the sales which have not materialized, and as an under-absorption of fixed and semi-fixed costs due to consequent low output value. They are really principally the responsibility of the Sales Department.

Profit variations due to sales fluctuations may be analysed by causes and locations, according to—

Variations in selling prices
Variations in sales volume
Variations in varieties sold
Variations in selling expenses.

One method of computing the effect of selling variations where the standard cost is known is to decide on the standard percentage margin of profit which should be carried in each product group. For example, assume this to be 20 per cent on *cost*. Then if—

|  | £ |
|---|---|
| Actual Sales | 920 |
| Standard Cost of Actual Sales | 800 |
| Profit | £120 |
| *Percentage profit 15 per cent* | |
| Profit at Standard Percentage (20%) | 160 |
| Variation due to fluctuation in Selling Prices | £40 Loss |

When the above calculation is carried out, the variation in profit due to volume of turnover should be calculated at the standard profit margin.

|  | Actual £ | Budget £ |
|---|---|---|
| Standard Cost of Sales . . . . | 800 | 900 |
| Profit at Standard Profit Margin . . | 160 | 180 |
| Variation due to fluctuation in Sales Volume . . . . . . |  | 20 |

In this case the Total Profit Variation—£60 (£180 — £120) is made up of—

|  | £ |
|---|---|
| Sales Price Variance . . . . | 40 |
| Sales Volume Variance . . . . | 20 |
|  | 60 |

With care, similar calculations can be made from the standard percentage profit margin on *sales*.

Variations in profit due to the proportion of different products making up the total sales can similarly be made up if need be (i.e. Sales Mixture Variance). This should be calculated at the standard percentage margin of profit for each product as for the volume variations. Price variations should be found for each product.

## Revisions to Standard Cost of Stocks

A revision of standard cost will usually entail a revision of the value of stocks held at standard cost. This will result in a Stock Price Revisions Variance appearing in the Profit and Loss Account which will offset or augment previous variances.

There are several methods of dealing with the revision to the standard price of stocks, e.g.—

(a) The entire stock of a given item may be revalued, the procedure being to revise a different section of stock each month, or (*b*) Two values may be allowed to exist till the earlier standard price is cleared out, on a first in first out basis.

There is some evidence that not a few companies prefer to keep raw material stocks at actual or average prices and confine standard values to manufactured parts, work in progress and finished stocks.

A complete revision of the standard price of stocks could have a marked effect on monthly accounts where the stocks are in excess of the monthly turnover, as in the following example. The effect will not be so marked on annual figures where the reverse position may hold good.

## REVISION OF STANDARD STOCK PRICES
### CONTROL ACCOUNT

| | £ | | £ |
|---|---|---|---|
| To Sales, 200 at £10 (A) . | 2,000 | By Stock, 600 at £7 (s) . | 4,200 |
| „ Stock, 600 at £8 (s) . | 4,800 | „ Purchases, 200 at £9 (A) | 1,800 |
| | | „ Profit      .     .     . | 800 |
| | £6,800 | | £6,800 |

### STOCK ACCOUNT

| | £ | | £ |
|---|---|---|---|
| To Balance, 600 at £7 (s) . | 4,200 | By Issues, 200 at £8 (s) . | 1,600 |
| „ Stock Price Revision, 600 at £1 . . | 600 | „ Balance, 600 at £8 (s) . | 4,800 |
| „ Purchases, 200 at £8 (s) | 1,600 | | |
| | £6,400 | | £6,400 |

### PROFIT AND LOSS ACCOUNT

| | £ | | £ |
|---|---|---|---|
| To Cost of Sales, 200 at £8 (s) . . . | 1,600 | By Sales, 200 at £10 (A) . | 2,000 |
| „ Materials Price Variance | 200 | „ Stock Price Revision Variance . . | 600 |
| „ Profit    .    .    . | 800 | | |
| | £2,600 | | £2,600 |

*Note.* (A) means at Actual Cost; (s) means at Standard Cost.

# PART III
## BUDGET AND COST REPORTS
## AND ACCOUNTS

# CHAPTER XV

## BUDGET AND COST REPORTS

THE information provided by budgetary control and by the cost system is presented to the management in the form of statements or reports. It is axiomatic that such reports should state clearly what they intend to convey. They should be so drafted that the salient features stand out—and they should be prompt.

The time-lag between a happening and the notification of its effect in one of the reports will vary according to its relative importance and the recording methods employed, but reports on matters which can be influenced by prompt action should receive priority, and be issued in time for such action to be taken.

Detailed reports will be issued most frequently to the persons having responsibility for, or in direct control of, the reportable events. Summarized reports will be issued to the higher executives, who will require explanations of any variations from the persons responsible.

Reports on certain matters may be issued daily, others weekly, and some monthly or annually.

Usually all members of the Budget Committee (see Chapter II) will receive summarized copies of all the principal reports, together with detailed reports relating to their own particular functions.

Practically all reports will be issued in the most effective form of comparison between actual and budget, or actual and standard, stress being laid on the principal variations. Reports will be issued relating to each department.

Typical procedure might be on these lines—

DAILY REPORTS

    (a) Details of Orders Received.
    (b) Details of Orders Delivered.
    (c) Details of certain Excess Costs.

WEEKLY REPORTS

    (a) Summary of Orders Received.
    (b) Summary of Orders Delivered.
    (c) Summary of Orders on Hand.
    (d) Summaries of All Excess Costs.
    (e) Materials Cost and Variances.
    (f) Labour Cost and Variances.
    (g) Summary of Expenses and Variances.
    (h) Combined Summary Report of the above.

MONTHLY REPORTS

Full set of accounts, with full details available as regards sales, profits, and costs for each product or department. Summarized reports of these may be issued to members of the Budget Committee, together with full details to certain members regarding certain functions for which they are responsible.

    (a) Orders Received.
    (b) Orders Delivered.
    (c) Orders on Hand.
    (d) Work in Progress and Stocks.
    (e) Materials Cost and Variances.
    (f) Labour Cost and Variances.
    (g) Expenses and Variances.
    (h) Excess Costs.
    (i) Profits.

(*j*)  Outstanding Purchase Commitments.
(*k*)  Total Summary.
(*l*)  Financial Position.

Reports may be accompanied by any desired graphs or charts.  Any useful statistics may be incorporated, e.g.—

Number of Direct and Indirect Employees.
Number of Men on Night Shift.
Number of Men Absent, or Late.
Percentage of Operators on Piecework.
Number and Value of Overdue Orders.
Number of Inquiries.
Number of Complaints, etc.

Let us consider some of these reports.  The examples are examples only, and are not intended for direct adoption.  Each business will require to draw up the form of reports to meet its own particular needs, manufacturing procedure, and organization.

## Weekly Reports

(*a*)  Summary of Orders Received.  Fig. 5 shows a typical Summary of Orders Received.

Wherever possible, all orders received should immediately be priced.  Only in this way can work ahead be fully appreciated and true control effected.  A routine should be set up to adjust the figures for orders received and on hand, and to correct the balance for the relative value at which the orders are delivered.

(*b*)  Summary of Orders Delivered, and (*c*) Summary of Orders on Hand may be made out on very similar forms.

(*d*)  Summaries of Excess Costs.  Figs. 6A and B give examples of analysis of waiting time.  Immediate investigation of the fundamental causes thereof should be undertaken.

Fig. 7 shows an example of Analysis of Supplementary

Time as applicable to the engineering trade (see Chapter XIII).

Fig. 8 is an Analysis of Rectification Costs.

Fig. 9A is somewhat similar to Fig. 8, save that this refers to goods which are actually scrapped. A single summary combining Figs. 8 and 9A may be found sufficient in certain cases.

Fig. 9B shows the method of analysis required for charging scrap to responsible departments.

(e) Materials Cost and Variances. Figs. 10A and B show one method of setting out material variances. This would apply particularly in the case of process costing.

This type of report will be more usually issued monthly. Where material price and material usage variances are not required to be separated, the statement will appear simply as a comparison of budget and actual as set out under monthly reports figures.

(f) Labour Cost and Variances. Fig. 11A gives an example of wages grade or rate variances. The method illustrated would be applied to such cases as girls working in the textile trade.

Fig. 11B shows one method of recording labour time

### SUMMARY OF ORDERS RECEIVED

Week ended...............................

| Product | Budget for Week | Actual for Week | Budget to Date | Actual to Date |
|---------|-----------------|-----------------|----------------|----------------|
|         | £               | £               | £              | £              |
| A       |                 |                 |                |                |
| B       |                 |                 |                |                |
| C       |                 |                 |                |                |
| D       |                 |                 |                |                |
|         |                 |                 |                |                |

FIG. 5

SUMMARY OF IDLE TIME

Dept. No.....................................

Week ended...............................

| Class | Reason | Hours | Rate | Cost |
|---|---|---|---|---|
| 1 | Waiting for Machine Repairs . . | | | |
| 2 | ,, ,, Transmission Repairs . | | | |
| 3 | ,, ,, Power . . . . | | | |
| 4 | ,, ,, Materials . . . | | | |
| 5 | ,, ,, Drawings . . . | | | |
| 6 | ,, ,, Tools . . . . | | | |
| 7 | ,, ,, Jigs . . . . | | | |
| 8 | ,, ,, Instructions . . | | | |
| 9 | ,, ,, Inspection . . . | | | |
| 10 | ,, ,, Work . . . . | | | |
| 11 | ,, ,, Toolsetter . . . | | | |
| 12 | ,, ,, Unclassified . . . | | | |
| | | | | |
| | *Budget Allowance* . . . . | | | |

FIG. 6A

## SUMMARY OF MACHINE IDLE TIME

Dept. No.....................................

Week ended...............................

| Machine Number | Description | Reason | Hours | Rate | Cost |
|---|---|---|---|---|---|
| | | Under Repair . | | | |
| | | No Tools . . | | | |
| | | No Work . . | | | |
| | | No Operator . | | | |
| | | | | | |
| | *Budget Allowance* . . . . | | | | |

FIG. 6B

ANALYSIS OF SUPPLEMENTARY TIME

Dept. No.......................................

Week ended................................

| Class | Reason | Hours | Rate | Cost |
|---|---|---|---|---|
| 20 | Extra-hard Material . . . | | | |
| 21 | Excess Material on Casting . . | | | |
| 22 | Welded Material . . . | | | |
| 23 | Substituted Material . . . | | | |
| 24 | Using Machine other than Planned . | | | |
| 25 | Using Grade of Operator other than Planned . . . . . | | | |
| 26 | Using Tools other than Planned (Planned Tools Not Available) | | | |
| 27 | Using Jigs other than Planned . . | | | |
| 28 | Breaking Down of Batches . . | | | |
| 29 | Experimental Work. . . . | | | |
| 30 | Unclassified . . . . . | | | |
| | | | | |
| | *Budget Allowance* . . . . | | | |

FIG. 7

ANALYSIS OF RECTIFICATION COSTS

Week ended................................

| Class | Reason | Cost |
|---|---|---|
| 40 | Faulty Workmanship . . . . . | |
| 41 | Faulty Machines . . . . . . | |
| 42 | Incorrect Drawings . . . . | |
| 43 | Incorrect Instructions . . . . | |
| 44 | Faulty Materials: (a) Hardness . . . | |
| 45 | (b) Flaws . . . | |
| 46 | (c) Finish . . . | |
| | (e.g. Welding, Hardening) | |
| 47 | Incorrect Inspection at Previous Point . . | |
| 48 | Testing for Faults . . . . . | |
| 49 | Unclassified . . . . . . | |
| | | |
| | *Budget Allowance* . . . . | |

Fig. 8

ANALYSIS OF MACHINE SHOP SCRAP

Week ended...............................

| Class | Reason | Week | Cumulative |
|---|---|---|---|
| 60 | Incorrect Instructions from Clients . . | | |
| 61 | Incorrect or Ambiguous Drawings . . | | |
| 62 | Faulty Patterns . . . . . | | |
| 63 | Moulding . . . . . . | | |
| 64 | Coremaking . . . . . | | |
| 65 | Faulty Castings: (a) Blown . . . | | |
| 66 | (b) Cracked . . | | |
| 67 | (c) Degree of Hardness | | |
| 68 | (d) Sandy or Scab . | | |
| 69 | (e) Porous . . . | | |
| 70 | Annealing . . . . . . | | |
| 71 | Hardening . . . . . . | | |
| 72 | Forge . . . . . . | | |
| 73 | Stores . . . . . . | | |
| 74 | Internal Transport . . . . | | |
| 75 | Inspection . . . . . . | | |
| 76 | Planning . . . . . . | | |
| 77 | Machining[1]: Carelessness and Errors . | | |
| 78 | Lack of Skill . . . | | |
| 79 | Man in Course of Training | | |
| 80 | Unsuitable or Defective Machine . . . | | |
| 81 | Unsuitable or Defective Tools . . . . | | |
| 82 | Unclassified . . . . . | | |
| | *Budget Allowance* . . | | |

Fig. 9a

[1] See Form 9B also for Analysis by Machining Departments, e.g. Turning, Milling, Drilling, Boring, Planing, Grinding, etc.

## ANALYSIS OF RECTIFICATION AND SCRAP COST
## BY DEPARTMENT RESPONSIBLE

Week ended...............................

| | Chargeable to Department | | | | | | |
|---|---|---|---|---|---|---|---|
| | I | 2 | 3 | 4 | — | — | Total |
| INCURRED BY Department I | | | | | | | |
| ,,　　　2 | | | | | | | |
| ,,　　　3 | | | | | | | |
| ,,　　　4 | | | | | | | |
| ,,　　　— | | | | | | | |
| ,,　　　— | | | | | | | |
| ,,　　etc. | | | | | | | |
| | | | | | | | |
| *Budget Allowance* | | | | | | | |

FIG. 9B

## MATERIALS PRICE VARIANCE

Week ended...............................

| Type | Class of Material | Actual Quantity | Value at Standard Cost | Value at Actual Cost | Plus | Minus |
|---|---|---|---|---|---|---|
| | | | | | | |
| | | | | | | |
| | | | | | | |
| | | | | | | |

FIG. 10A

## MATERIALS USAGE VARIANCE
Week ended................................

| Type | Class of Material | Standard Quantity | Actual Quantity | Standard at Standard Cost | Actual at Standard Cost | Plus | Minus |
|------|------|------|------|------|------|------|------|
|      |      |      |      |      |      |      |      |

FIG. 10B

## WAGES RATE VARIANCE
Week ended................................

| Dept. No. | Department | Hours Worked | Cost at Standard Rate | Actual Cost | Plus | Minus |
|------|------|------|------|------|------|------|
|      |      |      |      |      |      |      |

FIG. 11A

LABOUR EFFICIENCY VARIANCE

Week ended.................................

| Dept. No. | Department | Time Allowed | Deduct Excess Bonus Margin | Standard Time | Actual Time | Differ-ence[1] | Standard Rate | Cost[1] |
|---|---|---|---|---|---|---|---|---|
| | | | | | | | | |
| | | | | | | | | |

FIG. 11B

[1] Credits in red.

## ANALYSIS OF VARIABLE EXPENSES

Week ended................................

| | Dept. 1 | | Dept. 2 | | Dept. 3 | | Total | |
|---|---|---|---|---|---|---|---|---|
| | Budget | Actual | Budget | Actual | Budget | Actual | Budget | Actual |
| **INDIRECT LABOUR** | | | | | | | | |
| Labourers. | | | | | | | | |
| Storekeepers | | | | | | | | |
| Inspectors. | | | | | | | | |
| Supervision | | | | | | | | |
| Apprentices | | | | | | | | |
| Overtime Allowance. | | | | | | | | |
| Miscellaneous | | | | | | | | |
| | | | | | | | | |
| **INDIRECT SUPPLIES** | | | | | | | | |
| Small Tools | | | | | | | | |
| Oils and Grease | | | | | | | | |
| Miscellaneous | | | | | | | | |

FIG. 12

## WEEKLY BUDGET AND COST SUMMARY

Department No............          Week ended.............................

|  | Budget | Actual |
|---|---|---|
|  | £ | £ |
| Orders Received . . . . . . | | |
| Orders Delivered . . . . . . | | |
| COMPARISON OF BUDGET AND ACTUAL COST | | |
|     Direct Materials . . . . . | | |
|     Direct Labour . . . . . . | | |
|     Indirect Materials . . . . | | |
|     Indirect Labour . . . . . . | | |
| VARIATIONS FROM STANDARD COST | Above | Below |
|     Material Cost Variance . . . | | |
|     Wages Variance . . . . . | | |
| EXCESS COSTS | | |
|     Idle Time . . . . . . . | | |
|     Supplementary Time . . . . . | | |
|     Rectification . . . . . | | |
|     Scrap . . . . . . . | | |
| *Difference* . . | | |

FIG. 13

variations where a bonus scheme is allowed and times are set for each operation.

Detailed tabulations may be available for issue by check number.

In its most simple form this variation would merely be stated as a detailed comparison of budget with actual labour costs for departments.

(*g*) Expense Variances. Fig. 12 furnishes an example of a comparison of budgeted and actual expenses. A separate copy might be furnished to the head of each department concerned.

(*h*) Combined Weekly Summary. Fig. 13 gives a simple form of weekly summary. Cumulative totals might also be included.

## Monthly Reports

(*a*) Orders Received will be summarized by product and compared with budget. Analysis and similar comparison will also probably be required by area or by salesmen.

(*b*) Orders Delivered will be similarly summarized.

(*c*) Orders on Hand for the various product groups will be ascertained.

(*d*) Work in Progress. If the cost system functions on the basis of monthly accounts, a calculated value of work in progress in each section will be available at each period end.

### MONTHLY PRODUCTION SUMMARY

Period ended.................................

| | Product A | | Product B | | Product C | | Total | |
|---|---|---|---|---|---|---|---|---|
| | Budget | Actual | Budget | Actual | Budget | Actual | Budget | Actual |
| Orders Received . | | | | | | | | |
| Orders Delivered | | | | | | | | |
| Orders on Hand . | | | | | | | | |
| Work in Progress . | | | | | | | | |
| Adjustment in Work in Progress . . | | | | | | | | |
| Output . . . | | | | | | | | |
| Standard Cost . . | | | | | | | | |
| *Manufacturing Profit* . | | | | | | | | |

FIG. 14

*Stocks.* A return should be made showing the balance of stock on hand for the principal classes of material together with the receipts and issues for each period.

Fig. 14 illustrates one possible form of combined Summary of Orders Received and Production, analysed by product group.

(*e*) Materials Cost and Variances may be available in similar form to Figs. 10A and B.

(*f*) Labour Cost and Variances may also be available in detail as in Figs. 11A and B.

Both the above, however, may only be in the form of a total comparison of actual with budget, and will appear in a summary statement comparing budget and actual.

PROFIT AND LOSS SUMMARY

| Standard | | Budget | Actual |
|---|---|---|---|
| £ 30,000 | Invoiced Sales . . . . | £ 27,200 | £ 26,750 |
| 30,000 | Sales at Standard Price . . | 27,180 | 26,800 |
| 26,700 | Standard Cost of Sales . . . | 24,150 | 23,810 |
| 3,300 | Standard Profit (*a*) . . . | 3,030 | 2,990 |
| | *Variances from Standard Cost* | | |
| — | Materials Cost . . . . | — | 80 |
| 60 | Specific Excess Costs . . . | 370 | 400 |
| — | Op. Efficiency . . . . | 30 | 100 |
| — | Labour Rates . . . . | 60 | 92 |
| — | Volume of Activity . . . | 1,060 | 1,247 |
| 60 | | 1,520 | 1,919 |
| — | Overhead Expenses (Gain) . . | 820 | 909 |
| 60 | Total Cost Variances (*b*) . . | 700 | 1,010 |
| 3,240 | Mfg. Profit *a* — *b*. . . . | 2,330 | 1,980 |
| — | Sales Price Variance . . . | + 20 | — 50 |
| 3,240 | *Net Profit* . . . . . | 2,350 | 1,930 |

FIG. 15

Fig. 15 (based on Fig. 17) shows a Statement suitable for general use. To give a sense of proportion it is useful to express variances in each class as a percentage to the standard for actual output for that category.

(*g*) Expenses. Figs. 16A and B give a typical example of expense analysis.

## ANALYSIS OF WORKS OVERHEAD

Period ended..................................

| | Dept. 1 | | Dept. 2 | | Dept. 3 | | Total | |
|---|---|---|---|---|---|---|---|---|
| | Budget | Actual | Budget | Actual | Budget | Actual | Budget | Actual |
| **INDIRECT LABOUR** | | | | | | | | |
| Labourers | | | | | | | | |
| Storekeepers | | | | | | | | |
| Truckers, Cranemen, etc. | | | | | | | | |
| Foremen, etc. | | | | | | | | |
| Inspection | | | | | | | | |
| Miscellaneous | | | | | | | | |
| **INDIRECT SUPPLIES** | | | | | | | | |
| Small Tools | | | | | | | | |
| Oils and Grease | | | | | | | | |
| Miscellaneous | | | | | | | | |
| **REPAIRS AND MAINTENANCE** | | | | | | | | |
| Machines, etc. | | | | | | | | |
| Buildings, etc. | | | | | | | | |
| **SHARE OF SERVICES** | | | | | | | | |
| Power, etc. | | | | | | | | |
| Lighting | | | | | | | | |
| Heating | | | | | | | | |
| Stores, Receive and Dispatch | | | | | | | | |
| **FIXED CHARGES** | | | | | | | | |
| Depreciation | | | | | | | | |
| Rent and Rates | | | | | | | | |
| Insurance | | | | | | | | |
| Miscellaneous | | | | | | | | |
| Total Works Overhead | | | | | | | | |
| Departmental Administration | | | | | | | | |
| Grand Total | | | | | | | | |
| **SUMMARY** | | | | | | | | |
| Variable | | | | | | | | |
| Semi-variable | | | | | | | | |
| Fixed | | | | | | | | |

FIG. 16A

ANALYSIS OF ADMINISTRATION AND SELLING
EXPENSES

Period ended...............................

|  | Budget | Actual |
|---|---|---|
| **ADMINISTRATION** | | |
| Secretarial . . . . . . | | |
| Financial Accounts . . . . . | | |
| Cost Accounts . . . . . . | | |
| Buying . . . . . . . | | |
| Correspondence . . . . . . | | |
| Design . . . . . . . | | |
| Planning . . . . . . . | | |
| General Management . . . . . | | |
| | | |
| **SELLING** | | |
| Central Sales Offices . . . . . | | |
| Advertising and Publicity . . . . | | |
| Estimating . . . . . . . | | |
| Branch Offices . . . . . . | | |

FIG. 16B

Analysis should also be provided by Salaries, Stationery, Rent, Rates, Sundries, etc.

It is interesting to note the different forms in which such an analysis could be made up. Supposing there were several departments, the layout might be—

(i),

|  | Dept. 1 | Dept. 2 | Dept. 3 | Total |
|---|---|---|---|---|
| Indirect Labour (detail) . . | | | | |
| Indirect Supplies (detail) . . | | | | |
| Repairs, etc. (detail) . . . | | | | |
| *Total* . | | | | |

or (ii),

|  | Period 1 | Period 2 | Period 3 | -13 | Total |
|---|---|---|---|---|---|
| Dept. 1 | | | | | |
| „ 2 | | | | | |
| „ 3 | | | | | |
| Total . | | | | | |

or (iii),

|  | Works Overhead | Administration Overhead | Selling Overhead | Total |
|---|---|---|---|---|
| Dept. 1 | | | | |
| „ 2 | | | | |
| „ 3 | | | | |
| Total . | | | | |

or (iv), each department on a separate sheet—

| Dept. 1 | Period 1 | Period 2 | Period 3 | -13 | Total |
|---|---|---|---|---|---|
| Indirect Labour | | | | | |
| Indirect Supplies | | | | | |
| Repairs, etc. | | | | | |
| Total . | | | | | |

The method adopted will depend on practical usefulness. A loose-leaf book having one expense sheet for each department covering 12 months or 13 periods, together with total and subtotal sheets as necessary, should be considered. This sheet will state the standard for the year at the left-hand side and comparisons of budget and actual throughout the year.

(i) Profits. Where there is a large number of products, a Profit Summary comparing output and profits with budget for each commodity should be made up.

Where the accounts are in departmental form, a similar sheet will be set up.

(j) Fig. 17 gives more complex set of figures for a certain business.

In this case the transfer of excess costs between departments and their reallocation to specific products is thought by management to be significant.

It is assumed that there are three main products which pass through two departments in the course of manufacture. The standard cost or long-term budget (on which the detailed standard costs for the individual articles are built up) is shown, and also the budget for the immediate future and the actual costs. The assumption is that it is a new business in the course of development, expensive preliminary experiments are still being carried out in department 1, and standard is still considerably above budget.

Fig. 18 is a simple Profit Statement abstracted therefrom. This should be compared with the Profit and Loss Account in Chapter XVI and with Fig. 15.

Fig. 19 is a detailed analysis of reasons for non-attainment of standard profit. Some of the variations are shown only in total or simply by comparison with budget. In this instance it has been assumed that it has been possible to allocate excess costs from departments to particular products, but this can only sometimes be carried out.

| | Product A | | | Product B | | |
|---|---|---|---|---|---|---|
| | Stan-dard | Budget | Actual | Stan-dard | Budget | Actual |
| Sales . . . . | 15,000 | 13,000 | 12,400 | 6,000 | 6,200 | 6,300 |
| (Standard Margin of Profit) | 1,500 | 1,300 | 1,240 | 900 | 930 | 945 |
| STANDARD COST OF SALES | | | | | | |
| Material . . | 3,750 | 3,250 | 3,100 | 1,200 | 1,250 | 1,266 |
| Labour. . . | 3,030 | 2,630 | 2,520 | 1,200 | 1,225 | 1,247 |
| Works Overhead . . | 3,720 | 3,220 | 3,060 | 1,200 | 1,225 | 1,247 |
| Administration Overhead | 3,000 | 2,600 | 2,480 | 1,500 | 1,550 | 1,580 |
| *Total* . . | 13,500 | 11,700 | 11,160 | 5,100 | 5,250 | 5,340 |
| Balance . | 1,500 | 1,300 | 1,240 | 900 | 950 | 960 |
| *Less* Excess Costs. . | 60 | 50 | 90 | | 320 | 250 |
| Efficiency Variances . | | 30 | 50 | | | 60 |
| *Manufacturing Profit* . | 1,440 | 1,220 | 1,100 | 900 | 630 | 650 |

| | Department 1 | | | Department 2 | | |
|---|---|---|---|---|---|---|
| Material . . . | | | | | | |
| Direct Labour . . | 3,510 | 3,440 | 3,440 | 1,970 | 1,800 | 1,840 |
| Works Expenses . | 3,500 | 3,440 | 3,410 | 2,030 | 1,820 | 1,884 |
| Administration Expenses . | | | | | | |
| Total Cost . | 7,010 | 6,880 | 6,850 | 4,000 | 3,620 | 3,724 |
| Transfers of Excess Costs . | | | + 25 | | | − 35 |
| *Deduct* Excess Costs . | 60 | 300 | 260 | | 70 | 130 |
| Efficiency Variances . | | 30 | 80 | | | 20 |
| Absorption at Standard | 6,950 | 6,550 | 6,535 | 4,000 | 3,550 | 3,539 |
| Rates . . . . | 6,950 | 6,300 | 6,100 | 4,000 | 3,600 | 3,624 |
| Loss on Absorption . | | 250 | 435 | | | |
| Profit on Absorption . | | | | | 50 | 85 |
| *Net Profit (Mfg. Profit* less *Loss on Absorption)* . . | | | | | | |

FIG.

136

| Product C | | | | | | Total | | |
|---|---|---|---|---|---|---|---|---|
| Standard | Budget | Actual | Standard | Budget | Actual | Standard | Budget | Actual |
| 9,000 | 8,000 | 8,050 | | | | 30,000 | 27,200 | 26,750 |
| 900 | 800 | 805 | | | | 3,300 | 3,030 | 2,990 |
| 4,500 | 4,000 | 4,050 | | | | 9,450 | 8,500 | 8,416 |
| 1,210 | 1,070 | 1,110 | | | | 5,440 | 4,925 | 4,877 |
| 590 | 530 | 540 | | | | 5,510 | 4,975 | 4,847 |
| 1,800 | 1,600 | 1,610 | | | | 6,300 | 5,750 | 5,670 |
| 8,100 | 7,200 | 7,310 | | | | 26,700 | 24,150 | 23,810 |
| 900 | 800 | 740 | | | | 3,300 | 3,050 | 2,940 |
| | | 60 | | | | 60 | 370 | 400 |
| | | Cr. 10 | | | | | 30 | 100 |
| 900 | 800 | 690 | | | | 3,240 | 2,650 | 2,440 |

| Administration | | | Material | | | Total | | |
|---|---|---|---|---|---|---|---|---|
| | | | 9,450 | 8,500 | 8,496 | 9,450 | 8,500 | 8,496 |
| | | | | | | 5,480 | 5,240 | 5,280 |
| | | | | | | 5,530 | 5,260 | 5,294 |
| 6,300 | 5,850 | 5,750 | | | | 6,300 | 5,850 | 5,750 |
| 6,300 | 5,850 | 5,750 | 9,450 | 8,500 | 8,496 | 26,760 | 24,850 | 24,820 |
| | | + 10 | | | | 60 | 370 | 400 |
| | | 10 | | | | | 30 | 100 |
| 6,300 | 5,850 | 5,750 | 9,450 | 8,500 | 8,496 | 26,700 | 24,450 | 24,320 |
| 6,300 | 5,750 | 5,670 | 9,450 | 8,500 | 8,416 | 26,700 | 24,150 | 23,810 |
| | 100 | 80 | | | 80 | | 350 | 595 |
| | | | | | | | 50 | 85 |
| | | | | | | 3,240 | 2,350 | 1,930 |

17

PROFIT STATEMENT

|  |  | £ | £ | £ |
|---|---|---:|---:|---:|
| PRODUCT **A** |  |  |  |  |
| Sales . . . . . . |  |  | 12,400 |  |
| *Less* Standard Cost . . . | 11,160 |  |  |  |
| Excess Costs . . . | 90 |  |  |  |
| Efficiency Variances . . | 50 |  | 11,300 | 1,100 |

|  |  | £ | £ |  |
|---|---|---:|---:|---:|
| PRODUCT **B** |  |  |  |  |
| Sales . . . . . . |  |  | 6,300 |  |
| *Less* Standard Cost . . . | 5,340 |  |  |  |
| Excess Costs . . . | 250 |  |  |  |
| Efficiency Variances . . | 60 |  | 5,650 | 650 |

|  |  | £ | £ |  |
|---|---|---:|---:|---:|
| PRODUCT **C** |  |  |  |  |
| Sales . . . . . . |  |  | 8,050 |  |
| *Less* Standard Cost . . . | 7,310 |  |  |  |
| Excess Costs . . . | 60 |  |  |  |
| Efficiency Variances . . | 10 *Cr.* |  | 7,360 | 690 |
|  |  |  |  | £2,440 |

|  | £ | £ |  |
|---|---:|---:|---:|
| *Deduct* Volume Variances (Activity below Standard) |  |  |  |
| Standard Absorption . . . | 17,250 |  |  |
| Actual Absorption . . . | 15,394 | 1,856 |  |
| Offset by Cost Variances |  |  |  |
| Standard Conversion Cost . . | 17,250 |  |  |
| Actual Conversion Cost . . | 15,824 | 1,426 | 430 |
|  |  |  | 2,010 |
| Material Cost Variance . |  |  | 80 |
| *Net Profit* . . |  |  | £1,930 |

FIG. 18

Let us consider the analysis set out in Fig. 19 on pp.
140–1 in detail.

### PROFITS AND LOSSES DUE TO VARIATIONS OF BUDGET FROM STANDARD

A standard profit of £3,240 has been set. The profit
achieved is only £1,930. Of the difference £890 is
accounted for by the *variation between budget and standard*.
It will be seen that this loss is anticipated even before
production starts for the current period, and the reasons
are due to loss on sales not realized, together with the
under-absorption of costs due to work done being below
standard. The nature, analysis, and extent of this being
known, steps can be taken to remedy the situation.

### PROFITS OR LOSSES DUE TO VARIATIONS BETWEEN BUDGET AND ACTUAL

The variations between budget and actual are designed
to show current efficiency in sales and in production.

### REDUCTION IN STANDARD PROFIT

Net profit at the standard margin of net profit will fail
to be realized whenever there is a fall from the standard
volume of sales. This variance from standard profit
should not be confused with the Volume Variance
referred to in the paragraph next but one.

### VARIATION IN PROFIT MARGIN

This is usually referred to as the Sales Price Variance
and will arise where standard or catalogue price has
been deviated from, and, in the case where selling prices
are estimated for individual orders, where there has been
a deviation from the normal percentage profit taken. It
will be the responsibility of the Sales or Estimating
Departments to prove that these are justified.

## ANALYSIS OF VARIANCES FROM STANDARD PROFIT

| | Gain | Loss | Net Gain | Net Loss |
|---|---|---|---|---|
| | £ | £ | £ | £ | £ |
| **A.** LOSSES DUE TO VARIATION OF BUDGET FROM STANDARD | | | | |
| 1. *Loss due to Budgeted Sales under Standard* | | | | |
| REDUCTION IN STANDARD PROFITS | | | | |
| Product A. Standard Sales £15,000 Profit . 1,500 | | | | |
| Budget ,, £13,000 ,, . 1,300 | | 200 | | |
| Product B. Standard ,, £6,000 ,, . 900 | | | | |
| Budget ,, £6,200 ,, . 930 | 30 | | | |
| Product C. Standard ,, £9,000 ,, . 900 | | | | |
| Budget ,, £8,000 ,, . 800 | | 100 | | 270 |
| 2. *Variation in Margin of Profit* | | | | |
| Product B. Standard Profit on Budget Sales 930 | | | | |
| Budget ,, ,, ,, ,, 950 | 20 | | 20 | |
| 3. *Loss due to Budgeted Production under Standard* | | | | |
| Dept. 1. Loss on Absorption . . 650 | | | | |
| *Less* Reduction in Costs . . 400 | | 250 | | |
| Dept. 2. Loss on Absorption . . 400 | | | | |
| *Less* Reduction in Costs . . 450 | 50 | | | 200 |
| 4. *Administration Cost Variation* | | | | |
| Loss on Absorption . . . . . 550 | | | | |
| *Less* Reduction in Costs . . . 450 | | 100 | | 100 |
| 5. *Variations in Efficiency* | | | | |
| Dept. 1. Excess Costs . {Budget 300 | | | | |
| {Standard 60 | | 240 | | |
| Efficiency Variance {Budget 30 | | | | |
| {Standard — | | 30 | | |
| Dept. 2. Excess Costs . . {Budget 70 | | | | |
| {Standard — | | 70 | | 340 |
| — | | | 20 | 910 |
| *Total Variation of Budget from Standard* . . | | | | £890 |
| LOSSES DUE TO VARIATIONS OF ACTUAL FROM BUDGET | | | | |
| 1. *Loss due to Actual Sales under Budget* | | | | |
| REDUCTION IN STANDARD PROFIT | | | | |
| Product A. Budget Sales £13,000 Profit . 1,300 | | | | |
| Actual ,, £12,400 ,, . 1,240 | | 60 | | |
| Product B. Budget ,, £6,200 ,, . 950 | | | | |
| Actual ,, £6,300 ,, . 945 | | 5 | | |
| Product C. Budget ,, £8,000 ,, . 800 | | | | |
| Actual ,, £8,050 ,, . 805 | 5 | | | 60 |
| 2. *Variations in Profit Margin* | | | | |
| Product B. Standard Profit on Actual Sales 945 | | | | |
| Actual ,, ,, ,, ,, 960 | 15 | | | |
| Product C. Standard ,, ,, ,, ,, 805 | | | | |
| Actual ,, ,, ,, ,, 740 | | 65 | | 50 |
| Carried forward | | | | 110 |

| | Gain | Loss | Net Gain | Net Loss |
|---|---|---|---|---|
| | £ | £ | £ | £ | £ |
| Brought forward | | | | | 110 |
| 3. *Loss due to Actual Production under Budget* | | | | | |
|   (a) Variation in Absorption | | | | | |
|     Dept. 1. Budgeted Absorption  .  6,300 | | | | | |
|              Actual   ,,    .  .  6,100 | | 200 | | |
|     Dept. 2. Budgeted    .  .  3,600 | | | | | |
|              Actual    .  .  3,624 | 24 | | | |
|   (b) Variation in Expenditure | | | | | |
|     Dept. 1. Budgeted Expenses  .  6,550 | | | | | |
|              Actual   ,,   .  6,535 | 15 | | | |
|     Dept. 2. Budgeted    .  .  3,550 | | | | | |
|              Actual    .  .  3,539 | 11 | | | 150 |
| 4. *Administration Cost Variation* | | | | | |
|   (a) Variation in Absorption .    {Budget 5,750 | | | | | |
|                       {Actual 5,670 | | 80 | | |
|   (b) Variation in Expenses .    {Budget 5,850 | | | | | |
|                       {Actual 5,750 | 100 | | 20 | |
| 5. *Variation in Materials Cost* | | | | | |
|   Standard Cost for Actual Production .  . 8,416 | | | | | |
|   Actual  ,,  ,,  ,,     ,,   .  8,496 | | 80 | | 80 |
| 6. *Variations in Efficiency* | | | | | |
|   Dept. 1. Excess Costs .    {Actual 260 | | | | | |
|                    {Budget 300 | 40 | | | |
|     Efficiency Variance    {Actual 80 | | | | | |
|                      {Budget 30 | | 50 | | |
|   Dept. 2. Excess Costs .    {Actual 130 | | | | | |
|                    {Budget 70 | | 60 | | |
|     Efficiency Variance    {Actual 20 | | | | | |
|                      {Budget — | | 20 | | |
|   Administration Excess Costs    {Actual 10 | | | | | |
|                      {Budget — | | 10 | | 100 |
| | | | 20 | 440 |
| Total Variation of Actual from Budget  .   .   . | | | | £420 |
| GRAND TOTAL VARIATION OF ACTUAL FROM STANDARD | | | | £1,310 |
| *Standard Profit*  .  .  .  .  .  .  . | | | | 3,240 |
| *Actual Profit*  .  .  .  .  .  .  . | | | | 1,930 |
| | | | | £1,310 |

FIG. 19

VARIATION IN ABSORPTION

In the analysis and in Fig. 18, presentation E shown on page 107 is used for simplicity to give "All-in" Volume Variances. Similarly Cost Variances (Variation in Expenditure) are shown on an "All-in" basis after extracting certain specified excesses.

If, however, it is assumed that Excess Costs and Efficiency Variances of £500 comprising labour £357, overheads £143, and that the Absorption at "Standard Rates" in Fig. 17 (excluding Materials) is made up—

|  | Standard Absorption £ | Actual Absorption £ | (Actual Cost) £ |
|---|---|---|---|
| Direct Labour . . . | 5,440 | 4,831 | 5,280 |
| Works Overheads . . | 5,510 | 4,893 | 5,294 |
| Administration . . . | 6,300 | 5,670 | 5,750 |
|  | £17,250 | £15,394 | £16,324 |

then the presentation can be converted to a variant of presentation B (page 107) to produce the Profit and Loss Account in the form shown in Fig. 15, where the Volume Variance is limited to overheads, the labour element being regarded as variable and net. In Fig. 15 these variances are made up—

| | | £ |
|---|---|---|
| Volume | $(5,510 + 6,300) - (4,893 + 5,670)$ | = 1,247 |
| Expenses | $(5,294 + 5,750 - 143) - (5,510 + 6,300)$ = | 909 |
| Labour | $(5,280 - 357) - 4831$ | = 92 |

Variances in Labour Efficiency will also affect the volume produced and it is possible to sub-divide the Volume Variance into the portion attributable to Labour Efficiency, the balance sometimes being referred to as the capacity variance. The split of the Materials Cost Variance between Materials Price Variance and Materials Usage Variance has not been illustrated.

## Graphs

Many of the salient features of the foregoing reports can be shown in the form of graphs. Graphs are the best available media for showing broad general trends and are invaluable for giving a lucid impression of the current general situation.

Simple line graphs are most useful for general purposes and can be adapted to most budget and cost figures.

Logarithmic charts can be used to express ratios, but the plain chart with any percentages marked thereon has the advantage of usually being more easily understood by the management. Alternatively, the percentages may be graphed and the figures marked thereon.

Bar charts, vertical or horizontal, may serve to give further stress to certain facts. The Gantt type of chart may be used for production statements, and also to give a concise summary of the ratio of periodic and cumulative achievements to budgeted figures.

Comparison is the most effective method whereby efficiency can be controlled, and comparison of budget and actual should supply this need.

Suitable colours should be chosen to render graphs clearly legible.

Graphs suggested for submission to Budget and Cost Committee meetings might be—

ORDERS. Three lines on one sheet, showing trend of—
Orders Received, Delivered, and On Hand.

PRODUCTION. Graph showing relationship and trends of—
Output, Work in Progress, and Manufacturing Profit.

COSTS. Graph showing relationship and trends of—
Output, Direct Material Cost, Direct Labour Costs, and Works Overheads.

EXCESS COSTS. Comparisons may be made with budget.

Single items of interest may be given separate graphs, or graphs may be given for separate departments, or submitted for temporary illustration only of particular items of interest. Graphs may be drawn to show cumulative results, and graphs showing the Moving Annual Total may also prove very useful. The Z-type graph, too, showing period, cumulative, and moving annual total figures, is ideal for giving a comprehensive picture of the total position of single principal factors, such as orders received or output.

Another dramatic form of presentation is to develop a "Control Panel" containing gauges with dials of the speedometer or pressure gauge type. Such diagrams can show, say, three comparisons, one hand pointing to results of this period, another to those of last period, and an indicator on the external circumference can point to budget. Deliveries, purchases, expenses and key ratios of the type given in Chapter XIX can be presented. Balance Sheet figures and Orders on Hand can be incorporated but they are best shown on vertical gauges of the thermometer type with external pointers to comparative figures.

Charts in general serve to give a clear impression of outlines and trends, and to direct managers' thoughts into proper constructive channels. When it comes to details the figures themselves must be considered.

### Cost Comparison and Measurement of Output

When comparing costs over any considerable period it will often be found that the most orthodox method of comparing them in terms of percentage to output can be rather misleading owing to fluctuations in selling price. If the volume of output has increased over a previous period, and yet owing to reductions in selling price the total value of the output has fallen, then, when comparing costs in terms of percentage to output, unless this fact is clearly borne in mind, it might be assumed that costs had increased!

When making any such comparisons it will usually be well to show cost items as, say, percentages to direct labour and as percentages to total costs, as well as showing them as percentages to output, if a true picture of cost fluctuations is to be shown.

Wherever possible, costs should be shown as cost per unit of output. As was pointed out in a previous chapter, this can be done where output can be stated in terms of comparable numbers, say, 1,000 standard bricks, or by weight (cost per ton, etc.). Here again, though, difficulties may arise in comparing like with like.

In some cases it may be worth while to set some standard unit of output, and evaluate all production in terms of this unit to give a total *volume* of production. This may be possible and specially suitable where the bulk of the production can be stated in terms of common units and the balance of the production as proportional units of standard.

In other cases where sales price fluctuations will have marked effect, it may be possible to set up index numbers of price levels for each product group for different periods, and with the aid of these to adjust the value of total output to a common base indicating the true relative volume of output.

The measurement of output in terms of "effort" within the factory can also be calculated on a time basis.

Where *efficiently* set standard times are known for each operation or product, and are accumulated for all work produced, output can be expressed as so many "standard hours." This gives a useful comparable index of total factory production in any period and excludes monetary fluctuations. Such statements are useful for submission to foremen. "Standard Hours" done or produced can be compared with "Standard Hours" which ought to have been done or are budgeted for. A measurement of efficiency both departmental and individual can be given by expressing actual time taken as a ratio to standard.

Costs can also be evaluated in terms of "Cost per Standard Hour."

For special circumstances and for particular cost items, there are other units of measurement which are often worth while adopting, and in addition to forming a truer measure of particular costs they may serve to give a clearer impression of cost incidence. Costs per hour worked may prove valuable in certain cases. Certain costs (e.g. welfare, Wages Department, etc.) may be shown as costs per man employed. Office work can be measured in terms of numbers of documents handled.

Productivity measurements can often usefully supplement cost measurements. Comparative figures in total or by process of output per man-hour, per 1,000 sq. ft. floor space, per £1,000 fixed assets, etc., may be valuable. Figures of percentage capacity employed give an index of the productive use of equipment, and may be expressed as the ratio of hours worked to available hours at different process points. Indices of man-hours lost through lateness or absenteeism to possible man-hours with all engaged operatives serve a similar purpose.

Many other units of measurement may be adopted for special circumstances and may be profitably used, if only to emphasize a point in some report.

# CHAPTER XVI

## COST ACCOUNTS

THE Cost Ledger co-ordinates the figures given in the Cost Reports. All the total figures in the Cost Reports should agree with the relative figures in the Cost Ledger, as it is from this source that the figures for the Cost Reports should be abstracted. Though the reports themselves may give much more detailed analysis of certain items than is available from the Cost Ledger, yet the total of any such analysis should be in direct agreement with a similar total stated in the Cost Ledger. In other words, the form of the Cost Ledger should be dependent on the Cost Reports and the information which it is desired to show therein, and not vice versa.

Once all the figures to be shown in the Cost Reports are decided upon, it should be easy for any competent accountant to devise a scheme of double-entry cost accounts which, with various "Control Accounts," will reconcile with the financial accounts and give the necessary figures required for inclusion in the Cost Reports.

The Cost Ledger should be designed so that it may be easily interpreted, and all totals and transfers directly ascertainable from the accounts themselves. The double-entry principle must be retained, though interlocking schedules may replace a book.

The amount of clerical work attached thereto should be kept at an absolute minimum, consistent with showing all vital totals. Detailed analysis will not be given in the Cost Ledger, as much of it is of only temporary interest. The cost account totals will be supplemented with detailed Analysis Statements which should be systematically filed, say, in a loose-leaf book. These analyses must definitely tie up with the cost account totals.

If possible, inter-account transfers in the Cost Ledger should be able to be clearly followed from the ledger itself without reference to any subsidiary books or sheets. The ideal to aim at is to design the Cost Ledger so that the accountant is able to read the main facts of the business history of the firm from the Cost Ledger itself. It should be possible quickly to draw graphs of any of the principal trends by merely turning over the pages of the Cost Ledger.

The Cost Ledger will, of course, link up with the financial accounts through the total control accounts. The financial accounts should be so designed that this is directly possible without any further analysis or investigation. Reconciliation between the Cost Ledger and the financial accounts should be almost automatic.

Interlocking accounts are thought to be preferable to the integration of detailed cost and financial analysis in the same ledger. Any temporary breakdown in the detailed analysis, say through sickness, should not tend to interfere with the flow of main totals through the backbone of the system. Already some firms tend to regard the financial accounts as simply an additional summary of the cost accounts.

The following is a simple example of cost accounts according to Method 2 of Chapter XIV. The figures used are those shown in Fig. 17 (pages 136–7). To simplify the example, labour and works overhead absorption are taken as being combined and no balances have been shown on Work in Progress Accounts or in Stock.

*Note.* Neither standard nor budgeted costs, as such, are actually shown in the Cost Ledger, except for standard costs of actual production.

It will be appreciated that the entries appearing in the

Control Account should agree with the corresponding accounts in the Nominal Financial Ledger.

The possibility of analysing excess costs by products is envisaged in Fig. 17, but this has not been shown in the set of accounts, nor has analysis been given by the final fundamentals of time and rate, price and quantity. The example shows rather analysis of "excesses." The methods of obtaining complete analysis are indicated in the text, and the cost accounts will follow the same lines.

WORK IN PROGRESS ACCOUNT—Product A

| | £ | | £ |
|---|---|---|---|
| To Materials (at Standard) | 3,100 | By Mfg. A/c Product A(s). | 11,160 |
| „ Labour and Works | | (Cost of Sales) | |
| Overhead(s)[1] . . | 5,580 | | |
| Administration(s) . | 2,480 | | |
| | £11,160 | | £11,160 |

WORK IN PROGRESS ACCOUNT—Product B

| | £ | | £ |
|---|---|---|---|
| To Material(s) . . | 1,266 | By Mfg. A/c Product B(s). | 5,340 |
| „ Labour and Works | | (Cost of Sales) | |
| Overhead(s) . . | 2,494 | | |
| „ Administration(s) . | 1,580 | | |
| | £5,340 | | £5,340 |

WORK IN PROGRESS ACCOUNT—Product C

| | £ | | £ |
|---|---|---|---|
| To Material(s) . . | 4,050 | By Mfg. A/c Product C(s). | 7,310 |
| „ Labour and Works | | (Cost of Sales) | |
| Overhead(s) . . | 1,650 | | |
| Administration(s) . | 1,610 | | |
| | £7,310 | | £7,310 |

[1] *Note.* (A) means at Actual Cost; (s) means at Standard Cost.

### PROCESS or DEPARTMENT 1 OPERATING ACCOUNT

| | £ | | £ |
|---|---|---|---|
| To Wages from Control A/c (A) . . . | 3,440 | By Absorption A/c(s) . | 6,100 |
| „ Expenses from Control A/c (A) . . . | 3,410 | „ Excess Costs A/c . | 260 |
| „ Excess Costs t/f from Dept. (2) . . | 25 | „ Efficiency Variance A/c | 80 |
| | | „ Balance Under-absorbed transferred to P. and L. A/c . | 435 |
| | £6,875 | | £6,875 |

### PROCESS or DEPARTMENT 2 OPERATING ACCOUNT

| | £ | | £ |
|---|---|---|---|
| To Wages from Control A/c (A) . . . | 1,840 | By Absorption A/c(s) . | 3,624 |
| „ Expenses from Control A/c (A) . . . | 1,884 | „ Excess Costs A/c . | 130 |
| „ Over-absorbed Costs transferred to P. and L. A/c . . . | 85 | „ Efficiency Variance A/c | 20 |
| | | „ Excess Costs transferred | 35 |
| | £3,809 | | £3,809 |

### ADMINISTRATION EXPENSES ACCOUNT

| | £ | | £ |
|---|---|---|---|
| To Expenses from Control A/c (A) . . . | 5,750 | By Work in Progress A/c, Product A(s) . . | 2,480 |
| „ Excess Costs t/f from Dept. (2) . . | 10 | „ Work in Progress A/c, Product B(s) . . | 1,580 |
| | | „ Work in Progress A/c, Product C(s) . . | 1,610 |
| | | „ Excess Costs A/c . . | 10 |
| | | „ Balance Under-absorbed transferred to P. and L. A/c . . . | 80 |
| | £5,760 | | £5,760 |

## MATERIALS—STOCK ACCOUNT

| | £ | | £ |
|---|---|---|---|
| To Purchases from Control A/c (A) . . . | 8,496 | By Work in Progress, Product A(s) . . | 3,100 |
| | | ,, Work in Progress, Product B(s) . . | 1,266 |
| | | ,, Work in Progress, Product C(s) . . | 4,050 |
| | | ,, Materials Cost Variance A/c . . . | 80 |
| | £8,496 | | £8,496 |

## MATERIALS COST VARIANCE ACCOUNT

| | £ | | £ |
|---|---|---|---|
| To Materials Stock A/c . | £80 | By Profit and Loss A/c . | £80 |

## EXCESS COSTS VARIANCE ACCOUNT

| | £ | | £ |
|---|---|---|---|
| To Dept. 1 . . . | 260 | By Profit and Loss A/c . | 400 |
| ,, Dept. 2 . . . | 130 | | |
| ,, Administration . . | 10 | | |
| | £400 | | £400 |

## EFFICIENCY VARIANCE ACCOUNT

| | £ | | £ |
|---|---|---|---|
| To Dept. 1 . . . | 80 | By Profit and Loss A/c . | 100 |
| ,, Dept. 2 . . . | 20 | | |
| | £100 | | £100 |

## MANUFACTURING ACCOUNT—Product A

| | £ | | £ |
|---|---|---|---|
| To T/f from Work in Progress A/c(s) . . | 11,160 | By Sales Control A/c . | 12,400 |
| ,, Profit and Loss A/c . | 1,240 | | |
| | £12,400 | | £12,400 |

## MANUFACTURING ACCOUNT—Product B

| | £ | | £ |
|---|---|---|---|
| To T/f from Work in Progress A/c(s) . | 5,340 | By Sales Control A/c . | 6,300 |
| „ Profit and Loss A/c . | 960 | | |
| | £6,300 | | £6,300 |

## MANUFACTURING ACCOUNT—Product C

| | £ | | £ |
|---|---|---|---|
| To T/f from Work in Progress A/c(s) . . | 7,310 | By Sales Control A/c . | 8,050 |
| „ Profit and Loss A/c . | 740 | | |
| | £8,050 | | £8,050 |

## PROFIT AND LOSS ACCOUNT

| | £ | | £ |
|---|---|---|---|
| To Excess Costs . . | 400 | By Mfg. Profit, Product A . | 1,240 |
| „ Efficiency Variances . | 100 | „ „ „ „ B . | 960 |
| „ Under-absorbed Costs, Dept. 1 . . . | 435 | „ „ „ „ C . | 740 |
| „ Under-absorbed Administration . | 80 | „ Over-absorbed Costs, Dept. 2 . . . | 85 |
| „ Materials Variance . | 80 | | |
| „ Total Control A/c net Profit transferred . | 1,930 | | |
| | £3,025 | | £3,025 |

## TOTAL CONTROL ACCOUNT

| | £ | | £ |
|---|---|---|---|
| To Sales, Product A Mfg. A/c (A) . . . | 12,400 | By Wages, Dept. 1 (A) . | 3,440 |
| „ Sales, Product B Mfg. A/c (A) . . . | 6,300 | „ Expenses, Dept. 1 (A) . | 3,410 |
| „ Sales, Product C Mfg. A/c (A) . . . | 8,050 | „ Wages, Dept. 2 (A) . | 1,840 |
| | | „ Expenses, Dept. 2 (A) . | 1,884 |
| | | „ Materials (A) . | 8,496 |
| | | „ Administration (A) . | 5,750 |
| | | „ Net Profit . . . | 1,930 |
| | £26,750 | | £26,750 |

## ABSORPTION TRANSFER ACCOUNT

| | £ | | £ |
|---|---|---|---|
| To Labour and Works Overhead, Dept. 1 (s) | 6,100 | By Work in Progress, Product A(s) . . | 5,580 |
| „ Labour and Works Overhead, Dept. 2 (s) | 3,624 | „ Work in Progress, Product B(s) . . | 2,494 |
| | | „ Work in Progress, Product C(s) . . | 1,650 |
| | | „ For Labour and Works Overhead transferred . | |
| | £9,724 | | £9,724 |

One feature of standard costing should be appreciated. As long as activity is below standard and there are unabsorbed overheads, work in progress and finished stocks will show at a value below actual factory cost. Where activity is above standard and there is an over-recovery they will appear at a value in excess of actual factory cost, due to more overheads having been absorbed in work in progress than have actually been incurred. In the latter case this in effect means that certain "factory profits" may be taken *at the time of production*. As long as selling prices are in excess of standard costs and there is a regular flow of business this may be legitimate. If desired a year-end stock reserve can be created to offset this excess value. If only to obviate a situation arising where work in progress can show a value in excess of *total* costs it is advisable in practice to employ one group of recovery rates for works' overheads (to be included in work in progress) and one for distribution and a proportion of administrative expenses. This latter overhead group will be excluded from stock values and will be absorbed in total costs by separate rates applied *at the time of delivery*.

(Somewhat similarly material price variances are sometimes held in suspense and brought in as a cost at the time of delivery.)

# PART IV
# ADVANCED BUDGETING

# CHAPTER XVII

## ADVANCED BUDGETING

THERE are many modifications in budgeting and costing technique which can be introduced. These follow the lines of (a) simplification at all points where the information is found to be of little help to management as a guide to profitable action, and (b) elaboration and refinement where such a development seems of value. Such modifications can be made temporarily to meet special circumstances, or if found useful may become permanent features. There is scope for much wider use of sampling techniques in cost analysis. No system should remain static.

### Budgeting from Standard Costs

Where standard costs have been established for the bulk of the product range, or for volume of departmental process output, the cost of production budget can be built up by multiplying the quantities of the budgeted total, or departmental output, by the standard cost for labour, overheads (sub-divided by departments), and materials. (Final output will have to be adjusted for projected changes in stock-holding.)

Having worked out the standard cost of budgeted output, variances from standard will require to be budgeted for. These may be arrived at from past experience of variances and anticipated trends, or better still they may be ascertained by building up another complementary interlocking budget on the lines indicated in Chapters IV to VIII, e.g. foremen's estimates of requirements for labour, maintenance, etc., in the forthcoming short-term budget period.

Where standard costs are in existence, the preparation of short-term budgets may be considerably simplified and made more accurate. This technique is known as "budgeting for a variance." It is at this point that management can probably take the most effective controlling action, for, if practicable, steps can be taken to eliminate or reduce at least some of the adverse variances revealed before (and after) the budget is finally agreed.

As far as possible, standards for Materials, Labour and Overhead expenses should be developed in terms of quantities as well as values, if effective control is to be achieved.

## Simplified Applications of Standard Costing Technique

It is not always essential to embody standard costs in double-entry book-keeping. In some factories and mills where there is merely a flow process of a uniform product, a statistical version of standard costing analysis techniques may be applied. This is illustrated in simplified form in a later section of this chapter. For particular cost elements such as direct labour or materials, and for key process points this statistical analysis may be supplemented by other reports elaborated in some detail.

Under conditions of this nature another simplification will be to concentrate attention on variances between the standard cost of budgeted output and the short-term budgeted cost of budgeted output, and to take steps to endeavour to minimize these variances. Thereafter a tabulation of actual costs alongside budgeted costs merely is prepared and no detailed analysis is undertaken unless there are major variations, i.e. no detailed attempt is made to analyse actual costs against standard.

This approach can be successfully employed where there has been some considerable experience of budgeting and where there are no wide short-term fluctuations in output, and short-term budgets can be prepared to which actual costs will closely approximate. This is based on the clear recognition that the "control" aspect of budgetary control operates at two points: (1) control before the event, at the time plans are laid down, and (2) control after the event. It is recognized that the former is by far the more important and that the latter cannot cure extravagances or wastes which have taken place but can only help steps to be taken to prevent their continuance or repetition. It is also recognized that the most effective form of cost control is the use of the most efficient production methods.

For this approach to be successful, the budget must be based on, or be broken down sufficiently to provide, a detailed quantitative programme, and a mature, informed and responsible but decentralized organization should be in existence which it is known will endeavour to put the programme into effect, e.g. the pattern of consumable stores requirements will have been studied and appropriate arrangements made for programming issues, the maintenance programme will have been set down, and the labour staffing will have been arranged for the programmed output.

### Flexible Budgeting

Perhaps it should be emphasized that budgetary control is a technique for ensuring considered foresight and for securing co-ordination of all the various phases of a firm's activities and the collaboration of the responsible parties in achieving the objectives. Sales planning and pricing, output programming, stocking policy and planning for financial stability are important features. The target aspect of orders and output must not be forgotten. Accurate reporting of expense variances is but one, and not always the most important of the features of budgeting. Advanced forms of flexible budgeting are in the main designed to provide a closer check on expenditure.

Short-term budgets for the immediate future should be prepared on the basis of conditions which it is considered are capable of achievement. Should conditions change, e.g. a marked change in programmed output, new short-term budgets for the future should be prepared as quickly as possible thereafter. (A permanent change of conditions, e.g. wages agreements, should entail a revision of the long-term budget.) Charts and tabulations of the level of the expense groups and items anticipated at varying levels of activity should be computed as a helpful background guide to preparing such budgets, but they should not supersede or override mutually agreed figures for actual requirements in current conditions.

To the extent to which short-term or progressive budgets are in part derived from the previous, or from the long-term budget, they may be said to be flexible variants of the latter. Where flexible budgets are advocated, however, a step further than this is usually being thought of, i.e. that budgets for expenses should again be adjusted to the level of output actually attained. This might be referred to as fully flexible budgeting.

The Anglo-American Productivity Team on "Management Accounting" reported: "Rather than use elaborate flexible budget techniques it is the practice to set long-term budgets for cost ascertainment and prices, and during the lifetime of this budget to set up many short-term budgets which are used for control purposes."

Flexible budgeting can cover many modifications in technique, and in certain, and not always satisfactory, circumstances, can be a useful accessory in the accountant's tool kit.

At one extreme it can be used as a rudimentary form of budgeting and at the other as a complex refinement. Where top management is very secretive and unwilling to have figures discussed at lower levels, or where very little collaboration exists and no standard costs have been developed, the accountant may have largely to do his own budgeting and may use a simple form of flexible budgeting as a guide to excess costs and for management reporting. The same may apply where orders and production are virtually hand-to-mouth. At the other extreme more elaborate forms of flexible budgeting may be introduced where it is argued that production is so diversified and far-flung that the effort of achieving co-operatively prepared short-term budgets is too difficult or costly. (On the other hand this may merely be evidence of over-centralization and failure to delegate responsibility.) Similarly, where management is very mathematically-minded and can fully use and appreciate the mass of detailed figures, a more elaborate system may be worth while.

Should a scheme of fully flexible budgeting be thought desirable there are several dangers to be guarded against.

(1) In its most analytical form, a complexity of figures is produced. Top management is generally interested in salient features and for such purposes figures must be condensed.

(2) Budgets automatically adjusted to the level of activity actually attained, if not actually unrealistic, may appear to be so at lower management levels, for it is not easy to adjust consumption immediately to rapid changes in activity levels. Care is required if, for example,

freed production staff are held for policy reasons, and even usefully put on cleaning or maintenance work deferred for such an occasion.

(3) Even if expense curves appear to have been mutually agreed there is likely to be a feeling that automatically adjusted expense allowances are imposed rather than agreed. This may act as an irritant rather than as an incentive.

It is felt that in some forms fully flexible budgeting tends to depart from the principle that a business should endeavour to operate according to plan, and that while fully flexible budgets can form a useful starting point, or a helpful refinement, they are a poor substitute for an agreed programme where this is possible. Close liaison is often more important than mathematical perfection.

## The Mathematics of Variance Analysis

The following illustration is given as a simplified example of the mathematics of variance analysis of which useful applications can often be found.

|  | Standard (S) | | Budget (B) | | Actual (A) | |
|---|---|---|---|---|---|---|
|  |  | Per unit |  | Per unit |  | Per unit |
| Units Produced . . | 100 | unit | 80 | unit | 76 | unit |
|  | £ | £ | £ | £ | £ | £ |
| Value Produced . . | 120 | 1·2 | 94 | 1·175 | 91 | 1·197 |
| Materials . . . | 50 | 0·5 | 42 | 0·525 | 41 | 0·539 |
| Labour . . . | 30 | 0·3 | 26 | 0·325 | 25 | 0·330 |
| Overhead . . . | 20 | 0·2 | 18 | 0·225 | 19 | 0·250 |
|  | 100 | 1·0 | 86 | 1·075 | 85 | 1·119 |
| Profits . . . | 20 | 0·2 | 8 | 0·1 | 6 | 0·078 |

For a firm specializing an even flow process on a uniform product the foregoing form of statement, elaborated in expense detail might be considered to supply adequate data for overall cost control. A close study of such a statement will certainly indicate the starting point for investigations particularly if units can be expressed in quantities, tons, gallons, etc.

To enable variance analysis to be undertaken, what in effect is done is to interpolate one or other of a series of figures. These may be as follows—

| | Standard for Actual (SA) | | Standard for Budget (SB) | | Budget for Actual (BA) | |
|---|---|---|---|---|---|---|
| | | Per | | Per | | Per |
| Units Produced . | 76 | unit | 80 | unit | 76 | unit |
| | £ | £ | £ | £ | £ | £ |
| Value Produced . . | 91·2 | 1·2 | 96 | 1·2 | 89·3 | 1·175 |
| Materials . . . | 38·0 | 0·5 | 40 | 0·5 | 39·9 | 0·525 |
| Labour . . . | 22·8 | 0·3 | 24 | 0·3 | 24·7 | 0·325 |
| Overhead . . . | 15·2 | 0·2 | 16 | 0·2 | 17·1 | 0·225 |
| | 76·0 | 1·0 | 80 | 1·0 | 81·7 | 1·075 |
| Profit . . . | 15·2 | 0·2 | 16 | 0·2 | 7·6 | 0·1 |

These figures are computed by applying the predetermined standard (or budget) unit costs to the various volumes of output. The overhead line can be regarded as the overheads which would be absorbed by standard overhead rates at different activity levels.

It is now necessary to refer to the accompanying table. If a standard cost system alone is in operation and short-term budgets are not applied, variances would be extracted as in column (1) by interpolating the standard

cost of actual output. The Profit and Loss Account on a
standard costing basis would appear as

|  | £ |
|---|---|
| Output Value . . . . | 91 |
| Standard Cost of Output (SA) . . | 76 |
|  | 15 |
| Variances from Standard Cost . . | 9 |
| Actual Profit . . . | 6 |

If the story is to be completed, however, and as a
standard profit has been established, it is necessary to add
to the variances affecting the cost of production £9, the
sales price variance £0·2 and the unrealized standard
profit on lower volume £4·8, if the difference between
standard profit £20 and actual profit £6 is to be fully
explained. It should be noted that under this method
standards will be periodically revised, but their revision
(except as this affects stock values) will not be treated as
a variance.

(This technique may usefully be applied for the purpose
of analysing the results of two periods' trading accounts
compiled on an actual basis by treating the earlier period
as standard. If wages rates have been steady, direct
labour or labour hours can be treated as the index of
activity and the key factor to which other costs are
presumed to bear a standard relationship.)

Where management make use of short-term budgets,
(not embodied in the book-keeping) linked with standard
costs, and concentrate attention on the steps required to
reduce variances revealed by the difference between
budget and standard, the standard cost of budget output
can be interpolated giving variances as in column (2) of

the table. If the variances between standard and actual are extracted, the variances between budget and actual can in certain circumstances be obtained by deduction as in column (3). Where short-term budgets are regarded as overall figures and not as revised detailed standards for labour and materials, the form of analysis adopted may be that of column (6) which is a refinement of column (1).

Where output value is calculated from deliveries plus closing less opening finished stocks at cost, and with all variances related to production, the Sales Price Variance will be adversely affected by surplus production being put into stock at less than selling price and vice versa. An adjustment to give a Sales Price Variance on production valued at selling price can be created by inserting an (approximate) equal and opposite entry augmenting value produced (and thus sales price variance) on the one hand and showing a new Conservative Stock Movement Variance on the other, when finished stocks rise and vice versa.

It is important to realize the nature of the so-called volume variance and the assumptions and concepts on which it is based. It is intended to reveal the effect of changes in volume of activity on unit cost, and in effect arises through the fixed and semi-variable overheads having to be spread over a lesser number of units produced (where the variance is adverse). It can be thought of as the cost of under-utilization of the planned facilities.

It is dangerous, however, to think of the volume variance in isolation, for even so-called fixed costs can be reduced, and the offset of reduced overheads against an adverse volume variance must be kept in mind. The total effect of volume of activity on results is probably most clearly shown by charts of the "break-even" type.

With a detailed system it is of course possible to break

ANALYSIS OF VARIANCES BETWEEN STANDARD, BUDGET AND ACTUAL PROFIT

| | METHOD A | | | | | | METHOD B | | | | | | | | | METHOD C | | |
| --- | --- | --- | --- | --- | --- | --- | --- | --- | --- | --- | --- | --- | --- | --- | --- | --- | --- | --- |
| | (1) Variances between Standard and Actual (Interpolate SA) | | | (2) Variances between Standard and Budget (Interpolate SB) | | | (3) = (1) − (2) Variances between Budget and Actual Difference (1) − (2) | | | (4) Variances between Budget and Actual (Interpolate BA) | | | (5) = (2) + (4) Variances between Standard and Budget and Budget and Actual | | | (6) Variances between Standard and Actual (Interpolate SA + B) | | |
| | £ | £+ | £− | £ | £+ | £− | £ | £+ | £− | £ | £+ | £− | £ | £+ | £− | £ | £+ | £− |
| **COST VARIANCES** | | | | | | | | | | | | | | | | | | |
| Materials Cost Variance | 41·0A / 38·0SA | | 3·0 | 42·0B / 40·0SB | | 2·0 | | | 1·0 | 41·0A / 39·9BA | | 1·1 | | | (2) 2·0 / (4) 1·1 | 41·0A / 38·0SA | | 3·0 |
| Wages Variance | 25·0A / 22·8SA | | 2·2 | 26·0B / 24·0SB | | 2·0 | | | 0·2 | 25·0A / 24·7BA | | 0·3 | | | (2) 2·0 / (4) 0·3 | 25·0A / 22·8SA | | 2·2 |
| Volume Variance | 20·0S / 15·2SA | | 4·8 | 20·0S / 16·0SB | | 4·0 | | | 0·8 | 18·0B / 17·1BA | | 0·9 | | | (2) 4·0 / (4) 0·9 | 20·0S / 15·2SA | | 4·8 |
| Overhead Variance | 20·0S / 19·0A | 1·0 | | 20·0S / 18·0B | 2·0 | | | | 1·0 | 18·0B / 19·0A | | 1·0 | | (2) 2·0 | (4) 1·0 | 18·0B / 19·0A | | 1·0 |
| Overhead Variance (Budget Revision) | | | | | | | | | | | | | | | | 20·0S / 18·0B | 2·0 | |
| | | 1·0 | 10·0 | | 2·0 | 8·0 | | — | 3·0 | | — | 3·3 | | 2·0 | 11·3 | | 2·0 | 11·0 |
| **SALES VARIANCES** | | | | | | | | | | | | | | | | | | |
| Sales Price Variance | 91·2SA / 91·0A | | 0·2 | 96·0SB / 94·0B | | 2·0 | | 1·8 | | 89·3BA / 91·0A | 1·7 | | | (4) 1·7 | (2) 2·0 | 91·2SA / 91·0A | | 0·2 |
| Unrealized Profit on lower volume | 20·0S / 15·2SA | | 4·8 | 20·0S / 16·0SB | | 4·0 | | | 0·8 | 8·0B / 7·6BA | | 0·4 | | | (2) 4·0 / (4) 0·4 | 20·0S / 15·2SA | | 4·8 |
| | | 1·0 | 15·0 | | 2·0 | 14·0 | | 1·8 | 3·8 | | 1·7 | 3·7 | | 3·7 | 17·7 | | 2·0 | 16·0 |
| **PROFIT** | Standard · 20·0 | | | Standard · 20·0 | | | Budget · 8·0 | | | Budget · 8·0 | | | Standard · 20·0 | | | Standard · 20·0 | | |
| **PROFIT** | Actual · 6·0 | | | Budget · 8·0 | | | Actual · 6·0 | | | Actual · 6·0 | | | Actual · 6·0 | | | Actual · 6·0 | | |
| **DIFFERENCE** | 14·0 | | | 12·0 | | | 2·0 | | | 2·0 | | | 14·0 | | | 14·0 | | |

Fig. 20

down the Materials Cost Variance into Price and Usage, and the Wages Variance into Rate and Efficiency.

Sometimes a Calendar Variance is introduced to account for the change in the number of working days in the budget period. Though perhaps not academically sound, this variance can largely be avoided if the year's estimated and actual fixed charges are apportioned to budget periods in proportion to working and not calendar days.

## More Variances

By applying basic principles, one can devise specialized variances from standard (or budget) conditions to meet special local requirements, but, in reporting to management, proliferation of variances must not outpace management's understanding of their construction and significance. Often they can only act as a starting point for detailed studies or may be brought into use at irregular intervals when attention is being focused on particular problems.

PRODUCT MIX VARIANCES

The effects of changes from the standard proportion of different products can manifest themselves in complex repercussions within the organization with part of their effects seeping out in all other variances from standard. To be of real help to management, the likely effects of such changes in proportion are best covered by special studies of various permutations, undertaken in advance of their occurrence, as referred to elsewhere.

However, it is well for students to be aware of the approaches used for extracting sales mix variances after they have occurred, when this is called for.

Sales Volume Variance (Unrealized Profit on Lower Volume where adverse) is usually calculated after extracting the sales price variance. It is thus the Standard

Profit on the Standard Volume of Sales (at Standard Price and Standard Cost) less the Profit on the Actual Volume of Sales when calculated at Standard Price and Standard Cost for that volume.

In the preceding example this has been shown as

|  | Units | Sales Value | Cost of Sales | Profit |
|---|---|---|---|---|
| (a) Standard | 100 | 120 | 100 | 20 |
| (b) Actual at Standard Price and Standard Cost | 76 | 91·2 | 76 | 15·2 |
| Sales Volume Variance | | | | 4·8 |

Invoiced Sales Mix Variances are treated as a subdivision of the sales volume variance and are thus calculated by comparison of the standard (a), with the actual volume of sales at standard price (or standard mark up on standard cost) and at standard cost of actual sales (b).

If one now imagines the standard and the actual figures as being composed of a different product mix one might have, using slightly modified figures:—

STANDARD

|  | Units | Std Price | Total Std Sales Value | Std Cost | Total Std Cost Value | Profit at Std Unit Prices | % to Std Cost |
|---|---|---|---|---|---|---|---|
|  |  | £ | £ | £ | £ | £ |  |
| A | 100 | 30 | 3,000 | 24 | 2,400 | 600 | 25 |
| B | 200 | 20 | 4,000 | 18 | 3,600 | 400 | 11 |
| C | 125 | 40 | 5,000 | 32 | 4,000 | 1,000 | 25 |
|  | 425 |  | 12,000 |  | 10,000 | 2,000 | 20% |

ACTUAL

|  | Units | Std Price | Total Std Sales Value | Std Cost | Total Std Cost Value | Profit at Std Unit Prices | % to Std Cost |
|---|---|---|---|---|---|---|---|
| A | 20 | 30 | 600 | 24 | 480 | 120 | 25 |
| B | 220 | 20 | 4,400 | 18 | 3,960 | 440 | 11 |
| C | 103 | 40 | 4,120 | 32 | 3,296 | 824 | 25 |
|  | 343 |  | 9,120 |  | 7,736 | 1,384 | 18% |
| Sales Volume Variance |  |  |  |  |  | £616 |  |

How much of this sales volume variance is attributable to a change in the product mix?

One has first to decide what base one is going to use as representing the standard proportions and when one is dealing with product groups rather than product units, figures for unit quantities, (*a*) the most obvious in this case, will not always be available and some may decide to use either (*b*) Standard Sales Values or (*c*) Standard Cost Value though, if available, one might even use (*d*) the labour and overhead cost value embodied in the total standard cost value of standard sales, as representative of the standard proportions of capacity usage.

Using quantities, the effects of change in mix could be calculated.

Standard mix produces a profit of approx. £4·7 per unit. If the total units in the actual mix had been in this proportion they would have earned

$$343 \times 4\text{·}7 = \text{£1,612}$$

At Standard Cost and Price they only earned £1,384

Therefore Sales Mix Variance, Adverse    =    228

Therefore of the Sales Volume Variance £616, £228 can be attributed to change in mix on this basis.

Using standard cost values, with the standard mix, a total standard cost value has a mark up averaging 20 per cent or £2,000.

If the standard cost value of the actual mix £7,736 had been in the standard proportions it would also have produced a mark up of 20 per cent, i.e. £1,547, but only actually produced £1,384 a difference (adverse) attributable to mix of £163.

Therefore on this basis of the Sales Volume Variance of £616, £163 can be attributed to change of mix. In this case it should be pointed out to management that it arises from the fall off in sales of the high margin A and C, particularly A, though there is a growth in low margin B.

A similar approach can be applied to materials usage variances when one is concerned with blends of raw materials with changes in proportions at different standard prices.

## Production Efficiency—Effect on Overheads

(Volume *or* Fixed Overhead/Efficiency Variance)

It has already been pointed out, management can be provided with some indication of the cost of carrying resources not fully utilized by means of an adverse Production Volume (or Capacity) Variance.

The bulk of this can usually be attributed to the volume of business made available to the factory.

Where, however, the labour or machine hours actually required for jobs are more than the standard hours specified, excess resources require to be carried or viewed the other way; assuming orders available, a further volume (of standard hours) could have been produced had excess time not been spent on the first batch and part of an adverse volume variance might therefore be attributed to this inefficiency. An indication of such effects can be extracted from the total Production Volume Variance where the appropriate date is available.

Using method C (on page 107) the Capacity Variance was shown as

|  | Standard at Standard Activity | Absorbed by Actual Output at Standard Rates | Capacity Variance |
|---|---|---|---|
|  | (a) | (b) | (a)–(b) |
| Overhead Fixed | £1,200 | 912 | 288 Excess |

If one now elaborates on (b) and describes this as Standard Hours Actually Produced 912 at standard rate £1 = £912 (used as a basis for absorbing fixed overheads).

Hours actually taken for standard hours produced, 950, at standard rate £1 = £950.

| | | |
|---|---|---|
| Volume/Efficiency Variance (950–912) at £1 | £ 38 | Adverse |
| Balance, Capacity Usage Variance | £250 | Adverse |
| Total Capacity Variance | 288 | Adverse |

## Long-term Forecasts

Apart from the long-term budget on which standard costs are based, which will represent the best available computation of the "normal" position, it will often be worth while and even necessary to prepare other forecasts on varying assumptions. Often long-term Budgets of Capital Development are projected. For these to have validity they must be related to long-term forecasts of turnover and profitability and will be linked with forecasts of cash requirements. Irrespective of whether or not there is a capital development programme, it may be wise to prepare long-term cash forecasts, having in mind possible trends in volume of turnover, raw materials prices, selling prices, etc. More than one such forecast may be prepared on best and worst assumptions of high or low turnover, rising or falling raw materials prices, etc. "Time spent on reconnaissance is seldom wasted."

While short-term cash forecasts may be prepared on a receipts and payments basis, long-term forecasts for five or six years ahead are better set out in the form below, giving a columnar tabulation for, say, half-yearly periods, and carrying forward the cash balance at the end of one period to the beginning of the next. With the passage of time such forecasts will naturally have to be revised in the light of the then current estimate of changes in the forward situation.

*Period*......................................................

£

FORECAST OUTPUT . . . . .
  Cash at beginning . . . . .

FORECAST RECEIPTS
  Net Profit before Taxation . . .
  Provision for Depreciation . . .

FORECAST OUTGOINGS
  Taxation on Previous Profits . . .
  Dividends . . . . . .
  Capital Expenditure . . . .
  Financing Increased Stocks . . .
  Financing Increased Debtors . . .
  *Less* Increased Credit from Suppliers . .

  Cash at end . . . . . .

The foregoing wording assumes increased turnover and rising prices. Conversely decreased turnover or falling prices may initially release cash funds invested in debtors and stocks. A useful check can sometimes be applied, for debtors, creditors and stocks can often be held to a recognized percentage of turnover.

## Special Studies

While the Accountant or Budget Officer will do his best to ensure that standards of operation are based on careful studies of the best possible methods of utilizing the equipment available, and will build these into the framework of his costing and budget system of control for current routine operations, he should not be content with this. Other special studies are required outside the

framework of the system as such. Such studies, undertaken in conjunction with the technical staff, will deal
with the effects on costs and earnings of utilizing other
methods or other types of equipment coming on the
market; with the effect of changing the proportion of the
different products in the total output: with the effect of
changing their price or their volume or of introducing
new products. The Management Accountant should
make a practice of submitting special non-routine reports
on particular aspects of cost reduction and the potentiality
of maximizing earnings. Some firms adopt the practice
of forming teams for investigation projects dealing with
such aspects as materials handling, scrap reduction,
simplification of design, etc., in all of which the cost
reduction aspect holds foremost place.

## Budgeting for Inflation and Price Movements

This difficult problem can only be sketched here.
Orthodox net profits are based on the concept that no
net profit arises unless provision has been made for maintaining monetary capital intact, and it is widely recognized
that in a period of rising prices, inadequate provision may
have been made for maintaining physical capital intact
unless further sums have been held back from distribution,
in the form of reserves. This arises through depreciation
provisions being calculated on original cost and from the
fact that on a first-in first-out basis, closing stocks held
at higher prices than the corresponding opening stocks
have the effect of showing profits which are in fact locked
up in the higher priced stocks at the end of the period.

If it is an agreed policy that the finance required to
cover replacements is to be found from depreciation
provisions and reserves retained out of orthodox net
profits, then a basis has to be found for computing such
reserves, and selling prices have to be set as far as possible

to leave a profit which will enable not only a dividend to be paid but the desired reserves to be set aside after taxation. (Extant borrowed funds affect the answer.)

As far as replacement of fixed assets is concerned, it seems necessary to regard depreciation as a "Provision for Replacement of Depreciation computed at Current Values." The provision computed on original cost will require to be supplemented by the difference between this and the computation at current values. In a period of inflation it has to be recognized that provided the provision computed at current values is immediately invested in new fixed assets, on which provisions are also in turn computed on current values, no under-provision in previous years will arise, as would be the case if the provisions were held in cash when inflation is continuing.

As regards stocks, the simplest approach is to withhold from distributable profits the price rise between the opening and closing basic stocks, i.e. opening basic stocks are revalued at closing current prices and the difference between the opening and closing values is treated as a reserve. (Conversely, in periods of deflation, the difference is released from reserve.)

The concept behind such an approach to the problem would be on the lines that no "Current Operating Surplus" arises until provision has been made for maintaining productive capacity intact, and is based on an assumption that a business is a continuing business and will continue in the same line of business.

This utility concept comes somewhere between the concept that no surplus arises unless monetary capital is maintained intact, and that in which no surplus arises unless provision is made for maintaining intact the relative real exchangeable value of the business.

In compiling budgets an attempt should be made to cover these requirements.

## The Weekly Profit and Loss Account

Once the appropriate organization has been established and the techniques of compiling short-term budgets and actual results have been mastered, it becomes possible in some industries to compile reasonably reliable weekly profit and loss accounts or operating statements progressively corrected by running adjustments. This becomes a meaningful and practical proposition under conditions where there is a fairly steady flow of dispatches or finished production (see note p. 40); where selling prices are known at the time of delivery and where prices of main raw materials embodied in deliveries have been notified by the time finished goods are dispatched. (It is getting a fairly correct "cost of sales" that is significant— unconsumed purchases carried forward at cost in closing stocks do not affect profits nor do they influence them if they are unpriced and excluded from purchases and stocks.) In some contexts it may be helpful to work in terms of "margins" (sales values less direct materials costs, i.e. net output). When this is achieved the entire organization starts to think in terms of the budgeted income, costs and profit rates *per week* and actual results are similarly discussed in terms of rates per week, and cumulative totals. Arguments about monthly or 4, 5 weekly periods then become academic. Prompt weekly results provide advance danger signals in terms of profit —the activating figure for top management.

## The Limitations of Standard Costs and Budgetary Control

Whilst standard costing goes a long way towards measuring productive efficiency as compared with a predetermined standard, and budgetary control can provide a co-ordinated plan of action based on considered foresight, it is as well to realize their limitations.

Standards in general must be set with reference to a firm's own experience and knowledge of operating with its existing equipment, but if the standard itself is based on inefficient conditions, variances will only reveal a greater or lesser degree of inefficiency. In the long run, efficiency must be looked at from three angles.

1. *Past* success in achieving ends. Apart from holding shareholders' capital intact and maintaining a reasonable return on their investment, success must surely include the maintenance of a reasonably stable level of employment and wages, free from violent fluctuation, and provision of a sustained supply of goods of quality.

2. *Present* means for achieving ends.

3. *Future* plans and schemes in being for achieving ends over a continuing period.

It is not sufficient to think only of the negative aspect, the apparent absence of waste of space, time, machinery, materials and money. Much more will be achieved if the positive approach is followed, and efficiency is thought of in terms of the maximum balanced utilization of resources for the purpose of supplying exchangeable goods and services over a continuing period. These resources include brains and skill and the external resources of accumulated knowledge and educational facilities.

This leads up to the need for greater study of comparative costs within an industry and of the cost aspects of technical improvements and management techniques being developed elsewhere. Similarly the value of a budget forecast is limited if it is based on a lack of foresight or an inadequate knowledge and appreciation of the probable trends of demand and of supply and of the growth of competition.

CHAPTER XVIII

# FINDING THE BEST BUDGET

IF one would set bounds to the function of management accountancy (for lack of a better term), it is considered that it would cover anything related to the financial and economic evaluation of the outcome of events and plans—past, present and future—pertaining to an organization.

In this capacity the management accountant must be prepared to utilize any tools which are available, whether they be mathematical, statistical, or actuarial, or simply single, double, triple, or multiple entry; or any other appropriate means of compilation and analysis.

Whilst the largest firms may be in a position to subdivide this section between specialists with varying background training, in firms of less vast dimensions the accountant may be the only member of the staff capable of this type of work. In larger organizations he may co-ordinate it.

## Management Accountancy

The Management Accountant must have a sense of proportion and be well aware of the part played by Management Accountancy and similar information in the organization. Recently there have been many references to management decision making. The table overleaf may help to clarify the part played by accountancy in this.

Decisions must be based on information. It is in the multiplicity of these same basic decisions relating to multiple products, consumers, machines, materials, and men, and in their delegation, that much of the complexity arises. Nor is management an entirely free agent.

In effect, decisions once taken constitute a plan till a

## PRIMARY MANAGEMENT DECISIONS AND INFORMATION

| DECISIONS | | INFORMATION | |
|---|---|---|---|
| PRIMARY | SECONDARY | INTERNAL | EXTERNAL |
| What to make. | Designs and specifications to choose (How many kinds to make) | Specifications and designs available. Plant and know-how available. What we make profitably. | Under-satisfied consumers' needs and desires. What others are making or plan to make. What others make profitably. Locations available and suitability. |
| Where to make it. How to make it. | What machines, materials, labour, staff, power, transport. | Capacity and plant available. Plant, men, designs and machinery available. How efficiently we make it. How profitably we make it. | How others make it. How efficiently they make it. How profitably they make it. |
| To whom to sell it. | How to publicizei t. How to distribute it. When to deliver it. | Sales contacts available. Customers' status. | To whom are others selling it. How others are publicizing it. Others' capacity. |
| How much to sell. | | Plant capacity and rate of production. Own stocks finished goods. Sales orders on hand. Rate of receipt of orders and trends. Finance available and becoming available. | Others' stocks on the market. Others' orders on hand. Market potential. Others' finance. |
| What to charge. | What credit to give. | What we have been charging. Volume of stocks and cost. Cost to produce at varying volume. Profit at varying prices and costs. Who can or has supplied it. | What others are charging. Others' cost of production. Credit others are giving. Probable future costs of materials. Where are others getting it. What substitutes available. What are others paying. What prices are offered. Stocks held in the market. Current and estimated rate of production. What prices are offered. Price trends. |
| Where to get the materials. | Whom to get them from. | What price have we previously paid. What price will we sell at. Own stocks of materials on hand. Orders for materials outstanding. Production programme. Rate of consumption. Finance available. | |
| What price to pay. | What credit to ask for. | | |
| How much to buy. | When to buy it. How much to store. | | |
| How much to be established to make. | When to install it. | W.I.P. and Finished Stocks held. Sales orders on hand. Estimated orders receivable. Availability of materials, labour, machines and specifications. | Sales potential. Machines available. Price trends. |
| How much to make. | When to make it. How much to store. | | |
| How to divide the income. | What wage rates to pay. What salaries. What bonuses and pensions. What dividends. What retentions. What taxes. | Current rates and earnings. What future plans. What commitments. What finance available. What future income. What profit made and anticipated. Past profits. Future profit estimates. | What others are paying. |
| How to finance the production until it is sold. | Shares or borrowing. How to invest any surplus. | | Finance available. State of the market. Profitability of others. |
| How are the decisions to be co-ordinated. | Who is to make the decisions. | How are we organized. What talent do we possess. | How do others organize for co-ordination. Existing training facilities. |

**All decisions and information interlocking.**

fresh decision is required, and the real test then lies in getting the plan implemented and, when delegation arises, keeping a check that it is working correctly.

The Management Accountant should also be conscious of the part played by industry in the national and international scene.

Fig. 21 gives a grossly over-simplified picture of the participants at one stage of the cycle.

The combination of accumulated resources and organization represented by the firms sends goods moving off in one direction and stopping at the end consumer and sends off money circulating in the opposite direction and continuing round and round.

In the approach to budgeting already outlined, it is inferred that one is trying to arrive at the best co-ordinated budget for the 12, 6, or 3 months ahead and that in the process, conflicting aims between say sales, production, engineering, research, and finance have been reconciled. Sales may want variety and comprehensive stock, Production a few standard lines and long runs (which may also entail rather high stocks), Engineering may seek a lot of new equipment calling for funds which Sales may feel would be better devoted to advertising, and the Designers to research, whilst Finance may emphasize that if the various requirements are to be met, certain changes in the financial structure are inevitable and certain results will undoubtedly emerge.

Budgeting thus aims to convert the divisionally ideal into the jointly feasible. In this process more than one draft budget may have been amended and modified. Not a great deal has been said about long-term planning—some firms in some industries may find this more worth while or potentially significant than others.

Certain difficult problems relating to finding the "best budget" have to be referred to.

# RETURNS ON CAPITAL EMPLOYED

←——— Movement of Money          ———→ Movement of Goods

Fig. 21

| | | |
|---|---|---|
| Wage and Salary Earners | G  Government Departments | T  Taxes (Coy and PAYE) |
| Shareholders | B&I  Banks and Insurance Coys | D  Dividends (Net) |
| Forces, Doctors, Civil Servants and Pensioners etc | M  Materials | S  Savings |
| | W  Wages (Net) | NP  New Plant |

## The Long Term and the Short Term

In seeking the best budget one of the factors which the Management Accountant will often be faced with is that estimated long-term considerations are not always fully compatible with what may at first sight seem "best" in the short run.

Thus immediate profits may look better if research, maintenance, or advertising expenditure are scaled down or deferred, but the long-term repercussions may far offset the short-term profit increase.

The installation of a larger-type plant than is now necessary may incur added costs now, but if demand expands in the long run it may save exorbitant costs of changing everything round later.

The desirability of extensive new plant installations, probably accompanied by cost reductions and/or increased earnings now, may seem by some to be incontrovertible in a period of demand pressure, but others who feel that this is a short-lived boom may justifiably visualize it as a potential future "white elephant."

Considerations of this type will be found to arise in all questions of product selection and pricing, in relation to capital expenditure, to wage payment and labour relations policies, and in many other spheres.

## Product Mix and Product Pricing

Before one can talk about price fixing one must be conscious of the widely varying products and pricing situations in industry "of shoes—and ships and sealing wax—." Some face direct, some indirect substitutes. Some are made to individual customers' requirements, some for the taste of the mass market. Some supply a single buyer, some export throughout the world. For some products there will be an elasticity of demand which will be sensitive to minor price difference—for others there will not. For some, price changes will alter the share of the market. Firms may be dominant price leaders, small firms who fill the gaps; virtual tariff-protected national or local monopolies, or subject to strong competition at home or abroad. Sometimes there is a tradition of relative price stability and competition in quality rather than price, as with certain branded lines.

Nevertheless there are some general remarks with fairly wide application. For example, where there is significant elasticity of demand and a possibility of substitution one cannot fix both price *and* volume. Where demand is strong, prices set too high, if they do not dampen demand, will tend to attract new competition and new entrants to an industry. Though pushing up prices steeply in a boom may be quite practical, the long-term effects on customer relations may be quite damaging. Reducing established prices in what looks like being a short-term slump may produce temporary gains, but the time and difficulty and loss of goodwill in raising one's own (and one's competitors') prices once more to economic levels on a return to more normal trading may much more than wash this out.

If one is to attain the highest current profit, it may seem foolish to make and sell small uneconomic quantities of certain products, yet in the long run it may be these very products which offer most scope for profitable expansion.

## Price Volume Surveys

If one is in a large market which is price sensitive, and is backed by some sound market research, one can usefully carry out price/volume/cost surveys, particularly where one holds a dominant position. Such surveys perforce have a less sound basis where one has to assess the probabilities of uncertain reactions by significant competitors. The element of "Games" in management is now recognized. There can be boomerang effects.

Irrespective of this, their compilation can have an educative value as to the economics of the firm.

Where a firm distributes the same products in different markets insulated from each other, one may think in terms of differential pricing and differential costs.

The following are examples of this type of tabulation.

PRICE VOLUME SURVEY

SINGLE PRICING

| Quantity | Price | | Sales Value | Variable Cost 4s. | Contri-bution | Stepped Cost | Profit |
|---|---|---|---|---|---|---|---|
| | s. | d. | £ | £ | £ | £ | £ |
| 5,000 | 13 | – | 3,250 | 1,000 | 2,250 | 1,150 | 1,100 |
| 6,000 | 12 | – | 3,600 | 1,200 | 2,400 | 1,200 | 1,200 |
| 7,000 | 11 | – | 3,850 | 1,400 | 2,450 | 1,200 | 1,250 |
| 8,000 | 10 | – | 4,000 | 1,600 | 2,400 | 1,250 | 1,150 |
| 9,000 | 9 | – | 4,050 | 1,800 | 2,250 | 1,250 | 1,000 |
| 10,000 | 8 | – | 4,000 | 2,000 | 2,000 | 1,300 | 700 |
| 11,000 | 7 | – | 3,850 | 2,200 | 1,650 | 1,300 | 350 |
| 10,000 | 9 | 6 | 4,750 | 2,000 | 2,750 | 1,300 | 1,450 |

DIFFERENTIAL PRICING

| | | | | | | | |
|---|---|---|---|---|---|---|---|
| 7,000 | 11 | – | 3,850} | | | | |
| 1,000 | 10 | – | 500} | 1,600 | 2,750 | 1,250 | 1,500 |
| 7,000 | 11 | – | 3,850} | | | | |
| 2,000 | 9 | – | 900} | 1,800 | 2,950 | 1,250 | 1,700 |
| 7,000 | 10 | – | 3,500} | | | | |
| 4,000 | 7 | – | 1,400} | 2,200 | 2,700 | 1,300 | 1,400 |

The Total Unit Costs and Differential Costs are of interest.

## Orders to be Accepted

If there is any likelihood that some orders may have to be accepted at sub-standard prices, it is best for someone to have a fairly clear idea in advance of the set of circumstances where this might be policy—and, where appropriate, some form of contingency allowance may be inserted in the budget.

In some types of competitive industry there can on

occasion be a form of price fixing in reverse. A customer, for example, may offer to place a bulk order, but at a sub-standard price. Here we are passing into the realms of product selection.

Some of the questions are as before. What amount of cohesion exists between suppliers, and between customers? What reactions in these spheres if the sub-standard price gets mooted abroad? What is the length of order book and what, if any, the idle capacity? What is the state of the trade? What are the chances of soon getting a similar volume of orders from other sources at better prices? Are we sufficiently specialized to hold out for a better price? Can the customer afford to pay it? Will acceptance of this order lead up to better business later? Is he one of our good customers or a potentially good customer one has been after for years? What of our financial position? What relation does the price offered bear to standard or marginal costs and rates of production?

Although statistics of prices offered and cumulative profit trends on orders booked may be helpful, nevertheless it is on an almost subconscious permutation of such factors that a decision is reached. There is no simple answer.

### Target Price Fixing

Despite all that has been said, there are still innumerable cases where, within limits, prices can be set having a direct relationship with manufacturing costs—trade traditions of mark-ups, of live and let live, of special "know-how," reputation, patent rights—particularly where goods are made to customers' special requirements. Price leaders have to keep a constant eye on this.

In computing costs for pricing purposes it will help to keep one's feet on the ground if one thinks in terms of the costs with the plant ideally balanced to produce that one product. (It might be a competitor's plant.)

Where normal turnover averages twice capital employed, a 10 per cent mark-up on all products will produce roughly a 20 per cent return on capital employed; but this basis will not necessarily be the return on each individual product where the allocated capital employed and the rate of turnover may be widely different from the average. If one wishes to aim at the same percentage return on capital employed on all products, target prices will require to be established on the lines of the following formula.

Net current assets as well as fixed assets have to be thought of, and, of two products with the same ratio of profit to cost, the one for which there is a shorter period of holding materials and labour in stock will give the higher profit on capital employed.

The rate of production or movement as well as the cost of production must be taken into account. For example, if different products have steady but different rates of flow through the factory to give the same return on capital employed on each product, the required profit margin on total cost might be calculated on the lines—

$$P \times \left[ M \times \left( \frac{a - b + c + d + e}{50} \right) + \left( L + O \right) \times \left( \frac{\frac{c}{2} + d + e}{50} \right) + \frac{D}{X} \right]$$

When $P$ = Percentage return required on total capital employed.

$M, L, O$ and $D$ = Materials, Labour, Overheads and Depreciation per unit respectively.

$a$ = weeks' raw material held in stock.
$b$ = weeks' credit given by suppliers.
$c$ = weeks in process.
$d$ = weeks in finished stock.
$e$ = weeks' credit given to customers.
$X$ = the average percentage depreciation on fixed assets.
50 = approximate working weeks per annum.

## Selecting the Best Products

Fundamentally the success of a manufacturing business rests on the products it manufactures, and success lies in

finding products for which there is a sustained or expanding demand.

By considering both the mark-up which will attract the
customer or which the market will stand, and considering
the resultant rate of turnover, retailers generally have a
fairly clear idea as to what are their most profitable lines.
Manufacturers of multiple products appear to be less
conscious of the varying rate of turnover aspect.

Selecting the best products to make, out of a possible
range of products, is complementary to the price-fixing
problem even where a firm is in the fortunate position of
having a fair degree of latitude in its price fixing. It rises
in importance where prices are really competitively
determined in the open market, or where one is one of the
smaller fry and prices are largely determined by the
dominant producers.

The conventional profitability measures will usually
be helpful provided one bears in mind the rate of turnover
aspect and the saleability aspect.

When it comes to the question of the rejection of
apparently unprofitable lines, however (based on cost
computations of total cost), one must be wary, for unless
more profitable lines can certainly be substituted for
them, in a multi-product firm they may still be making
some contribution towards fixed overheads and profit.
Before taking action it is well to have a look at the marginal
cost and contribution aspect.

Thus what at first sight looks like—

|  | | | | Sales £ | Cost £ | Profit £ |
|---|---|---|---|---|---|---|
| Product A | . | . | . | 2,000 | 1,600 | 400 |
| Product B | . | . | . | 3,000 | 3,300 | − 300 (Loss) |
| Product C | . | . | . | 1,000 | 900 | 100 |
| Product D | . | . | . | 2,400 | 2,100 | 300 |
|  | | | | £8,400 | £7,900 | £500 |

may be shown up in another light as—

|  | Sales | Variable Cost | Contribution |
|---|---|---|---|
|  | £ | £ | £ |
| Product A  .   .   . | 2,000 | 1,300 | 700 |
| Product B  .   .   . | 3,000 | 2,800 | 200 |
| Product C  .   .   . | 1,000 | 700 | 300 |
| Product D  .   .   . | 2,400 | 1,700 | 700 |
|  | £8,400 | £6,500 | 1,900 |
| Fixed Overheads  .   .   . |  |  | 1,400 |
|  |  | Profit | £500 |

When "variable costs" are referred to, one may think in terms of "standard variable" (or "marginal") costs. It is, however, the former version which indicates that it would still be undesirable to go for B as a product worth cultivating at its present price or for which one would consider installing replacement plant, but unless the other products can be expanded to take its place, or a better substitute is found, it has a useful place in the overall pattern.

It must be clearly realized that the traditional measures on relative product profitability, e.g. percentage mark-up on (standard) total costs, percentage profit to sales value (computed from this cost basis), profit per unit produced, per cent profit to standard conversion cost (excluding raw materials), especially if merely taken from past results, must rest on the following assumptions when they are applied in isolation as a guide to the products on which to concentrate.

1. That the sales of the product can be expanded and expanded at the existing price, and without a disproportionate reduction in the sales or the price of other relevant products.

2. That its production can be expanded and expanded at no greater unit cost than at present, and without a disproportionate decrease in the production of other relevant products or a disproportionate increase in their unit costs or in the cost of idle capacity.

3. That any increase in the capital employed arising from its expansion is not disproportionately greater than it would be for the expansion of other products.

These assumptions are by no means unreasonable in the longer run for many situations, particularly in the distributive trades, in a factory with very flexible equipment or ample spare capacity, or even where a factory at full activity is prepared to expand its capacity.

They are not all, however, invariably fully valid even if forecast data are used on the sales side, especially where the information is applied as an argument for diversion of capacity to "better" products; for when a factory is already operating near to capacity diversion will almost invariably give rise to bottle-necks.

## Limiting Factors

In some industries using small machines, dealing with separate components and with spare floor-space, it may be simple to clear bottle-necks by sub-contracting, overtime working, or the installation of additional equipment. This is not so feasible in process plants with a continuous production flow through large, heavy and expensive plant, originally designed to be balanced for a particular production pattern.

The short- (and medium-) term problem here may become one of finding the most profitable product mix from the existing equipment.

Where there is only one significant bottle-neck affecting all products (different products being passable through the bottle-neck at different speeds), in the short run the most profitable product, provided it can be sold, will be that showing the highest "profitability factor"—

$$\frac{\text{Marginal Contribution}}{\text{per unit}} \times \frac{\text{Rate of Production at the}}{\text{Bottle-neck Process}^1}$$

It will be easier to devise the appropriate "unit" in some industries than others.

Since the labour and/or overhead cost per unit at this process is likely to be in inverse proportion to the rate of production, a similar scale of profitability factors can be derived from the formula

$$\frac{\text{Marginal Contribution}}{\substack{\text{Labour and/or Overhead Cost} \\ \text{at Bottle-neck Process}}}$$

Where there are two or even three main bottle-necks, one practical approximation method involves testing a range of possible combinations of a limited number of representative products working up from combinations of $\frac{1}{2}$ and $\frac{1}{2}$; $\frac{1}{4}/\frac{3}{4}$ to combinations down to $\frac{1}{8}$, e.g. $\frac{1}{8}$ $\frac{1}{4}$ $\frac{3}{8}$ $\frac{3}{8}$, then eliminating product quantity combinations which violate the bottle-neck including the capacity to sell, and seeking the combinations which make the most use of the main processes. (If there is a logical price structure in the trade related to cost of production and influenced by specialist producers, it is unlikely that the most profitable product mix will leave much idle capacity at any main process.)

The quantities of the products appearing in the surviving combinations are then extended by their marginal contribution to find by this organized trial and error method the mix making the best combined contribution to fixed overheads and profit.

Even in this situation, and more especially where the

---

[1] The limiting factor need not be machines. It may be labour at a process—when the applicable rates of production may be per operative; or it may be one raw material, when a similar technique can be applied.

situation involves a network of multiple bottle-necks (it being assumed that at many stages products are interchangeable between processes), finding the most profitable product mix from the existing capacity (it can also apply to the projected capacity) is rather complex. A more refined and promising method of solution is illustrated in Chapter XXII, and is one of the applications of the technique known as Linear Programming.

It should be noted that the most profitable mix from the existing capacity may not, however, be the most profitable mix to go for in the long run, if bottle-necks for potentially profitable products were to be removed. Long versus short term may be questions more of managerial philosophy than actuarial science.

## The Make or Buy Problem

In the "Make or buy?" problem one again moves into a field where marginal or differential costs are applicable.

Thus it is the difference in future costs which are relevant; depreciation charges on existing plant have generally to be regarded as sunk or dead. So that if an outside supplier offered to supply parts at £85 each, it would be foolish, other things being equal, for one to install plant to produce at an estimated cost of £95, made up say materials £40, operating costs £25, depreciation £30. But if one had existing spare capacity, *with no better alternative use*, where material costs were £40, operating costs (excluding depreciation) £35, it would be policy to make for oneself irrespective of the fact that this item of plant carried an amortization charge of £20.

## Stock Levels, Economic Batch or Order Quantities

Another aspect of seeking the best budget relates to the "best" level of stock holding, which is closely linked with the problem of most economic batch or order quantity.

It is readily seen that the larger the batch size, the larger the average stocks, and that annual holding costs therefore vary in some way directly with batch size. The smaller the batch size, the lower the average stocks and their holding costs, but the higher the annual cost of ordering and setting up. At some point the combination of these two curves will be at a minimum. In some circumstances the most economic order quantities can be set, provided the economic lot size for one item does not interfere with achieving the most economic lot size for other items.

Though still at the "pilot plant" stage, a lot of work has been done on more elaborate situations covering probabilities associated with certain trends and variations in the timing of demands, receipts, and in the inwards delivery ("lead") times, and even to cater for anticipated price rises aimed at, among other things, establishing "scientific" rather than "guestimated" minimum stocks, etc., which will leave negligible chances of shortages with their associated loss of profits which might otherwise be earned.

Patterns something like this may emerge—

| Probability of being out of stock when demand comes in | 1 in 5 | 1 in 10 | 1 in 20 | 1 in 100 |
|---|---|---|---|---|
| Minimum Quantities | 1,120 | 1,600 | 2,040 | 3,060 |

The mathematics of the formulas are generally valid, and it is the assumptions that have to be embodied in the costs to insert into them that tend to be shaky, and the mechanics of application that are in their infancy. Management accountants may be well advised to keep in touch with these developments. Further brief mention appears in Chapter XXII.

## Commercial Timing

It perhaps may be opportune to refer to commercial timing in relation to profitability because there is a significant element of truth in the belief that those who acquire raw materials when and where they are relatively plentiful and cheap, and produce and distribute them when and where they are relatively scarce and dear, thus preventing their becoming scarcer and dearer, receive more tangible thanks from the community than those who find themselves in the reverse position.

The best timing of policy price change in mass produced goods is in itself a complex subject involving stocks at the factory against and not against firm order and levels of stocks in distributors' hands. Inconsiderate timing of announcements of price changes may seriously react on customer goodwill.

One of the most difficult decisions required of management is judging when to cut one's losses. Book values have little relevance as to the timing of disposal of a stock item acquired for £3,000 which will now fetch only £1,000. An assessment as to whether if retained another twelve months it will then fetch £200 or £2,000, is the only relevant approach, bearing in mind that £1,000 now, turned over a few times, could well be augmented by then.

The accountant can find himself a participant, for his request that dubious stocks be written down to an estimated realizable figure seemingly partakes of a ritual value in lifting responsibility from other shoulders. Since deferment of release too often awaits this act, it demonstrates all too well the occasional power of numbers.

## Budgeting in Large Dispersed Organizations

Budgeting has several functions, among the most important of which is the provision of (a) targets for production and for deliveries, (*b*) plans for acquisition of materials and for stockholding and (*c*) sanction for incurring various costs in line with plan, etc. With the passage of time and with changes in circumstances, one or other of such functions will tend for a time to predominate over the others.

In far-flung organizations, budgets may be utilized to obtain a view at the centre of the forecasts and aspirations of their various divisions and groupings, and to obtain a consolidated picture of their financial requirements and perhaps also of anticipated inter-divisional transfers of materials and products and calls on inter-divisional capacity.

Though not invariably necessary or appropriate, the problems of obtaining approval of consolidation at different levels may lead to budgets being compiled further in advance, and covering longer periods than may be found in smaller organizations. They may thus tend to lose some of their sharpness in certain fields but still serve what is the dominant need in the circumstances.

Because of such features, the need may arise for short-term local supplementary forecasts on top of the basic budgeting procedure.

In course of time and perhaps with the aid of computers, means may be found of quickly preparing amended budgets with changes in circumstances initiated by making changes in some of the key variables certain materials costs, wage rates, sales prices, volume factors and rolling their repercussions through the data.

Because of such ramifications, however, a tactical need may also arise for superimposing short-term targets in certain areas as an overlay to the basic budgets.

## Head Office and Divisional Expenses

The best treatment of these within the organization and possibly at establishment level in budgets, in actual results, in product costs and in target prices, is a problem which has not been widely discussed.

The scope and scale of such centralized functions will vary widely between organizations and there might seem to be a long-term cycle between heavy centralization and radical decentralization. As to treatment, at one extreme there is the school which holds that all general central services should be allocated out to establishments, or that specialized consultative services should pay for their keep on a fee-receiving basis for the services. At the other extreme, knowledge of central costs is top secret and unallocated, and, whether selling prices are or are not centrally controlled, cover for the central costs is sought by calling for a high enough return on establishment capital employed, or a high enough mark-up on establishment costs to cover this.

If allocation is to be the principle, and it is to be seen to be fair, its basis should be disclosed, and for this it would seem necessary to break down the central services into functional segments such as finance, accounts, buying, personnel, work study, marketing, research, etc., and seek what is probably a different but appropriate allocation base for each. Even then, it can only be rough justice, and good public relations will have to emphasize that in many cases the allocated charge will have to be regarded by establishments as an insurance premium, for it is in the nature of many such central services that they will have to concentrate on trouble spots.

The main argument against allocation of costs is its effect on morale. Since viewed from the periphery its benefits may seem to take a very intangible form, allocation may only produce ill-informed comment and irritation, and in extreme cases where sections are doing badly, may spread alarm and despondency.

The arguments in favour are (a) that dissemination

of knowledge of the total costs of running the organization will help to emphasize the need for efficiency in its various branches, (b) will influence proposals on selling prices and on volume, (c) will promote a greater sense of participation, and (d) that healthy criticism will contribute to effectiveness.

## Transfer Prices

Another thorny problem which may affect budgeting arises in large-scale organizations where one division transfers goods or work done to another, and where in some cases there may also be competing known open market prices for the same or similar goods. In one form this problem will be avoided, where all goods, or nearly all, are transferred to another division or to a central selling agency at standard or actual cost. Controls on the manufacturing unit will then develop into measures of success in achieving targets set for volume, stocks, unit costs, etc.

On the other hand, though inconvenient, it may be considered stimulating to embody a standard "mark up" on such transfers to provide the conventional profit measure, though in fact this may not be meaningful in such circumstances and the real control must still be in the terms of targets.

Where, however, there is an active open market in which one division is expected to trade at a profit, whilst also serving another division, which in turn may or may not also be allowed to buy in the open market, further complications and stresses arise.

Apart from other things, it may be policy to apply equal non-discriminatory prices both for external sale and internal transfer, for customers for the former may be lost if they become aware the latter are more favoured, and on the other hand internal divisional customers may be starved if there appears to be a higher paper profit on the former.

Again, policies differ, ranging from one extreme in which it is insisted that the acquiring division must buy from the supplying division and the supplying division must sell and strive to supply the other division in absolute priority over the open market, to the other in which complete freedom is given to both divisions to deal in either market, despite marginal cost arguments in periods of temporary slackness.

The compromise solution offers some flexibility, in that the buying division may acquire up to say 20 per cent of its requirements in the open market if the price and service is favourable, and that the selling division satisfies policy if it meets say 80 per cent of the buying division's requirements, and this arrangement commends itself to some, because it enables those concerned to keep in touch with the open market, prevents thereby complacent in-breeding and is in the interests of long-term efficiency.

## Uniform Accounting and Costing

The very large organizations with multiple factories engaged upon the production of similar articles are in a position to take advantage of some of the uses of uniformity in accounting, which some of the pioneers of uniform costing within a Trade Federation rightly foresaw as potentially obtainable but who had only limited success in practice, partly due to inadequate supporting statistical data, and the inability to correlate means (the balance of forces applied) with success in achieving ends.

Particularly where some common physical units of measurement can be found (tons, gallons, etc.) there is a basis for inter-establishment comparison which will provide a starting point for more detailed investigation with a view to improving performance.

# PART V

# FINANCIAL CONTROL

# CHAPTER XIX

## FINANCIAL CONTROL, GRAPHS, AND STATISTICS

PRIMARILY, any business must be in a reasonably sound financial position before it can successfully and efficiently carry on its operations. If the current position is unsatisfactory, the trend must be towards a sounder position.

The older form of two-sided Balance Sheet is very unsatisfactory from the point of view of giving a clear statement of a company's financial position, and before it can be intelligently interpreted and its true significance grasped, the figures usually require to be set out in a more practical form and compared with previous figures.

What directors, managers, and shareholders really want to know from a Balance Sheet are—

(1) Are their interests adequately safeguarded?

(2) Is the company able to meet all its current obligations?

(3) Will the company be able to meet all its long-term obligations?

(4) Is the company making the best use of its assets?

(5) Is the company earning an adequate return on the money invested?

(6) Is the position from these angles improving, or the reverse?

In order to be able rapidly to grasp the answers to these questions the Balance Sheet should be set out somewhat on the lines as given on page 196.

The corresponding figures for the previous Balance Sheet should be inserted alongside.

It should be remembered that a business showing the greatest financial stability is not necessarily the most profitable or efficiently conducted one. Surpluses should be profitably utilized, and a happy medium must be struck between a wide balance of financial stability and a profitable (though perhaps rather speculative)utilization of funds.

Written-down original cost will rarely represent contemporary fixed asset real values. A worked-back analysis of dates of acquisition may give some clues.

A valuable supplement to any Balance Sheet is a "Movement of Funds Statement" showing the changes between two periods. This may follow the same lines as the long-term cash forecast on page 169, though cash at beginning and end may be netted to show increase or decrease of funds. Such a statement taken back to cover a period of five or ten years can be an illuminating document. A matrix form of combined Trading and Profit and Loss Account, Balance Sheet and Movement of Funds Statement is given on page 197.

Cost control does not lie solely in the hands of management. One aspect of securing co-operation of supervisors and operatives is the provision of information. Figures showing the breakdown of the Sales £ form one published approach. For this to be true and fair, if dividends are shown "net" then wages should also be shown net of tax, and P.A.Y.E. tax treated as an outlay. Wages can also similarly be shown net after the deduction of national insurance.

## Financial and Operating Ratios

The basic financial ratios are fundamentally a concise running check to ascertain whether the funds due to flow

## A. B. & CO. BALANCE SHEET AS AT ————————

CURRENT ASSETS
    Cash on Hand and in Bank . . £
    Sundry Debtors . . . .
    Stocks and Work in Progress . .     £

*Deduct* CURRENT LIABILITIES
    Bank Overdraft (if any) . . £
    Sundry Creditors . . . £

               *Current Surplus* . . . . £

FIXED ASSETS
    Machinery and Plant, etc. . . £
    Furniture and Fittings, etc. . .
    Buildings . . . . .     £

*Deduct* LONG-TERM LIABILITIES
    Loans . . . . . £
    Debentures, etc. . . . £

               *Long-term Surplus* . . . £

INTANGIBLE ASSETS
    Goodwill . . . . . . £
    Patents, etc. . . . . . .
                        £
               *Total Net Assets.* . . . £

ORIGINATING FROM SUBSCRIBED CAPITAL
AND EARNINGS RETAINED IN THE BUSINESS
RECORDED AS
    Preference Shares . . . .     £
    Ordinary Shares . . . .
    Retained Earnings (Capital Reserves)
    Retained Earnings (Revenue Reserves)     £

                              £

## THE XYZ TRADING COMPANY LIMITED ANNUAL ACCOUNTS

| | Capital & Retentions Trading A/c | Capital & Retentions Balance | Creditors, etc. | Plant | Stock | Debtors | Cash | Total |
|---|---|---|---|---|---|---|---|---|
| Opening Balance . | £ — | £ 1,800 | £ 700 | £ 1,000 | £ 900 | £ 400 | £ 200 | £ 2,500 |
| Plant Installed . | | | + 100 | + 100 | | | | |
| Plant Paid for | | | — 60 | | | | — 60 | |
| Depreciation | | — 200 | | — 200 | | | | |
| Sales Invoiced . | + 5,000 | | | | | + 5,000 | | |
| Sales Paid for . | | | | | | — 4,600 | + 4,600 | |
| Goods Purchased . | | | + 3,000 | | + 3,000 | | | |
| Paid for Purchases . | | | — 2,800 | | | | — 2,800 | |
| Cost of Goods Issued . | — 2,700 | | | | — 2,700 | | | |
| Adj. Cost to Market Value. | — 100 | | | | — 100 | | | |
| Wages Paid . | — 600 | | | | | | — 600 | |
| Expenses Paid . | — 400 | | | | | | — 400 | |
| Provision for replacing Depreciation . | — 200 | + 200 | | | | | | |
| PROFIT BALANCE . | + 1,000 | | | | | | | |
| Dividend Provided . | — 80 | | + 80 | | | | | |
| Dividends Paid . | | | — 50 | | | | — 50 | |
| Balance Transferred . | | + 920 | | | | | | |
| Closing Balances . | | 2,720 | 970 | 900 | 1,100 | 800 | 890 | 3,690 |

in are adequate to meet the moneys soon due to be paid out to meet financial claims.

Broadly, a business may be considered to be financially sound if Liquid Assets (i.e. cash and marketable securities plus Debtors) are roughly equal to Current Liabilities, i.e. a ratio near 1:1. If this ratio is not met, however, a ratio of 2:1 for Current Assets (i.e. Liquid Assets plus Stocks) to Current Liabilities would still be generally accepted as indicating a sound position. The latter ratio is typical of British Industry. There is a tendency to regard ratios lower than this as a danger sign. Higher ratios than this give evidence of greater current financial soundness, but perhaps at the expense of profitability. Trends, however, may be more significant than absolute figures, and are worth recording and watching. Graphs marked with what are considered high and low tolerances may be helpful.

If liquid resources are drawn off and heavily invested in fixed assets, for a time the ratio of fixed assets to total assets may be abnormally high and the preceding "vulnerability" ratios rather low.

The ratio of Cumulative Depreciation Provisions to Gross Fixed Assets is also worth watching as indicative of Depreciation Policy. Long-term loan holders will be interested in the Net Assets cover for the lending.

An attempt can be made to link these with the Profitability Ratios (sometimes called Operating or Operating Efficiency Ratios). Fundamentally these latter are built up from the basic equation—

$$\frac{P}{C} = \frac{P}{S} \times \frac{S}{C}$$

Where $P$ = Profit, $S$ = Sales or Turnover, and
    $C$ = Capital Employed (i.e. Share Capital plus Reserves).

Thus where the ratio of Sales to Capital Employed is 2:1 (capital turned over twice a year) and the per cent profit to sales is 10 per cent, the profit to Capital Employed will be 20 per cent.  These ratios can be used for rough inter-firm comparisons.

A pyramid of other ratios building up to the foregoing formula as the apex can be developed.  Thus the ratio sales to capital employed can be sub-divided and analysed as:

Sales: Stocks (number of times stock turned over per annum).

Sales: Debtors is more often expressed in the reverse form, Debtors as a ratio of Sales.

When this is in excess of say 1:12 it may indicate slow settlement of customers' accounts.

For overall measurement and rough inter-firm comparison from the equity shareholders' viewpoint, in the foregoing formula, Profit might be defined as Profit after Interest receipts and payments, after Depreciation Provisions and before Tax, and Capital Employed as Share Capital plus Reserves at the end of the period.  If one wishes to turn to a measurement of the effective use of invested funds a version which includes Loan and Debenture Capital with Capital Employed and takes Profit before Interest paid may be brought into use.

When, however, it is desired to use this measure for (a) inter-divisional comparison within a firm: (b) product profitability comparison and price fixing; (c) new capital project comparisons and "efficiency" comparisons; and in general where allocations arise, it is advisable to use a modified and in some ways simpler version based on profit defined as Profit before all Interest Receipts and Payments, and perhaps before Depreciation Charges, and Capital Employed as "Trading Assets," viz. Tangible Fixed Assets Gross (i.e. at cost) *plus* Stocks *plus* Debtors only, preferably based on an average of the opening and closing figures or average figures for the year.  Where considered appropriate, Trade Creditors may be deducted.  This basis, which might be referred to as the "Works Manager's

Basis," avoids rather arbitrary attempts to allocate accumulated cash on hand or overdrafts, loans, dividend and tax provisions and the like (which may in fact be centrally controlled). It attempts to eliminate the effects of central policy matters related to source of funds (e.g. proportions financed by share capital, loans, debentures and policy depreciation provisions) and the allocation and investment of surplus cash; and by thus eliminating some items which really reflect a long history of past policies and performance rather than current responsibilities it helps to make the ratio a better current measure for this purpose.

It may be noted that Capital Employed, particularly in this version, has a fixed and a variable element.

Overall figures for the firm as a whole on the same basis should be available for comparison.

Whilst inflation has tended to play havoc with long-term assessments, it has not vitiated the value of such ratios for the comparison of shorter-term trends.

For special purposes "refined" versions which attempt to bring in "real" or "replacement" values of fixed assets (which need to be carefully defined) may be used, but if some replacement values are used it should be borne in mind that it is not only the depreciation content of the Trading Account which may be altered but the operating costs themselves may be radically changed if the most modern plant was employed.

There are other ratios in common use by investors, and managers and accountants are well advised to keep in touch with this viewpoint. Thus "dividend yield" is expressed in terms of the last dividend gross to the current market value of the total equity capital; "dividend cover" is the ratio Profit after Tax to Gross Dividends; Price/ Earnings Ratio refers to market value of equity capital to profit after Tax.

## The Use of Ratios

Whenever possible, ratios should be used as a supplement rather than as a substitute for the actual data, for, when used *en masse* divorced from the actual data they are tricky things to handle and interpret unless in, for example, comparisons between different periods, one of the bases is fairly stable or any two ratios are firmly interlocked by a third ratio. Thus to say that advertising has risen from 5 per cent to 10 per cent of turnover can either mean that advertising has doubled and sales are stable or advertising is stable and turnover is halved, or a combination of the two; and the translation of ratios showing 2 : 1 as compared with 1 : 1 might be used for such an interpretation as "In the so-and-so trade the horse power per operator in factory A is twice that in factory B," whilst when combined with the missing third ratio that output per horse power in factory A is the same as in factory B the correct deduction is that the operators per horse power in factory A are only half those of factory B (due to good organization of manpower not horse power).

## Cost Percentages

Tabulations should be regularly compiled of the relative proportion of the different items of cost and of cost absorbed in the various products and in the different departments. These relationships are best expressed as percentages to output, percentages to direct labour, or percentages to total cost, and are exceedingly useful in checking and comparing the general overall efficiency of different departments, and almost essential for explaining cost variations and building up balanced budget figures for different volumes of output. Figures should be tabulated periodically for the relationship in each department. (See example p. 31.)

This can be supplemented with detailed percentages for particular departments if required.

It is with the aid of such figures that the type of chart given in Chapter IV is compiled.

## Summary Monthly Board Report

Some managements like to see salient features of the situation condensed on two sheets of foolscap.

Good design will enable quantities or values to be set down with selected comparisons such as last period cumulative, budget, this period last year, etc. Details will be relegated to appendices. Other reports on prospects, problems and achievements may be circulated by functional heads. Headings of the summary might be—

> Net Profits.
> Orders Received, Delivered and On Hand.
> Cash and Short-term Loans and Deposits.
> Capital Commitments Outstanding and Installed.
> Labour Force and Labour Turnover.
> Price Changes—Cost Changes.

Occasional alterations in content and layout are desirable to bring out features requiring emphasis.

## Master Chart

It may be useful to supplement accounts by one or two master charts covering principal trends. Orders Received, Delivered, and On Hand can be graphed together with Net Profit on a Trading Chart (reading on two scales). A financial chart might cover Bank Balance, Stock Values (with percentage to Deliveries noted), Surplus of Current Assets over Current Liabilities.

# PART VI
# ACTION

# CHAPTER XX

## ACTION

FIGURES in themselves have no meaning; it is what they represent that is significant. A perfect budget or standard cost system is not a substitute for management. It is only a guide to management. For figures to be any use whatever from a management point of view, it is necessary to ensure that any variation in policy, any new methods, or the correction of any adverse tendencies indicated as necessary by the figures, be translated into *Action*.

Some organization must be devised to ensure first of all that any indications shown by the figures are brought to the notice of the proper parties, and secondly that the action indicated is carried out.

### Budget and Cost Committee  (See also page 17)

Probably the best form of organization (personalities permitting) that has been devised for this end is on the lines of a committee, meeting regularly to discuss the relevant questions arising from the budget and cost reports.

Why have a committee at all? Because much more is likely to be achieved by a well-run committee, meeting at regular times, with a specified personnel, and with agenda and minutes, if thought necessary, than is ever likely to be accomplished through haphazard conversations and discussion held any time ("if free"), any place, and anyhow.

The true nature of a committee, however, should be recognized; by itself it is consultative, not executive. Executive functions are carried out by individuals. The final authority lies with the General Manager, but the degree of authority carried by the various divisional chiefs will depend on the type of organization and on the personality and capacity of each individual.

As previously stated, the committee must be supplied with prompt and adequate reports, which may in fact form the agenda of the meetings. Summarized reports will be given to the higher executives, while more detailed reports will be furnished to the persons directly interested. The meeting will consider and discuss these reports (see Chapter XV) and decide on any steps that require to be taken.

One of the most effective methods of ensuring that any action decided on has been carried out is to ask the person responsible therefor to submit a report to a subsequent meeting on the effectiveness of any steps taken, or on the progress made with any particular scheme.

We would stress again the importance of having adequate figures showing the causes of inefficiencies and loss of profits, and also of potential profits. If a proper diagnosis cannot be given, how can we expect to effect a cure?

Action starts, and will be most effective, at the time the budget is being prepared and the programme set out for achieving the desired objectives. Action on consequent variances is the second line of defence.

### (1) **Decline in Orders Received** (Orders below Budget or Standard Level)

The value of orders received is the fundamental basis of carrying on business, and any variation is the first matter which should receive attention.

Causes of a decrease may be—

(*a*) Stronger competition:
> Better quality
> Better price
> Better service
> Better salesmanship
> Better substitute.

(*b*) Lack of demand:
> Change of requirements
> Change of fashion
> Lack of buying power.

(*c*) Lack of, or unreliable supply.

The investigation of such causes is most important and will usually be in the hands of the Sales Manager, and it is primarily for him to discover the reason and if possible suggest the remedy. (It is also for him to interpret such conditions and be forearmed against them.)

In this he will be aided by all necessary forms of sales analyses supplied by the Accounting Department, by salesmen's reports, and by reports on the investigation of national business trends and statistics.

Assuming the causes to have been correctly analysed, let us consider the possible remedies.

(*a*) STRONGER COMPETITION

*Quality.* If a better quality of product is being marketed by a competitor, the management will naturally turn at once to the Technical and Production Departments. Can their own product be improved? What are its faults? Where do their competitors beat them? Is it in the method of production? Is it the quality of the materials used? Is it in the design? Are the designing and technical staff the best men available?

It is in the courageous answering of these questions that the remedy will be found.

*Price.* Assuming the quality to be designed to meet the demand, and the method of manufacture to be as efficient as is currently possible, if it is considered that many sales are still being lost through high price, the margin of profit taken will then come under review. What extra sales will result from a reduction of price? This is an extremely difficult question to answer, and the Sales Manager will have to rely largely on common sense based on his personal experience and the reports from his salesmen, supplemented by market analysis reports as to the demand and buying power of certain sections of the public. The method of making up such estimates may vary tremendously, depending on the class of product. Once it is decided that a certain increase in sales is likely to result from a reduction in price, and assuming that the plant can efficiently cope with the increased production, a simple calculation will show what profits should result from such a step.

EXAMPLE

|  | £ |
|---|---|
| Present Sales (1,000 at £5) . . . . | 5,000 |
| Cost (1,000 at £4) . . . . . | 4,000 |
| Profit . . . | 1,000 |

After reduction in price and, say, some reduction in unit cost from increased output—

|  | £ |
|---|---|
| Anticipated Sales (2,000 at £4·50) . . | 9,000 |
| Cost (2,000 at £3·75) . . . . | 7,500 |
| Profit . . . | 1,500 |

If sales can be maintained at a 2,000 level, and production obtained at the reduced cost, such a reduction in price would be profitable. But it should be remembered that price reductions may simply start a vicious circle and competitors may follow with similar reductions, leaving the position worse than before.

The reverse situation may occur. Can more profitable business be done by increasing price and perhaps slightly reducing sales? Similar calculations will supply the answer.

"Dumping" is also a form of price competition, against which, if a good case can be made out, and technical superiority is of no avail, action may take the form of appeal for Government action, or extend even to political agitation for tariff adjustment.

*Service.* The question of after-sales service and the cost thereof, boldly tackled, can be readily solved, once the situation (inferior service to competitors) is fully realized.

*Salesmanship.* This should also be fearlessly dealt with by competent authority. Analysis of individual travellers' results should be referred to and steps taken to remedy any defects found. Salesmen's classes and conferences should be held, and regular encouraging letters sent. The quality of the publicity and advertising should be carefully reviewed, and the percentage cost thereof to sales considered.

*Substitutes.* Full reports should be made out regarding the effect on the market of competitive substitutes and where such competition is marked. Entire changes in production programmes may even have to be faced.

### (b) Lack of Demand

Probably more old-established businesses have sunk from this cause than from any other. In some cases the situation is almost uncontrollable, but in a large number the fault may be said to be in "failure to keep up with the times"—i.e. non-adaptability.

*Change of Requirements.* The requirements of the public are not static and change with social conditions, education, technical advances, etc. A firm specializing in the manufacture of press-bulb motor horns cannot expect to survive when electric horns are being installed in all cars, or a mill weaving very expensive tweeds if everybody decides that a factory-made suit will suffice. There is still a very real diehard conservatism in many sections of business, an unwillingness among old directors to adapt themselves to change, which, if persisted in, imposes severe strains on any firm.

It is for the Sales Department to forecast and foresee such changes and to appreciate their significance. Often real difficulties in adapting or converting plant will be encountered, but with a bold and courageous policy of facing up to facts they can usually be overcome. New products should continually be sought and those for which demand is likely to drop courageously abandoned. It is only by such a policy of meeting the public's current demands that a firm can keep in the front rank.

*Lack of Buying Power.* This situation is not so easily met, especially in the case of a nation-wide or world-wide slump, and the thing to watch is that adequate reserves are built up to meet depression and provision made for curtailing or diverting production at the proper time. Here again, adaptation to current conditions may enable the situation to be profitably met. Reduction in quality and price may be undertaken to meet the requirements of the new standard of living.

Where, however, the reduction of buying power is confined to one district or section of the community, the remedy is to be found in seeking new markets.

In certain extreme cases it may even involve the courageous transfer of the whole business to some new locality.

(2) **Decline in Output** (Output below Budget)

        (a) Lack of orders
        (b) Lack of raw material
        (c) Lack of labour
        (d) Uncoordinated planning
        (e) Excessive scrap and waste
        (f) Plant breakdowns
        (g) Power failures
        (h) Designing delays
        (i) Technical troubles
        (j) Lack of capital.

(a) has just been dealt with.

(b) LACK OF RAW MATERIALS FROM OUTSIDE SUPPLIES
    (See Materials, Usage and Volume Variances)

The baby in this case will undoubtedly be handed over to someone who is not even a relation. But excuses for lack of raw material—from the Buying and Stores Control Departments—should not be too readily accepted except in the case of ascertained exceptional circumstances. Where such difficulties regularly recur, the whole stores system and methods should be thoroughly investigated—maximum and minimum stock values may have to be revised and the purchase requisitioning system brought up to scratch.

The Buying Department's methods and systems may also require to be investigated, and the steps they take to ensure that suppliers keep to their obligations should be reviewed.

The method of notifying the Buying Department to obtain all special items not regularly stocked should be investigated, and it should be seen that the Planning Department or drawing office gives the Buying Department the maximum possible notice of requirements. It should also be seen that they have adequate records of all possible sources of supply.

And over and above all systems must be considered the enthusiasm and resourcefulness of the buyers themselves, it being amazing what can be almost miraculously produced at short notice by a resourceful buyer.

(c) LACK OF SUITABLE LABOUR (See Wages Rate, Labour Efficiency, and Volume Variances)

Responsibility in this case must be placed on the Personnel Department, provided production programmes and labour requirements have been properly planned. Usually suitable labour can be obtained, provided the management is prepared to pay a high enough price. This will, of course, depend on the urgency of the requirements, but this aspect of the matter may raise some thorny problems, for often it will be difficult to engage new men at high rates of pay without increasing the rates of pay of the existing workers.

Such difficulties may often be overcome by proper schemes of apprenticeship and unskilled labour training.

It should be seen that prompt notice is sent to the Personnel Department of all anticipated labour requirements.

Apart from wage levels, etc., another factor to be taken into consideration is welfare. Some works acquire an undesirable reputation for harsh or unjust treatment, or long hours or uncomfortable surroundings, while others have a reputation for considerate treatment and welcome amenities. Naturally workers will gladly leave the first and willingly join the second class. It may be necessary to consider the position from this angle.

(d) LACK OF CO-ORDINATED PLANNING (See Waiting Time, Extra Time, Supplementary Time, Shortages Reports and Volume Variances)

Probably this cause has more to do with low output than any other, especially in the case of complicated assembly work. Planning starts right from the preparation of the design or drawing to the final dispatch. Assemblies must be planned so that each individual component is completed just at the right time to fit into the assembly. Any assembled article cannot be completed so long as one part is missing.

Planning will include progressing materials from one section to another, and this must be so co-ordinated that all aspects are covered, e.g. progressing drawings to pattern shop, patterns to foundry, castings to machine shops, machine shops to inspection, inspection to dispatch, etc., together with provision of men, machines, and tools.

(e) EXCESSIVE SCRAP AND WASTE (See Scrap and Excess Costs)

In the case of a firm manufacturing a small number of large orders each period (e.g. a foundry specializing in very heavy castings), the scrapping of a single item may materially affect the output figures. In most cases, however, there will be a sufficiently wide range of manufacture to enable an average normal or standard scrap or waste figure to be set up. Any wide deviations from normal will naturally affect the output. In order that the precise effect of this on output can be ascertained it will be necessary to show the time taken in replacing work which has been scrapped (or the time spent on the work scrapped which will require to be replaced).

Together with this might be considered *excessive rejects by the Inspection Department*. This may or may not be scrap and may only require adjustment, but the inspection standards should always be under review in the light of current conditions.

(f) PLANT BREAKDOWN (See Waiting Time Report)

Responsibility here lies with the Maintenance Department. It should be seen that there is an effective routine system of plant inspection and replacement. The cost of avoidable breakdown should be set against the cost of additional maintenance men and a regular policy of replacement. The policy of plant replacement is considered later.

(g) POWER FAILURES (See Waiting Time Report)

These may be very expensive (the cost system should provide for showing the cost thereof), especially if a breakdown affects a whole department or the whole works.

It should be seen that all adequate steps and precautions are taken to avoid such failures and that wherever possible alternative sources of supply are made available.

Transmission failures are usually avoidable where there is adequate inspection and maintenance, and excuses should not be readily accepted.

(h) DESIGNING DELAYS

The avoidance of delay usually depends on an adequate and efficient staff, efficiently organized and supervised, with a proper system of allocating work.

(i) TECHNICAL TROUBLES (See Excess Cost Report)

Multitudinous difficulties peculiar to each trade arise in connexion with manufacture and cause delays. It can only be said that these should be recognized, and if possible classified, and steps taken to record the cost of such troubles and if possible to remedy them.

(j) LACK OF CAPITAL

All the aforementioned causes of output being below budget are controllable to some extent by works management. But another very real difficulty affecting many firms with no lack of orders is lack of capital. This usually manifests itself in inability to purchase sufficient raw material or plant, or to pay increased wages for which the cash return may not be immediate.

## (3) Cost of Production

This, of course, is probably the chief item for consideration at cost and budget meetings.

Quality of production affects cost of production as it does price. From this angle the ruling factor will be: Is the quality correct to fulfil the purpose of the product required by the customer, at a price he is prepared to pay?

Cost of production is vitally affected by methods of production, which cannot be entirely evaluated in terms of money. In the case of an engineering product the following should be considered. Are the designs and drawings such as to simplify pattern-making and moulding and minimize machining and assembling operations? Are details standardized? Would a reduction in the range of products supplied result in more economical working and more profitable results? Are the most suitable machines employed? Are suitable tools, jigs, and fixtures being used? Could more skilled tool-setters be employed? Could semi-skilled men or apprentices be profitably substituted on certain work? The general question, too, of plant layout and methods of handling will also affect the cost. And even though continual improvements are being made, a special investigation by experts on some particular section may enable a reduction in the costs of a particular product to be made to meet competition.

DIRECT LABOUR COSTS (See Wages Rate and Labour Efficiency Variances, Excess Cost Report, and Comparison of Budget and Actual)

In this country rates of payment are largely governed by the trade unions, but the question of the method of remuneration may still bulk largely in the matter of labour cost, particularly the cost per unit.

Consideration should be given to the methods of payment. Could a bonus or piecework system be introduced, or, if in force, could it be improved, subdivided, extended, or revised; or could a system of group bonuses or of labour grading under various classes with progressive rates of pay and encouraging prospects of promotion meet the case?

Are the methods of training men the most satisfactory? Is this left to foremen? Should a training school be set up or could special instructors be profitably employed? Is the right class of man employed for each type of job? Are the methods of recording labour efficiency sufficiently adequate and detailed to enable prompt steps to be taken to locate and improve poor workmanship? Is the ratefixing satisfactory? Is supervision efficient? Have the possibilities of applied motion study been investigated?

All excess costs, such as scrap, waste, and extra operations, of course, affect the total direct labour cost, and it should be seen that adequate analysed records of these are available so that corrective action may be taken. Finally, it should be seen that the most efficient methods are employed, not only by the individual (as shown by time studies), but as regards machines, equipment, and design.

DIRECT MATERIAL COSTS (See Materials Price, and Usage Variances and Comparison of Budget and Actual)

Are the materials used the *cheapest available* at the quality desired? The answer to this question lies with the Buying Office. Has its personnel sufficient knowledge of trade and market conditions to enable them to pick the best place and time for buying? Are the Buying Department's records adequate and their methods efficient? Are standard specifications kept for the principal material requirements?

*Buying Policy.* This should be examined. Is it better to buy in bulk and secure large discounts, or to keep to a hand-to-mouth buying policy? In this connexion the question of capital available and the storage space may have considerable weight.

*Stock Control.* The methods used should here be brought under review. Is an up-to-date recording system of bin cards or control ledgers employed, operating with maximum and minimum stock levels, and do the Buying Department get adequate notice of all requirements? Or is old stock allowed to accumulate till it is obsolete?

*Stores Organization.* This vitally affects direct material costs. Is the system of storing such that spoilage and scrap are reduced to a minimum? This question again arises in the overhead cost of handling. Are the stores layout methods such that it is reduced to a minimum?

*Quality.* Is the quality of material employed (or the price paid) the most suitable? Here the requirements of the customer are the paramount question. Profitable business does not necessarily result just from satisfying the æsthetic tastes of the management. The question is: Does the material fulfil the service demanded of it?

Consideration should be given to the question of alternatives: castings or fabricated sheet metal; forgings or die stampings; wood or metal; bakelite or wood, etc.

Would the all-over cost be reduced if a poorer quality of material were used, even after allowing for material process difficulties, extra scrap, and the cost of stricter inspection? (This question of the effect of quality of material on cost of machining operations is of considerable importance.)

The system of inspection employed directly affects the quality of material used. Could a poorer quality be used if stricter inspection were employed? The all-in cost of materials plus inspection must not be forgotten. Are laboratory and physical tests taken of all materials employed, or is the best available material always used and detailed inspection dispensed with? Finally, would it pay to install a department to manufacture materials which had previously been bought outside?

## EXCESS COSTS

*Scrap and Rectification Costs.* In order for effective steps to be taken to minimize the cost of scrap it is essential that such costs be separated and analysed by causes or departments responsible. Once the cost of scrap has been properly analysed and allocated, the first step to be taken is to discover if it is the human element that is at fault. Is inadequate training or experience the cause? If so, can proper training be given, or experienced men be substituted? If carelessness is the cause and admonitions have no effect, unsuitable workmen may have to be transferred. Or does the fault lie in the quality of the raw materials?

The procedure for notifying responsible parties of faults arising so that steps can be taken to eliminate them may be unsatisfactory.

Where technical difficulties are found, parties responsible will be consulted and the research department, or independent experts, called in.

But apart from these aspects, the question of scrap raises other problems. The cost of scrap might easily be reduced at one point, but this might involve higher costs at another (e.g. better quality material). It is the all-in cost that must be considered.

The question will arise: How much can a process be cheapened in one department without involving increased waste or increased work in another? Comparative costs for different methods of working will require to be got out.

*Waiting Time* will often be found to be due to inadequate planning. Detailed analysis must be available and regular investigation carried out.

## Idle Facilities

*Idle Space and Waste of Space.* This is of very frequent occurrence, and unless the cost system is designed to show the precise effect of this overhead, it can be very easily overlooked. First of all, trade prospects should be reviewed. (1) Is there likely to be expansion of production? In a progressive company this end should always be kept in view. (2) If not, could the idle space be put to profitable use? Could other lines of production be engaged in? (3) Could the idle space be let out? (4) Should it be sold?

*Idle Plant*, i.e. plant only intermittently used or idle owing to trade conditions. The same considerations apply. (1) Sales must be pushed with a view to providing work for these machines, or (2) new products should be developed, or (3) the machine should be sold. This sounds all right. But in how many cases is any direct action taken? Obsolete unused plant should, of course, be sold at once.

## Works Overhead Costs (See Comparison of Standard, Budget, and Actual Costs)

*Indirect Labour.* The cost of labourers and odd men has a surprising habit of jumping up unless a constant watch is kept on this item by way of the regular expense reports. The only way by which an authoritative statement on this matter can be made by the executives is to keep a record of previous accomplishments and be able to point out that such and such an output was achieved with so many labourers, therefore why is it necessary to employ more now?

*Overtime and Shift Allowances.* This is a very thorny problem and warrants detailed investigation, and apart from questions of cost, the ultimate value of the reputation of the firm for prompt deliveries must be given full weight.

The question of fatigue and discontent also has to be

considered, for it can definitely be stated that output will not increase in direct proportion to overtime, and certain occasions may even arise where it might be found that with suitable incentives output might be maintained by abandoning overtime entirely. The actual effect of the face value of overtime on costs should be investigated, and, except where deliveries are of first importance, its continuance should be questioned.

Where overtime is continuous the question of extension or new plant must be considered, and the overall cost of this compared with the cost of overtime. Future trade prospects will largely determine this matter. The substitution of shifts for overtime may relieve the situation.

Where, however, trade is seasonal, overtime at certain seasons may be considered part of the normal cost of the product, but in this case the possibility and cost of building up stocks should be looked into.

The degree of mechanization in the factory largely affects this matter. Where a great deal of very expensive plant is employed it will often pay to run double day-shifts and/or night shifts to keep it fully employed.

Much can be achieved by advance planning and budgeting to avoid overtime.

*Supervision.* The management must decide at what level of output it pays to employ or dispense with the services of another foreman or chargehand, or where a departmental superintendent is required. In times of depression there are levels of production where old and trusted staff members can be retained only by converting supervision officials into working officials, and this method should be borne in mind. A clear, tabulated analysis of staff responsibilities and duties will often help to keep the cost of staff within bounds.

*Indirect Supplies.* Regular expense comparison under this heading and careful analysis and investigation will help to keep this item at a minimum. Here again the Stores and Buying Departments must look to their laurels, and a judicious choice of quality may often effect considerable savings. Periodical notices regarding cutting down wastes will also help.

## WORKS SERVICES

*Internal Transport.* This is an item on which considerable cost reductions can often be effected, and should be regarded not merely from the angle of direct cost reduction, but of subsequent speeding up of production. All the most modern methods of handling should be constantly under review—different types of cranes, jack trucks, belt and overhead conveyors, chutes. The plant layout itself and the routing of work will have to be taken into account. The whole of the workshop and stores layout should be considered with the object of minimizing this expense and time factor.

*Stores.* Similar considerations apply to stores as to transport. Accessibility, methods of handling, receiving and dispatch, efficiency of records, safety—all should receive thought.

*Lighting.* Efficient lighting has been proved to have a surprising effect on the efficiency of workers, and the installation of modern systems of lighting often more than repays any capital outlay. Alternative methods should be studied, but a watch should be constantly kept to prevent waste.

*Heating.* The first step towards economy is to see if there are adequate records of boiler efficiency and total heating cost. A record of coal consumption is a minimum requirement. The existing system should be compared with the most up-to-date practice and expert advice sought if considered necessary.

*Power.* This is covered by a wide field of technical research. The cost and advantages of private generation as compared with public supply may be investigated. In respect of the former, the rival claims of steam, electricity, internal combustion engine, and even water power may have to be considered. On the transmission side there are the advantages of individual as compared with group drive to be investigated, and also belt, chain, or directly geared drives.

The efficiency of compressed air or hydraulic supplies should be checked. Where steam is employed, figures should be available for boiler efficiencies, coal consumption, $CO_2$ readings, pressure, flow, etc.

*Maintenance.* It should be seen that there is a properly organized system of maintenance in force, providing for regular inspection, cleaning, oiling, repair, and replacement of plant and transmission gear. In this department prevention is better than cure.

## FIXED OVERHEADS

As rent, rates and taxes, etc., are not so liable to fluctuation, this item of cost is not often subjected to detailed investigation. Once the details are checked as being correct, the factor that matters is to ensure that the space provided is profitably utilized to its fullest possible extent. The fact should not entirely be lost sight of that it might be possible to carry on business as effectively on another site bearing a far lower charge.

Insurance premiums should be checked to see that they supply adequate cover.

The cost of depreciation should be viewed in the light of plant utilization and the state of the plant generally and its fitness for the work required of it.

## ADMINISTRATION EXPENSES

The real question here often concerns the personal efficiency of higher executives, and it requires to be boldly faced. Is the company getting value for money?

On the office side, efficiency is to be sought from the angle of office organization. This applies to accounting, buying, sales, correspondence, stores, and other offices.

Routines should be checked, unnecessary forms and procedures eliminated. Increased efficiency may be found from a degree of mechanization.

SELLING EXPENSES

A proper analysis of costs is required here if the true effect of selling expenses is to be gauged. Their incidence and effect on the true cost and profits of the various products should be ascertained if their efficiency is to be judged.

Methods of advertising should be scrutinized, methods of remunerating salesmen and agents considered, and packing and transportation costs examined.

## (4) Stock and Work in Progress

Close watch should be kept on the amount of these items. They should bear a definite normal or standard relationship to the volume of production. Work in progress should be analysed under product groups, and the reasons for undue increases investigated.

Stocks should be analysed under class groups, and figures kept of the relationship of value on hand to the average issues each period.

It will usually be advantageous to keep graphs of these relationships in each group.

The resources of a company may even become seriously strained if stock and work in progress items are allowed to build up above a normal level.

Where departmental managers have control over the volume of work in progress, if a figure for interest on work in progress is included in the accounts, this will help to stress the cost of high work in progress and have the psychological effect of causing every effort to be made to keep it at a minimum.

### (5) Development and Research

The operating of a research and development department devoted to the improvement of products and the extension of their application may prove one of the most profitable forms of action that can be taken.

### (6) Plant Extensions

This is a matter which may often come up at cost and budget meetings and is discussed in Part VII.

### (7) Long-term Planning

Better forecasting and planning, better budgeting in fact, may be one form of action required. In many circumstances long-term planning will pay dividends. Though dominant companies may be in a better position to control the outcome, small companies can also benefit.

Budgeting principles apply when five to ten years' planning is attempted. Starting from evaluating the present position and its strengths and weaknesses, objectives are set, product developments and market strategies are considered, capital and organizational requirements are detailed and the phasing of these developments is set down as a time plan. This would periodically be revised.

Finally, the most all-round effective action that can possibly be taken is to develop a feeling of enthusiasm and co-operation among the men and with the men. This is the highest function of management.

# PART VII

# LONG RANGE PLANNING AND DECISION PROBLEMS

# CHAPTER XXI

## CAPITAL BUDGETING AND PROJECT EVALUATION

PROJECTS may range from a steady stream of relatively small scale replacements, to the acquisition of an existing business, or the widely spaced building and equipping of a new factory for new products.

The motivation which leads to projects was perhaps more clearly seen in the earlier owner-manager stage of the industrial revolution before finance and management tended to become divorced.

Almost all industrial projects are aimed at improving or maintaining either the costs and/or volume, quality, utility, or diversity of products or services. They are thus product centred. They entail the maintenance or improvement of product design, materials purchasing, production planning, warehousing, marketing, organization, research and so on. They will also aim to provide a surplus of income over costs, including costs whose benefits will only emerge over many years. The shorthand expression "capital projects" may thus give a distorted and unbalanced impression not only of the relative significance of the various means necessary to achieve the ends but even of the ends themselves. We are thus talking of projects which among other things involve capital outlay, the value of which stems solely from the products or services it contributes to producing.

In the foregoing context, initial asset life is therefore not necessarily synonymous with project life, even if ideally it would be desirable to be able to evaluate each item of capital spending in isolation and on its own merits.

The dual nature of the outlay under contemporary phraseology and modes of presentation has also to be taken into account. From one angle it is a cost of much the same nature as other costs, but embodying the labour costs of the engineers and others involved in its creation, and the measure of its worth when combined with other running costs is the combined income they produce in relation to the total costs involved. From another angle it can be regarded as an investment—a cost held in suspense, against which a specific share of the income has to be earmarked.

Once the product policy is settled and the relevant capital expenditure decisions are made, however, they will determine the track on which the wheels must perforce turn, possibly for many years to come.

It is against this background that we can examine the capital expenditure aspects of projects and the rewards of venture capital.

Most decisions contain an element of speculation, for the future is never certain. Market research can play a big part, but the development of substitutes and the actions of competitors can never be fully seen. Foresight is the key, and the over-riding factor to be considered is a reasonable assurance of a strong continuing demand for the products or services of the proposed new equipment. A major step will have been taken if all the foreseeable projects for some time ahead have been listed and discussed well in advance of the time when a decision is urgently called for. Adequate information relating to changes in the activities of customers and competitors ranks high in the requirements for successful capital budgeting. A measure of success may be conceded if major blunders are avoided.

## Sanction

In short-term budgets, the incidence of the capital budget will be its effects on the cash budget and on the budgeted balance sheet; longer term budgets will include the effect on earnings.

In large organizations, procedure may follow the lines of (a) a forecast, listing items for which approval is sought in the coming year and, (b) an outline of the major items envisaged for the following two or three years or more. Sums for unforeseen items will be included. After discussion a modified version of (a) will be given approval in principle for incorporation with the other budget details. This may act as formal approval for managers to proceed with smaller items when they so wish. Items over a certain amount appearing in (a) have usually to be submitted again in much greater detail to the approving body before formal actual authority is given. Very large projects involving figures equal to say 20 per cent of existing assets will certainly entail movement of funds forecasts for several years ahead.

## Evaluation

Sanctioning procedures are often the formal climax of an evaluation process which in the case of large scale projects may have included discussions going on for many years, in the course of which a deeper impression of prospects and environment may have been accumulated than is even likely to be committed to paper. Nevertheless, some summary will rightly be called for, which in the case of a profit-making firm will include initial capital outlays, anticipated running costs and anticipated income at least for the early years of the project's life. Examples are shown on pages 227 and 239.

In public services, the summary might cover the most economic ways of obtaining benefits.

Evaluation is essentially based on comparison and the simplest comparison will be between two alternative new ways of achieving much the same ends, on much the same scale, and over the same duration, for here one can assume that all the other things which can affect the project will be more or less equal for either alternative, and one will most naturally follow the basic principles of comparison.

At bed-rock, the most valid basis of comparison is probably the ratio of the total income to the total cost (including initial outlay) of the project over its entire life, for then one may dare to make the assumption that at least a portion of the difference will be available for savings to enable genuine further expansion to be effected somewhere.

In practice, when dealing with many mixed types of projects, a conscious effort is required if one is even to approach within striking distance of adhering to the basic principles of comparison, and features exist which render it difficult to reach what might seem ideal.

There will be a natural urge to try to reduce everything to a common denominator, and to treat each project in isolation on its own merits, but in practice one may be limited to getting the answer "that it seems good within its own class."

## Cash Rationing and Selection of Priorities

There will usually be some degree of cash rationing associated with proposed expenditure. Though there may be an inability to find or raise funds through lack of

FACTORY EXTENSION FOR NEW PRODUCT—SUMMARY EVALUATION
USING SHARE OF EXISTING FACTORY SERVICES
(ASSUMED FINANCED FROM UPLIFTED CASH DEPOSITS)

*Simplest Version*

Estimated Results of First Year's Full Working

|  | Project not undertaken £ | Project undertaken £ |
|---|---|---|
| *Capital Employed—* | | |
| Cash on Deposit . . . . | 20,000 | — |
| New Fixed Assets at Cost . . . | | 9,800 |
| Modification to Service Dept. Fixed Assets . . . . . | | 200 |
| Stocks *plus* Debtors *less* Trade Creditors | | 10,000 |
| | £20,000 | £20,000 |
| *Estimated Return before Tax—* | | |
| Sales . . . . . . | | 30,000 |
| Less Raw Materials . . . . | | 15,000 |
| Net Output . . . . . | | £15,000 |
| Operating Costs— | | |
| Variable . . . . . | | 6,900 |
| Fixed . . . . . | | 2,960 |
| Additional Service Dept. Costs— | | |
| Variable . . . . . | | 100 |
| Fixed . . . . . | | 40 |
| Provision for Depreciation 10% . . | | 1,000 |
| | | £11,000 |
| Profit before Tax . . . . | | 4,000 |
| Interest at 5% (Short Term) . . | £1,000 | |
| % Profit to Sales . . . . . . . . | | 13·3% |
| Ratio of Turnover to Capital Employed . . . . | | 1·5 |
| % Return on Capital Employed . . . . . | | 20% |
| Estimated % Capacity Utilized . . . . . | | 90% |
| % Activity to Break Even . . . . . . | | 46% |
| % Price Fall to Break Even . . . . . . | | 13·3% |
| Simple Break Even Period Fixed Assets . . . | | 10,000 |
| | | 4,000 + 1,000 = 2 years |
| "Additional Return" on Cash Reinvested (£3,000) . . | | 15% |

*Main Assumptions—*

1. Income and outlay to be sustained for at least 2 years for break even period fixed assets to hold good.

2. Original company Cash Balance reinstated, assuming gains retained after tax, in about 6½ years.

3. Continuity of 20 per cent return requires same income and costs for 10 years, all profits distributed. If in addition retained depreciation provisions invested to earn more than decline in earnings from deteriorating assets, return would rise above 20 per cent.

4. If part profits retained and earn 20 per cent, this ratio maintained; if retained but earn less, it will fall.

*Note.* If company's present total capital employed £200,000 and profit £30,000 (a 15 per cent return), after project undertaken capital employed £200,000 profit £33,000, making Return 16½ per cent.

proof of previous success, even for what appears to offer a good return, this can also be self-imposed through unwillingness to entertain even the remote possibility of wider spread of control or of outside interference should things fail to work to plan. Even where this element is absent, financial institutions will be reluctant to back fund raising for expansion on a scale where there can be a suspicion that management is trying to bite off more than it can chew. This might be placed at anything more than 15 to 20 per cent up on the existing scale of operations except in special cases, however good the prospects.

## The Quality of the Information

The initial outlay on projects, being the most imminent, should be the easiest to compute, but there has been public evidence of how far astray such estimates can be in complex construction projects. Here the application of Critical Path Techniques will be warranted. Careful co-operative studies should enable running costs at varying capacities to be estimated without undue error. It is the income element, which will be present in most major projects, which will be most subject to uncertainty, and which places the project at risk, though with adequate knowledge of the environment, figures for the early years need not normally be wide of the mark.

Check lists of the type shown on pages 229 and 230 are worth using even for small projects.

Short-term benefits will not only be more certain, but will be easier to calculate than long-term benefits, for among other things there will be a greater chance that "other things will remain equal."

It is not much use applying elaborate evaluation procedures if the basic data relating to capital, operating costs and income in the early years is wide of the mark.

## CAPITAL PROJECT CHECK LIST

ALL PROJECTS

During new or overhauled plant's (*a*) physical life, and (*b*) simple pay-off period—

Is demand for plant's products reasonably assured?
Are supplies of raw material for products reasonably assured?
Are supplies of labour for products reasonably assured?
Are supplies of fuel and power reasonably assured?
Any comments on price trends of foregoing.
Alternatives considered and rejected.
What teething troubles anticipated?
Could process be sub-contracted in emergency?
Main repercussions at other processing points.
Action in similar circumstances being taken by competitors if known.
Any substitutes likely to displace the plant's products.
Proposed plant rather small or rather big (*a*) for present, (*b*) for anticipated, requirements.
Next priority this department.
Other main company priorities if known.
Proposed running hours per week.
Estimated % activity.

NEW PLANT PROJECTS

What tests carried out on reliability and suitability of new plant?
Nothing known of new developments likely to make this plant soon obsolete.
Well tried model or new model.

IF OVERHAUL, REPLACE OR REVISED LAYOUT

How production to be maintained during change?
If not maintained, period of production drop and estimated loss of production.
How operatives to be employed during change-over?
Current running hours.
Last year's % activity.
How old plant to be disposed of. Alternative use.

1. MAINTENANCE OF PRODUCTION OR BOTTLE-NECK RELEASE ASPECT

(*a*) *Defective or Unsuitable Plant*—
Has good production already fallen due to plant defects?
If potential drop anticipated, when likely to arise.
(*b*) Is bottle-neck due to change in production pattern, design of product, quality of material, etc.?
If so, how long is change causing bottle-neck likely to last?
What other steps possible to maintain production, if bottle-neck exists?
What and how many other processes affected?
Are delivery dates and customers' expectations affected?

2. COST SAVING ASPECT

Changes in grade of (or substitute) raw materials (or fuel)?
Savings in scrap or waste.
Labour savings this process.
Labour savings preceding or subsequent processes.
Release of direct and indirect labour.
Any proposals for absorbing released labour.

Any higher rates for operating new machines.
Maintenance costs, old *v.* new (or overhauled).
Power and heating costs.  Insurance.

3. QUALITY OR DESIGN IMPROVEMENT ASPECT
Present quality defects and proposed improvements?
Primarily aimed (*a*) to stop decline in quality, or (*b*) to raise quality to higher levels than hitherto.
Ancillary effects at other processes
Any resultant sales price changes proposed.
What particular advantage has improved quality to customer?

4 and 5. EXPANSION ASPECT
Additional labour required?
Source of recruitment.
Training problems.
Repercussions at other processing points.
Storage and warehousing.  Internal and external transport.
Any expansion in service departments, power, heat, maintenance, etc.
Customers for additional volume.
Advertising necessary.
Additional Working Capital.

6. SOCIAL ASPECT
Better conditions?
Health or accident factors.

7. RISK SPREADING ASPECT
Flexibility and adaptability of plant to other products.

8. INTANGIBLE ADVANTAGES

9. INSTALLATION ASPECTS
Space and passage way O.K.?
Structure strong enough?
Big design changes after first sanction?
Services covered—power, lighting, switchgear, heat, compressed air water, gas, effluent, sanitation.
Handling and transport facilities.
Revised layout other plant.
Accessories wanted.
Tools and/or containers wanted.
Time required for delivery of new plant.  How long to instal.
Installation by own men?

10. EFFECT ON OUTPUT
(i) *Plant and Quality Improvement Projects*—
Approximate % by which current output below potential of existing capacity due to (*a*) machine defects and/or (*b*) product quality defects.
What further approximate % drop from current production level in next 12 months if no action taken?
(ii) Approximate % by which saleable output can be raised above present level as result of project.

11. RANGE OF PRODUCTS AFFECTED

12. OTHER COMMENTS

Always assuming continuing income, where no turnover changes are envisaged, "annual cash gains" will represent the difference in operating costs between the old and the new method (excluding depreciation and interest charges).

Where income changes are programmed, it will be income less operating cost of a proposed expansion, or if replacement, the difference in this, between the new and the old method. Whilst allowing for teething troubles, one must avoid duplicating contingency allowances at many points.

## Types of Projects

Projects may be classified in many ways to facilitate management judgement. They may be graded according to size, or sub-divided between defensive replacements to maintain or improve existing products and offensive projects to expand existing products or introduce new ones. Some projects may be classed as vital, e.g. replacing a broken down machine forming a part of a line producing a profitable product, or seizing a transient golden opportunity and some will be regarded as social, e.g. safety and amenity projects.

For evaluation purposes it would seem necessary to distinguish between dependent and independent projects.

(a) Fully independent projects can be classed as those capable of producing and distributing their own products with most of their services and working capital, e.g. acquiring an established limited company, creating and equipping a new factory.

(b) Semi-independent projects will be capable of being converted into independent projects or will have a readily available alternative use, or be in demand in an active second-hand market.

(c) Dependent projects generally form part of a large whole, and their measure of success will depend on all supporting plant and services being kept in being to sustain the project (and that product demand continues).

(d) Interdependent projects will refer to equipment totally incapable of producing a saleable article or service, except in conjunction with one or more associated items of plant. One might add multi-phase projects where the full benefits of the earlier phases only emerge after completion of later phases.

Dependent projects can usefully be sub-divided into classes primarily aimed at the maintenance or improvement of (1) output, (2) quality, (3) costs, (4) safety and amenities, (5) cars and communications, (6) external transport and distribution, (7) buildings.

Few projects are likely to fall wholly into one of these categories and replacement projects form a special sub-section.

## Principles of Comparison

These first principles of comparison of like with like include—

### (1) *Method with Method*

It is meaningless to state that "Project B shows a 20 per cent return," unless all interested parties are aware of the exact basis on which the 20 per cent is calculated, and will only make mental comparison with other data calculated on the same basis.

### (2) *Future with Future*

Whilst past history can be used as reference to provide a standard for projects whose success lies in the future, one must compare the effects of doing it against not doing it, deferring it, or doing something else. For example, one might show a profit of £50,000 before the project and £40,000 after doing it. What has been omitted is the profit if the project were not undertaken of £10,000.

The English Language is still short of adequate terminology to deal with this subject. Among the terms required is one to cover "the avoidance of loss of profit," or "loss of contribution to profit," which would otherwise occur were a project not undertaken. The term "pull backs" is suggested to distinguish this avoidance of a fall in profit from "additional cash gains" which will be used to refer to contribution to profit (before depreciation, interest and tax) which will raise these above current levels. "Cash gains" will be applied to the combined figure.

### (3) *Magnitude with Magnitude*

Is a project costing £20,000 and showing a 17 per cent return, however calculated, better or worse than a project costing £10,000 and showing a 20 per cent return, other things being equal?

This question must be answered in terms of what could be done by spending another £10,000 in the latter case. If this could only be invested at 8 per cent giving an average of 14 per cent, the first proposition is better. If it could be invested at 20 per cent the first proposition is the worse, in a situation involving consideration of how £20,000 is best invested.

This form of mental adjustment is always involved in comparisons and rationing of projects of different magnitudes.

### (4) *Time Span with Time Span*

Strictly speaking, no percentage returns or other indices of relative advantage should ever be quoted without also quoting the time span over which they are expected to apply. Often there is a query as to whether the figures represent the effects of the first year only or whether they may even represent a perpetuity.

Again the answer to the question "Is a project outlay of £20,000 showing a 17 per cent return per annum for 10 years, better or worse than a £20,000 outlay showing a 20 per cent return per annum for 7 years?" must lie in what opportunities would exist for investing £20,000 for 3 years at the end of 7 years. If at that time 20 per cent could still be obtained, the second proposition is the best, but if one takes the view that one might be lucky to get 5 per cent, bringing the average below 17 per cent, then the first proposition is superior.

Although considerable thought has been given to finding means of circumventing this problem, which is particularly relevant to the timing of replacement of maintainable plant where the comparison is between the effects of retaining the old for a further period against the new, this has only met with partial success, for one may be faced either with considering the introduction of successors or introducing residual values at some point (where "values in use in association with other complimentary plant" may be substantially removed from open market values).

(5) *Trend with Trend*

How would one compare the following two estimated income series?

| Year | 1 | 2 | 3 | 4 | 5 |
|------|------|------|-------|-----|-----|
| A | 1,000 | 800 | 600 | 400 | 200 |
| B | 400 | 700 | 1,000 | 900 | 500 |

The most obvious answer is (a) to add them up and/or (b) to average them.

Matters are not quite so simple, for even with equal totals, it can be argued that all or part of the receipts could be invested at an interest rate and the series with its highest receipts in the earlier years would accumulate to a higher total.

## Single Venture versus Perpetuity

A more basic conceptual difficulty is whether projects should or can be treated as single ventures locked to the life of their initial basic assets with their income (and working capital) fading out as these assets deteriorate, or whether, as say in the case of the purchase of an existing business, or the creation of a new factory, they should be treated as a perpetuity involving initial products and initial assets and their successors, though possibly scaled down in later years to cover the contingency of risks and uncertainty or the effects of interest rates. If one rules out progressive replacement/substitution and rigorously applies the single venture concept, this would on occasion logically entail jettisoning the values derived from developed designs, markets, organization and customer contacts associated with some major projects.

## The Simpler Evaluation Methods

Even apart from the question of uncertainty, taken together, the foregoing make rather formidable demands which have proved difficult to satisfy and any lengthy evaluated schedule of mixed projects which purports to do so must be viewed with no little degree of reservation.

Thus in the case of dependent projects, one has either to make the bold assumption, that in some way or other all supporting plant and services will be kept in being, or one has the difficult task of making a long-term study of a complete sector of the business.

Simpler approaches take two forms. Either the initial impact in the early years (say up to five) is taken as being indicative of the relative advantage of the eventual outcome, or, taking a leaf out of the theory of games, the problem is inverted and instead of asking which projects are most likely to show the maximum gains, one asks which projects are most likely to show the minimum losses.

The answer to the latter question is easier to answer with conviction, since shorter time spans are involved, and there can be some confidence that other things will remain more or less equal. Such techniques can of course be criticized as offering a rather negative approach.

## Income Based and Savings Based Evaluations

Income based evaluations will take the form Product Income less Costs equals Gains. Gains are then generally related to Outlays. Independent projects are generally presented in this complete form and dependent projects can be forcibly squeezed into it by allocating a portion of income.

Savings based evaluations represent an incomplete form, for they make the assumption that product or service demand continues and exclude this from the calculation. This is quite legitimate when considering alternative ways of providing the same service, provided the basic assumption is correct. The return is an additional return and not the return itself.

## Pay-off Periods

The most commonly applied short-term evaluation is the "Pay Back" or "Break-even Period." This must not be scorned as a method of assessing relative advantage for comparing projects, with, as far as is known, similar lives, similar trends of gain, similar tax treatment and with most of the capital outlay falling in one year.  In its simplest form it is merely

$$\frac{\text{Outlay on New Plant (less Salvage Value Old)}}{\text{Additional Annual Cash Gains plus } \textit{Pull-backs}} = \frac{\text{Number of years to}}{\text{run to break even}}$$

or better, where gains are uneven, the number of years before the cumulative gains match the initial outlay.

Even in this simple form it may be used (a) as a basis for assessing relative advantage, (b) as an indication of when a firm can actually achieve a return to its original liquidity and manœuvrability (gains retained).

Although taxation charges are not allowed for above, because the effect of balancing allowances on plant sold or scrapped permits its total cost to be charged against income, it does produce the point at which one cannot lose in this event.

In this simple form it does not really tell when one gets one's money back if the plant continues to run.  It is not difficult, however, to construct a chart which will convert either annual cash gains expressed as various percentages of capital employed, or as simple break-even periods as calculated above, into genuine cash recovery periods at current rates of tax and current capital allowances and grants, an assumption being made that the balance of gains after tax is retained in the organization. One could also compute pay-off periods after interest and tax, say on the assumption of borrowing money and using all available surplus gains, after tax and interest on the balance of outstanding borrowing, to repay borrowing until the original pre-installation cash position is restored. Where gains have uneven trends as between projects for which comparison is sought, figures discounted at commercial rates can be used in the numerator of the pay-off period fraction if felt necessary.

It may be noted that pay-off periods can become rather artificial when applied to plant replacement if they emerge as being longer than the maintainable life of the old plant.

In the major new plant projects involving additional stocks and debtors (less creditors) it is usual to apply the pay-off period concept only to the fixed assets portion of the new investment, it being assumed that current assets could, in case of need, be converted to cash on cessation.

The tentative conclusion may be reached that a simple pay-off period of up to 4 years can produce satisfactory profitability where profitable life is likely to extend to $2\frac{1}{2}$ to 3 times this. For longer pay-off periods, a long profitable life must be looked for, as may well be the case with major fully independent projects. Short-life risky projects will probably entail shorter pay-off periods.

## Initial Accounting Return on Initial Assets

This is the basic model from which other more advanced models have been developed, for it involves the examination of all income and expense categories.

In the case of projects of any size it is just as well to view it in the context of the whole in order to keep a sense of proportion. One condensed version might appear as on p. 239.

This presentation only commits itself to an estimate of the position for the first year fully operational. It is deliberately non-committal as to long-term results, for the continuity of the indicated percentages will depend on continuity of the relationship between income, costs and capital. The existence of depreciation provisions infer that they will be re-invested in the business to keep the new level of capacity intact. The assessment of a 10-year economic life points to the belief that attributable

## PROJECT TYPE—DEPENDENT—REPLACEMENT—BOTTLENECK RELEASE

| | Present Year (reference only) (1) £ | Estimated Future Project not Undertaken (2) £ | Estimated Future Project Undertaken (3) £ | Change (3) V (2) (4) £ |
|---|---|---|---|---|
| Fixed Assets—General | 77,000 | 68,000 | 68,000 | |
| Fixed Assets—New Plant | | | 12,000 | +12,000 |
| Working Capital—(excluding Cash and Loans) | 90,000 | 89,100 | 91,800 | +2,300 |
| Working Capital—From Present Year's Depreciation Provisions | | 9,000 | 9,000 | |
| CAPITAL INVOLVED | 167,000 | 166,100 | 180,800 | 14,300 |
| INCOME/COSTS | | | | |
| Invoiced Sales | 350,000 | 346,500 | 357,000 | +10,500 |
| Less Materials Used | 175,000 | 173,250 | 178,500 | +5,250 |
| | 175,000 | 173,250 | 178,500 | +5,250 |
| Operating Costs excluding Interest | 135,000 | 134,650 | 135,500 | +850 |
| Depreciation Provisions General | 9,000 | 9,000 | 9,000 | |
| ,, ,, New Plant 10% | | | 1,200 | +1,200 |
| | 144,000 | 143,650 | 145,700 | +2,050 |
| ESTIMATED PROFIT | 31,000 | 29,600 | 32,800 | +3,200 |
| % Initial Profit to Initial Assets | 18·6% | 17·8% | 19·1% | |
| % Initial Additional Return to Additional Assets | | | | 22·3% |
| Simple Pay-Off Fixed Assets | | | 12,000 / 4,400 | = 2·73 yrs |

Est. Minimum Life of Product Demand on Project Process 7 yrs. Replaced Plant assumed written off. No salvage value.

income will still cover related running costs at the end of 10 years. In this sense only can it be said that it partially moves towards a long-term evaluation.

For the project to be satisfactory, in reading this form of presentation an initial return on additional assets would be expected to be higher than a normal commercial interest rate, representing either loss of interest on funds switched from cash into fixed assets, or an additional borrowing to finance the project.

## Uncertainty, Risk and Probability

Even with short-term evaluations there will be an element of uncertainty particularly with forecast income changes, and especially with quality/design improvement projects, where the evidence may virtually be limited to consolidated judgements as to the extent to which customers can be wooed to the improved product, or an accelerating flight from an inferior one be reversed. In the long run, the major uncertainties will usually stem from uncertain actions by competitors.

"It is most likely that sales will run at 10,000 units per annum, there is a slight chance that they could be as low as 6,000, but I would tend to be twice as optimistic as pessimistic and suggest that there is a not unreasonable chance that they could run at 11,000 a year." If such a statement is translated into subjective probability terminology, where the total probability is unity, the following table could emerge.

|  | Annual Sales | Probability |  |
|---|---|---|---|
| "Pessimistic" | 6,000 | ·1 | 600 |
| "Most Likely" | 10,000 | ·7 | 7,000 |
| "Optimistic" | 11,000 | ·2 | 2,200 |
| "Expected Value" |  | 1·0 | 9,800 |

This kind of approach to the immediate future, mid-term and longer term outcome can in practice provide some refinement in forecasting.

## Sensitivity Tests

According to their varying capital/income/cost structure, the success of projects will, in varying degree, be sensitive to changes in selling price, volume, running costs and length of unchallenged economic life. At least in larger projects, it will be worth while indicating in the data presented the effects of even minor changes in such factors as percentage falls from expected values in price or volume.

Where there is some doubt as to the life of special purpose products allied with special purpose tools for their production, the cumulative income test can be applied in a tabular or graphed form, which will indicate the area of loss which might be incurred by a premature collapse, and it is possible to combine two of these tests in one presentation as follows on page 242.

Where there are various ways of achieving the same output at different capital costs, those with heavier capital costs showing progressive reduction in running costs, similar cumulative outlay tests for life sensitivity can be applied, and here one is also interested in the incremental capital cost of the heavier outlay in relation to the incremental income which it produces. Sometimes this is subject to the law of diminishing returns, e.g.

| Alternative Method (same output) | Annual Running Costs | Capital Outlay | Av. Annual Total Cost if 10 yr life | Cumulative Outlay Years in Use | | | | |
|---|---|---|---|---|---|---|---|---|
| | | | | 1 | 2 | 3 | 4 | 5 |
| A | 77 | — | 77 | 77 | 154 | 231 | 308 | 385 |
| B | 50 | 80 | 58 | 130 | 180 | 280 | 280 | 330 |
| C | 38 | 120 | 50 | 158 | 196 | 234 | 272 | 310 |

The foregoing also shows a cost test on specific assumptions and cost per unit test will be one of the usual tests where unit measurements are available.

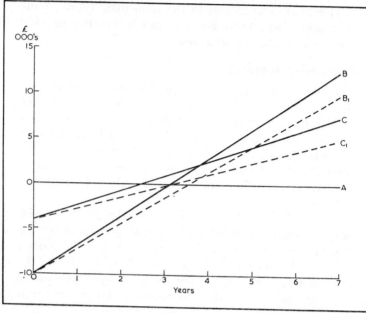

FIG. 22.  Cumulative Cash Gains less Outlays—Alternative Methods

A  No change
B  Method 1
C  Method 2
$B_1$ and $C_1$: Methods B and C at lower selling prices

## Long-term Evaluation

### The Accountants Approach to Major Fully Independent Projects

Some of the inherent problems associated with long-term evaluation have already been referred to. Accountants associated with the purchase or sale of businesses have traditionally primarily based their ideas of valuation in terms of the purchase of "so many years after tax profits," but have also borne in mind the prospects for the firm and the industry, the state of the assets and the quality of the management. Share prices of public companies also reflect this but also reflect dividend distributions and the effect of market forces.

Accountants thus think of the earning power of existing products, conglomerate assets and their successors, and this line of thought can also be applied to other similar type projects, visualizing earnings retained from distribution by way of depreciation provisions, finding their way from interest earning cash, via profit earning additional circulating stocks of goods, into successor plant which in simplified diagrammatic form might look as follows on page 244.

If this were regarded as a standard model with standard trends and standard profit, a project which came up to standard as evidenced by the ratio AC to AD in the early years would be regarded as acceptable. Abnormally good projects would show an early profit of AG (GCB might be regarded as super profit). There is an assumption in this model that profits are distributed and depreciation provisions retained.

The decline in original assets does not represent deterioration in itself, it represents a decline in earning power associated with the slow emergence of more modern machines in competitors' hands, and the appearance of rival and substitute products at more competitive prices. Depreciation provision would be regarded as going into a common pool for general asset replenishment.

When combined with a project's successor assets within its lifetime built up from its retained depreciation provisions, a project with an initial or peak return of say 30 per cent would thus on a continuing basis be assumed to revert to the standard return of say 15 per cent as it is faded out, and its successor assets step in giving an average return of $22\frac{1}{2}$ per cent.

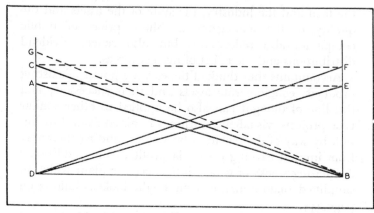

FIG. 23

| ADB Initial Project Assets | DEB Successor Assets |
|---|---|
| ACB Initial Project Profits | DFE Successor Asset Profits |
| AEBD Total Assets | ACFE Total Profits |

Another form of presentation of a Semi-Independent Expansion project appears on page 227 and read in this light can be regarded as a long-term evaluation.

## Asset Life. Depreciation and Obsolescence

Both the continuing business concept and the single venture concept introduce the element of asset life, but from different angles. In the former case, this will not necessarily be synonymous with project life and in the latter, it will, although for plant used for specialized products, life may be shorter than operating capability if product life is the shorter of the two.

Assets may function in a primary capacity and then be displaced for use in a lower grade secondary capacity but because of unreliable evidence it will be usual in practice to adopt a somewhat arbitrary standard life for each main type of equipment.

A continuing concept, regarded as maintaining capital intact, implies not necessarily replacement with similar machinery but the retention from distribution and the holding in some common pool of amounts adequate to compensate for the disappearance of the assets originally acquired. Viewed from this angle, the deterioration may be thought of as a loss of share capital and of assets which have to be replenished before profits are declared, and the entry in the Profit and Loss Account as a debit, the opposite credit of which goes to replenish the capital lost. As to the incidence of this, if one pays deference to the "costs matching benefits" principle one may subscribe to some diminishing provision as the years progress. One may note that 20 per cent on the diminishing balance leaves a residual balance of 5 per cent of the original cost after $12\frac{1}{2}$ years or 10 per cent after 9.

Depreciation provisions can, however, possess some of the properties of an optical illusion, for they can also be viewed as an amortization of cost.

## Residual Book Values

It is sometimes put forward that the true value of a business lies in its future earning capacity and that theoretically, this should in some way be reflected in its book values, as to some extent it is reflected in share prices. But how and by whom are these to be decided? Such difficult problems tend to rule out this valid-sounding proposition.

Nevertheless a decision, if soundly made, that future earnings less capital and running costs of new equipment will be greater than future earnings less the out of pocket running costs of continuing to use the old, does improve the value of a business unless it leaves it in a dangerously tight cash situation, and those responsible do not or cannot convince finance suppliers that earning power is markedly improved. Unfortunately of course, increased earning power will not be immediately reflected in the books other than as additional equipment.

One should not be surprised that residual book values of old equipment, though truly irrelevant to sound decision (though they may act as a signalling system for outlays regarded as recurrent costs) can be a deterrent to proper decision timing, for this balance has to be written off, possibly showing previous misjudgements in timing and understatement of costs. Special provisions may be built up to cover this.

## The Timing of Replacement of Maintainable Plant

When one owns a reasonably sound machine which, though subject to more frequent stoppages for repair or adjustment, or less consistently precise, or slower than the latest model, can more or less do its job, one is faced with the problem of whether to replace now, or next year, or in five years time.

A deferment now and a replacement later may in turn allow deferment of replacement of the replacement and comparison could be against replacement now with an earlier replacement of this replacement.

An adequate comparison, if it could be calculated, would be of the effects of replacing now as against replacing one year later but this in turn means making a whole series of comparable assumptions as to what is likely to happen subsequently in either case.

Unless there are some associated and self-evident gains, e.g. added capacity or radical cost saving features, this represents one of the most awkward theoretical problems in project evaluation, for one can be faced with unequal lives and leapfrog effects, and even if one creates equal lives for comparison purposes by introducing the cost of major overhauls of the old, one can end up with an evaluation showing the advantage of replacing now as compared with replacing ten years rather than with one year hence. One may also want a second calculation showing the return one expects to obtain once one has replaced. Facts regarding loss of custom through quality defects or delivery delays and losses of production through stoppages for adjustment or spoilt material are hard to come by and may be insidious.

Some clues may be gleaned from the following.

## The Peculiar Viaduct Problem

If one imagines the capital outlays as building bricks forming the piers of a viaduct, they could be spaced well apart or close together. These spaces are spanned by uniformly shaped right-angled concrete triangles ($\triangle$) representing maintenance costs, rising steadily across each gap to a peak and a span size determined by how widely the bricks are placed apart.

OR

FIG. 24. The Peculiar Viaduct Problem

The problem is to determine how widely apart the bricks should be placed to obtain the minimum use of materials.

"Maintenance" may have to be used in a special sense to include the loss of income arising from quality deterioration and interrupted production arising with progressive deterioration.

It is assumed that the structure of the "arches" is repetitively uniform. Where $x$ is the distance apart at which the bricks are placed costs are minimized when

$$x = \sqrt{\frac{C}{M}}. \quad x \text{ being in terms of years.}$$

| Replacement Cost in any year £8 (C) | | 1 | 2 | 3 | YEAR 4 | 5 | 6 | 7 . . . n |
|---|---|---|---|---|---|---|---|---|
| | | £ | £ | £ | £ | £ | £ | £ |
| (a) Year's Maintenance cost if retained | | 0 | 1 | 2 | 3 | 4 | 5 | 6 |
| (b) Cum. Maintenance cost | | 0 | 1 | 3 | 6 | 10 | 15 | 21 |
| (c) Annual Aver. Maint. Cost. (b) ÷ year | | 0 | 0·5 | 1·0 | 1·5 | 2 | 2·5 | 3 |
| (d) Annual Aver. Capital Cost. C ÷ year | | 8 | 4 | 2·67 | 2·0 | 1·6 | 1·33 | 1·14 |
| (e) Combined Annual Aver. Cost if retained (c) + (d) | | 8 | 4·5 | 3·67 | 3·5 | 3·6 | 3·83 | 4·14 |

The levelling off of the slope of series (d) is worth noting. The lowest combined average annual cost appears to be around the 4th/5th year and thus would be about the time to replace, since all subsequent sequences are presumed to follow the same repetitive pattern.

Mathematically these approximations of trends can be expressed in equations in terms of, cost $= y$. For capital cost the slope of the curve (d) is

$$y = \frac{C}{x} = \frac{8}{x}$$

(c) is a rising straight line expressed in the form

$$y = k + Mx$$

(see page 266). In this case it will be found to be

$$y = -0.5 + 0.5x$$

The time to replace will be when the combined curve

$$y = \frac{8}{x} + (-0.5 + 0.5x)$$

is at a minimum.

This can be found using elementary differential calculus, i.e. differentiate $x$ with respect to $y$.

$$\therefore \frac{dy}{dx} = -\frac{8}{x^2} + 0 + 0.5$$

Set the derivation to equal zero giving—

$$-\frac{8}{x^2} + 0.5 = 0$$

$$\therefore \frac{8}{x^2} = 0.5,$$

$$\therefore x^2 = \frac{8}{0.5},$$

$$\therefore x = \sqrt{16},$$

$$\therefore x = 4$$

This example also has some relevance to consideration of economic life.

## The Single Venture Approach

If full life appraisals are to be tackled in the form of relating gains to capital outlays, and if one is treating each project in isolation and eliminating any effects of its potential successors, one must adopt some version of the single venture approach.

Applied to income based, major fully independent projects, this raises difficulties in correctly envisaging the pace at which income would fall, costs rise and working capital decline as assets deteriorate and better made competing equivalents begin to enter the field.

Applied to dependent projects, one has to reach an assumption as to whether this pace should or should not be regarded as being affected by decline in supporting equipment if not assumed to be self-renewing.

This is a theoretically valid approach, and one can assume that one starts with no funds and no assets, borrows to finance the project, repays borrowing at interest out of project gains, as the project proceeds, and ends up with no funds and no assets but with surplus gains earned in the process.

## Formalized Gain Profiles

Where "full life" evaluations are called for, especially in large far flung organizations with major projects and evaluations emanating from different sources, it would seem necessary to categorize projects into types, and to formalize "standard lives" by type, and issue a limited number of standard gain trend profiles with known properties for application beyond the point reached, say after the first 4 to 5 years, if any degree of uniformity of treatment is to be obtained.

## Taxation

The basis of taxation is liable to change with Government policy. There are, however, differences in tax treatment between different types of assets, incomes and locations.

Notice must be taken of this when company projects are subject to different tax treatment. It is possible to devise weighting factors to apply either to outlays or to income which will modify the basic figures to bring them to a more comparable basis.

## Interest

In a search for principles, the question of interest has been studiously avoided, for until one gets fundamentals straight at an interest or discount rate of zero, the introduction of interest charges may add little to the value of evaluations.

One may not go far wrong in thinking in terms of commercial interest rates, but in this context economists prefer to discuss the concept of "the cost of capital," whilst business men may prefer to introduce this in the form to represent the average return considered available from average alternative investment opportunities. Projects which offer returns equivalent to this will be regarded as acceptable, those showing higher figures will be looked on as exceptionally good.

There are varying methods of introducing this into calculations and figures will only be comparable when the method of their compilation is the same.

Space does not provide room for discussing the complex effects of inflation.

## Compounding, Discounting, Uniform Annual Equivalents, Sinking Funds, Present and Terminal Values

Economists and accountants operating in large corporations, faced with differences in tax treatment in different localities and many large scale construction projects, and seeking to improve evaluation and reduce diverging income trends for different projects to a common denominator, have turned to the well-known and readily manipulated mathematical properties of compound interest and discounting formula.

As a model, it may be conceded that they contain some degree of artificiality, in the assumption that all gains accrue in this form, but this does not prevent their use for establishing a better scale of relative advantage. The basic compound interest series takes the following form—

$$1, (1 + i), (1 + i)^2, (1 + i)^3 \ldots (1 + i)^n$$

Discount formula are the inverse of compound interest formula, thus the present value of an annuity of £1 to commence one year hence, which will be receivable for 4 years at a 20 per cent interest/discount rate is

$$\frac{1}{1 \cdot 20} + \frac{1}{(1 \cdot 20)^2} + \frac{1}{(1 \cdot 20)^3} + \frac{1}{(1 \cdot 20)^4}$$

$$= 0 \cdot 833 + 0 \cdot 694 + 0 \cdot 579 + 0 \cdot 483 = £2 \cdot 589$$

i.e. $0 \cdot 833 + 20\% = £1$

$$0 \cdot 694 + 20\% = 0 \cdot 833 + 20\% = £1.$$

From such basic series, formulas have been worked out for the Present Value of a series at the beginning of its term, the value of its sum at the end, etc. In practice such work is carried out from published tables such as the one on page 253. Discount Tables can be converted to compound interest tables by inversion. The calculation for say £20 is merely the table for £1 times 20.

The magnitude of the effects of applying such rates to sums receivable or payable in future years is worth studying from tables before one applies them indiscriminately.

Whilst discounting and compounding can properly be applied to Net Profit figures, the case has been advanced for applying them to Cash Flows (i.e. Profit after tax, before depreciation provisions).

PRESENT VALUE OF £1—COMPOUND INTEREST
COMPOUNDED ANNUALLY

| Years hence | 6% | 8% | 10% | 12% | 15% | 20% | 25% | 30% |
|---|---|---|---|---|---|---|---|---|
| 1 | 0·943 | 0·926 | 0·909 | 0·893 | 0·870 | 0·833 | 0·800 | 0·769 |
| 2 | 0·890 | 0·847 | 0·826 | 0·797 | 0·736 | 0·694 | 0·640 | 0·592 |
| 3 | 0·840 | 0·794 | 0·751 | 0·712 | 0·657 | 0·579 | 0·512 | 0·455 |
| 4 | 0·792 | 0·735 | 0·683 | 0·635 | 0·572 | 0·482 | 0·410 | 0·350 |
| 5 | 0·747 | 0·681 | 0·621 | 0·567 | 0·497 | 0·402 | 0·328 | 0·260 |
| 6 | 0·705 | 0·630 | 0·564 | 0·507 | 0·432 | 0·335 | 0·262 | 0·207 |
| 8 | 0·627 | 0·540 | 0·467 | 0·404 | 0·327 | 0·233 | 0·168 | 0·123 |
| 10 | 0·558 | 0·463 | 0·385 | 0·322 | 0·247 | 0·161 | 0·107 | 0·012 |
| 12 | 0·497 | 0·397 | 0·315 | 0·257 | 0·187 | 0·112 | 0·069 | 0·043 |
| 15 | 0·417 | 0·315 | 0·239 | 0·183 | 0·123 | 0·065 | 0·035 | 0·079 |
| 20 | 0·312 | 0·214 | 0·149 | 0·104 | 0·061 | 0·026 | 0·011 | 0·005 |

There are several contending versions of how the formalized compound interest/discounting formulae are best applied to arrive at some index of relative profitability, and there has been some argument as to interpretation, which can only be resolved when there is a clear statement of how the project is formally assumed to be financed, how, if, and when finance is assumed to be repaid and how inflowing funds are used for repayment, distribution or reinvestment.

The Discounted Cash Flow Yield (D.C.F.Y.) Method is the best documented. This has been described "as showing the highest rate at which one could borrow on bank overdraft to finance the scheme and still break even," and is primarily based on a single venture concept assumed to be financed by a loan repayable by changing

254 BUDGETARY CONTROL AND STANDARD COSTS

instalments over the life of the asset at an interest rate on the outstanding balance of the loan. The discount rate which brings the forecast cash flows to a present value equal to the initial outlay is found by a trial and error interpolation method. Here the cash flow is split between interest on the outstanding balance of the loan and the balance used for loan repayment.

Where the project is assumed to be financed by a fixed loan repayable at the end of the project life in a lump sum, the cash flows can be envisaged as being divided between an annual simple interest charge on the full loan, the balance of the cash flow being placed in a sinking fund, which when accumulated at the same percentage rate as above, but compounded, provides the exact lump sum at the end of the life, to meet loan repayment.

Where permanent finance is assumed, the first version can have an abstract interpretation of the interest being on the unamortized balance of the project as reduced by the instalments and the second as a sinking fund available for asset replacement.

In contra distinction from the above, which bases its evaluation on the resultant emerging discount rate, the Present Value Method and the Terminal Value Method both employ previously established known discount/ interest rates (usually at average commercial opportunity levels) to "equalize" the cash flow. The former discounts the cash flow to a Present Value, which is expected to show an acceptable surplus on the initial outlay or whose ratio to the initial outlay may be calculated.

The latter compounds the cash flow to a Terminal Value, which is compared with the initial outlay compounded to a terminal value at the same rate. The former is usually expressed as a ratio to the compounded outlay, or to its original value.

The last named lacks the attractive neatness of the D.C.F.Y. method but would appear to avoid some of its anomalies, and its mechanics, and inbuilt assumptions are perhaps more readily understandable by industrialists and more readily permit an assumed extension of the shorter of unequal lives to a longer equal period.

A study of the problem of trend comparison shown earlier, using a capital outlay of £1,850 for both A and B and applying different methods and different interest rates, will reveal that it is only when one is forced to borrow, or is able to re-invest, at rates above a certain level that relative advantages become reversed.

## Note

It may be interesting to note that with flat rate gains and high discount rates there is a close correlation between D.C.F. Yield and simple pay back periods when life is taken into account.

| Simple Pay Back Period in Years | 1 | 2 | 3 | 4 | 5 | 6 |
|---|---|---|---|---|---|---|
| Inverse as a percentage | 100% | 50% | 33% | 25% | 20% | 17% |
| Life Years of Project | 3 | 6 | 9 | 12 | 15 | 18 |
| D.C.F. Yield | 92% | 45% | 30% | 23% | 18% | 15% |

These correlations may not be materially disturbed even with high tax rates where there are significant capital allowances for wear and tear, and grants.

Research is likely to continue in this field and formulae containing dual rates seem likely to emerge.

## Check

Only a half check can be made that the actual outcome matches up to plan, for although one can fruitfully check expenditure and income with lessons to be learned for further projects, one cannot check on what otherwise would have happened had the project not been proceeded with.

## Conclusion

The depth of the investigation and the number and complexity of evaluation tests applied to projects should be proportionate to their significance to the organization.

It should be stressed again that in major projects, the vital over-riding feature in a profit or cash flow profile, will be related to the future of the plant's products, and that in incurring capital expenditure, what one is really doing is staking one's resources on the future of certain products or services.

For long range planning it will primarily be necessary to take a broad look at the forecast and planned changes in turnover pattern and alterations in product mix which, for most firms, will be the dominant factor. Allied with this will be the combined anticipated benefits and outlays of whole series of varied capital projects when establishing the probable financial outcome of long range plans.

# CHAPTER XXII

# MATHEMATICS AND MANAGEMENT

MATHEMATICS applied to business problems appear in several gradings.

(*a*) Simply as a shorthand method of expression, e.g. $\Sigma$ for "the sum of."

(*b*) As a neater, speedier or more precise way of performing calculations which can also be done perhaps more laboriously or less precisely by less sophisticated methods.

(*c*) As a means of getting answers which are virtually unobtainable by other means.

(*d*) As a new type of mathematics, emerging under the title of "simulation," which is applied to problems which are too complex, too long drawn out, too subject to "interference" or to chance (within certain limits) for conventional mathematics to deal with.

Here the mathematical skill lies in the ability to translate transactions or a flow of events in time within a stipulated environment into homogeneous sets of units related to each other, in such a form that they can be fed into a computer (or used for manual experiment). These formulations are then subjected to what is in effect a high speed trial and error approach to ascertain their interactions, then, by modification to the environment or to the constituents of the input, the best combinations for producing the required effects are sought. From studies of such models guiding lines for practical applications may be deduced.

Comparatively simple mathematical formulae can play an important role in clarifying the inter-relationship

and interaction between changes in dominant factors or
their effects over varying time spans.

The development of formulae of this type is valuable,
in that they entail seeking out the dominant factors and
discarding what appear to be irrelevances. Then for each
dominant factor, setting down what is considered to be
a sufficiently realistic approximation of its degree of
variability under certain changes or pressures within
certain ranges, in a form which can be easily manipulated
in mathematical terms—often sloping straight lines or
smooth curves or standard frequency or probability distributions with known characteristics.

Mathematics deals in numbers, and their use as a
medium of clarification serves to enforce the quantifica-
tion of relevant data (though it may permit upper and
lower limits of tolerance and even varying degrees of
probability).

Optimization techniques such as some applications of
differential calculus or linear programming also demand
the clear specification of objectives, or of objectives subject
to certain specified constraints, e.g. maximizing profits
in the short run provided the labour force is not changed by
more than 10 per cent per month.

It is vitally important that the simplifying assumptions
—the other things which can safely be assumed to be
more or less equal—and which may be perfectly valid
for some particular study, are fully tabulated, if the danger
is to be avoided of having what has proved a very useful
technique under certain circumstances transferred to
situations where such assumptions no longer hold water.

Thus, significant relationships which are valid in cases
of stable demand, one product, one customer, one
machine, ample financial resources, limited range of
change, may have to be radically modified under conditions of variable demand, many products (interfering

with each other), many machines, limited resources, and marked degree of change.

Another feature relevant to some techniques and referred to as "sub-optimization" must be mentioned. Efforts aiming at perfection in one sector of an organization may be subject to the law of diminishing returns and with limited resources there will generally be a point, below the best in this sector, where efforts and resources could be more fruitfully switched to establishing improvement in another.

Thus optimization at one point may not be the best way of achieving optimization of the whole.

Finally it must be emphasized that the results emerging from the mathematical evaluation of complex factors will depend on the margins of error inherent in the basic data used in the formulations, but that nevertheless, they are often capable of producing significant and useful approximations. One may thus discover that there are plateaux where movement in one direction or other has no marked effect, but beyond which one finds oneself in a steep slope which is to be avoided if one does not wish to descend rapidly from the heights.

With these considerations in mind, and remembering that in science of business we are not only dealing with physics, but with the biology of life, one can proceed to the study of further techniques, which can usefully be employed to unravel some of the complexities of business operation and improve performance. Other examples of such mathematical models also appear in appropriate sections of the text.

Not infrequently the fruits of quite complex studies and mathematical calculations can be crystallized for everyday practical application in the form of tables or graphs.

Examples are logarithmic, discount and probability tables and those of the type called nomengrams which commonly enable a third value to be read off directly given known quantities for two other factors.

A type of nomengram is illustrated by the accompanying version of a multiple break-even chart actually used for approximate weekly profit calculations in a simple industry (see Fig. 25, p. 263).

Application of more sophisticated mathematics are no excuse for unhappy results arising from failure to apply simple arithmetic to everyday decisions, say on price and volume, or to make a check on hunches, e.g. it is not necessarily immediately obvious that $1,610 \times 14 + 810 \times 17$ is substantially less than $2,520 \times 13 + 420 \times 18$.

## The Mathematics of Length of Run

One aspect of this which has been widely discussed is the subject of batch size, which is more complex in practice than the basic theory allows for, another relates to the effects of short run "specialities" versus long run "bread and butter" lines and their effect on output and on required relative prices, e.g. given the information that a factory's weekly non stop capacity was 36,000 units and that the equivalent of 1,000 units of production were lost for every change over from one batch to another and that the factory running cost per week was £360,000, the mathematically minded accountant might usefully point out that for average batch sizes of 8,000 units the output would be 32,000 but if this fell to 500 units it would only be 12,000 and that the cost per unit for varying average batch size could be found from the equation for the conversion cost/output line of—

$$y = \frac{R}{a - \dfrac{ba}{x + b}}$$

where $y$ = cost per unit, $R$ = total factory running cost, $a$ = non stop capacity, $b$ = units lost per change over, and $x$ = length of run.

The cost per unit where each batch of "specialities" was 2,000, would thus be £15 (at an output of 24,000).

It could rightly be said that stock holding costs had been omitted in this formula. Whilst the above equation might be called a mathematical model, life is generally more complex.

Rather more can be learned from the accompanying simulation study which models the effects of constraints and interference of the best batch size for one product with the best batch size for another. This example is suited for manual experiment, and can be developed to include cost values and chance changes in demand. (Stock movements in products may be clearer on a graph.)

This problem can be made more involved if one thus asks how the programme might be modified if, say, materials cost per unit of B is twice that of the other products and is four times its conversion cost. The factory may be assumed to cost £240 per day to run.

## SIMULATION STUDY OF FACTORS AFFECTING VOLUME VARIANCE

Maximum stocks permitted each product 10 days (or weeks) usage. "Run outs"—completely out of stock permitted one day's supply after reaching nil.

Change over time on machine from one product to another equivalent to loss of one day's production.

Two machines available P & Q.

All products A, B, C, D, and E, run out of stock from Maximum to nil in ten days (i.e. 10 days supply in stock runs out to nil in 10 days) when no replenishment. When machines are running on products the number of days required to build up stocks (10 days supply) including usages during period of replacement are—

A. 6 days. B. 5 days. C. 4 days. D. 3 days. E. 2 days.

Starting point say, C, D and E not in production with 2, 3, and 6 days stock in hand respectively. A in production on Machine P with 4 days stock accumulated and B in production on machine Q with 5 days stock in hand.

Devise an economic and workable production programme with guiding rules bearing in mind batch sizes, machine stopped time, level of stock holding, stock run outs etc.

*Example for first 5 days*

*Days and products on Machines*

| Days (End) | 0 | 1 | 2 | 3 | 4 | 5 |
|---|---|---|---|---|---|---|
| Machine P on | A | A | A | — | C | C |
| Machine Q on | B | B | B | — | D | D |

*Stocks of products held (number of days supply)*

| | | | | | | |
|---|---|---|---|---|---|---|
| A | 4 | 5·2/3 | 7·1/3 | 6·1/3 | 5·1/3 | 4·1/3 |
| B | 5 | 7 | 9 | 8 | 7 | 6 |
| C | 2 | 1 | 0 | OUT | 2½ | 5 |
| D | 3 | 2 | 1 | 0 | 3·1/3 | 6·2/3 |
| E | 6 | 5 | 4 | 3 | 2 | 1 |
| | —— | | | | | |
| | 20 | | | | | |

*Supplementary*

(1) Should the maximum stock level be (*a*) raised, (*b*) lowered?

(2) Within the terms, could the programme be modified—

   (*a*) If in a financial crisis, the sole objective was minimum average stocks.

   (*b*) The sole objective was maximum output?

(3) Could Produce F, with the same rate of usage as E but twice E's production rate be introduced into the programme—

   (*a*) without change in the stipulations.

   (*b*) If permissible maximum stock levels were raised?

# The Profit Grid

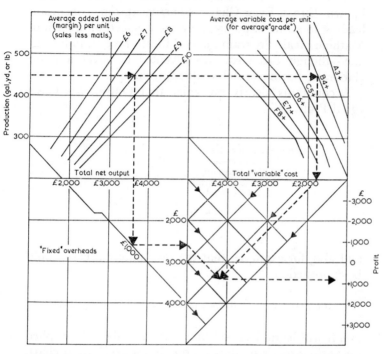

The "profit grid" is a device which is a dissected version of the familiar break-even chart designed in such a way that various permutations of sales volume, price, and variable costs can be readily worked out. It can allow different product mixes (shown here as "average grades."

Whenever conditions permit some unit of output to be devised, the profit grid can be used in this simple form to arrive at the results of recent activity, or to forecast future results.

Two straight-edge rulers are used and starting with volume of production one moves horizontally till one strikes the appropriate diagonals for added value and for "grade"; one then proceeds vertically to the next diagonal, when one again changes direction—the diagonal acting as a reflector or lead.

Such graphs can be used to apply multiplication, division, subtraction or addition.

FIG. 25. The Profit Grid

**Break Even Analysis** (See also page 32)

Accountants will realize that when they use the well-known "Break Even Chart" to arrive at some conclusion leading to a line of policy, they are engaged on a form of Mathematical Programming—Linear Programming in fact—though this term was invented to cover a more elaborate, but nevertheless allied, technique.

Accountants clearly recognize that Output *less* Costs equal Profit or—

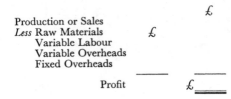

and also, for example, that the raw materials costs could be expressed—

Cost per unit × Units *produced* per hour × Hours in period

and it will be understood that when the above is graphed for various levels of activity, one has a break even chart. It is not so widely recognized that the questions answered by the break even chart in its simple form can also be given by the solution of a simple equation, one particular form of which is—

$$P = xaf - xae - xb - xd - c$$

where—

$P$ = Profit on one week's output expressed in pence.
$a$ = The hourly production of the factory, department,

or process, expressed in units—tons, lb., yards, gallons, units. The units could be standard hours (or even direct labour hours).

$b$ = The total variable hourly wage bill (at single shift rate) expressed in pence per hour.

$c$ = The fixed weekly overheads expressed in pence per week (including any fixed element in hourly wages).

$d$ = The variable hourly overheads expressed in pence per hour.

$e$ = The raw materials cost per unit of output ($a$) expressed as pence per unit.

$f$ = The selling price per unit of output expressed as pence per unit ($f - e$ = net output value per unit).

$x$ = The hours worked (at basic single-shift rate), used as a measure of activity and expressed in terms of factory working hours per week, e.g. 45, 30, 20, 50, etc.

The above may be averages.

In break even chart presentation $x$ would be the terms in which the measure of activity would be shown along the horizontal axis of the chart.

The level of activity is recorded in the above form in this particular version of the general equation (other versions can be developed) for a particular purpose. Thus $x$ is expressed in hours, but can readily be converted into percentage activity, e.g. if 45 hours full working is taken to represent 100 per cent activity, 50 per cent activity = $22\frac{1}{2}$ hours, 200 per cent activity equals 90 hours; or if 90 hours is taken as 100 per cent activity 45 hours equals 50 per cent activity.

For formula purposes any semi-variable expenses have to be split into a fixed and a variable portion appropriate to the range of activity under consideration[1] (the latter strictly proportional to the volume of saleable goods produced). To find the profit which will emerge at a certain volume of activity the general equation is used to solve for $P$, other values being known.

To find the activity at which a given profit will emerge, insert the desired value for $P$ and the other known values, and solve for $x$. Questions of the effect of price and cost changes can also readily be solved within the limitations of the equation.

---

[1] If one estimates that a heterogeneous collection of semi-variable over-heads, say "Consumable Stores" will change from say £200 p.w. to £250 p.w. for an increase in activity from 450 to 750 units produced, or 60 per cent to 100 per cent capacity, or 45 to 75 hour working week or similar activity measure (which could appear on the horizontal or $x$ axis on a break even chart), one can mathematically split the expenses into their theoretical fixed and variable elements within this range of activity. The cost change might alternatively be derived from observed experience at various activities, which could be plotted as points on such a chart and a best (rising) straight line $PQ$ drawn through them, (or being very refined, the best fit straight line could be obtained by regression analysis).

Where $y$ is regarded as the vertical, cost or value, axis (of a break even chart), $k$ the fixed cost element in the semi-variable expenses, and $M$ the variable expenses per unit of output or of activity (in effect referring to the slope of the line), then the value of the fixed and variable elements can be obtained by the equation—

$$y = k + Mx \text{ (which describes the line)}$$

In the above example the value of $M$ is obtained thus

$$M = \frac{250 - 200}{75 - 45} = £1.666 \text{ per hour of activity}$$

Fixed element, $k$, can be found by substitution in

$$y = k + Mx$$

(working from any specific points on the line, say end positions $P$ and $Q$, e.g. when $y = 200$, $x = 45$) thus—

$$200 = k + 1.666 \times 45$$
$$200 = k + 75$$
$$\therefore k = £125$$

or—

$$250 = k + 1.666 \times 75$$
$$\therefore k = £125$$

The break even activity point is found by inserting known values and solving for $x$ in the equation

$$xaf = xae + xb + xd + c,$$

or where

$$xa(f - e) = x(b + d) + c$$

A form of this equation can be used for solving the problem of at what level of activity would a double shift at a shift premium equal the single shift profit and start to pass it.

For this one uses: let

$y =$ hours worked at shift rate (basic rate plus shift premium) expressed in the same terms as $x$

$g =$ the fraction of shift (premium) rate per hour to basic (single shift) rate per hour, e.g. $\frac{110}{100}$

Solving for $y$ in the following equation, other values being known

$$yaf - yae - ygb - yd - c = xaf - xae - xb - xd - c$$

gives the activity value for $y$ (perhaps 55 hours) when the profit equals and passes the profit at $x$ activity (say 45 hours). (The maximum value of $y$ might be 90 on a two-shift basis.)

This equation can be expressed—

$$y[a(f - e) - (gb + d)] = x[a(f - e) - (b + d)]$$

It may be noted that $c$ drops out unless changed in value.

Similar type equations will give the activity at which the cost per unit is equal.

## Linear Programming (An introduction)

As referred to on page 185, when one approaches as it were to the maximum activity point on the break even chart (the full capacity level) one runs into a series of fresh problems; bottle-necks start to appear.

The products might be regarded as a growing army advancing without difficulty over a flat plain (as long as there is ample capacity available), then moving into broken ground where boulders and trees impede the progress, but where there are winding tracks, broad and narrow, if they can be located. The problem is how best to re-deploy the forces to get the most effective units through quickly. (If permanent occupation of this territory is anticipated it may later be policy to blast away the obstacles and level the ground.)

Until fairly recently there has been no satisfactory method of tackling this problem in industry other than by trial and error, organized or otherwise. A method of systematically approaching and finding the best and most profitable products and routes has, however, lately been devised.

In these circumstances the older techniques of measuring relative product profitability, e.g. per cent profit to sales, profit per unit, per cent profit to (standard) total or conversion cost of product, though still having relevance as a starting point for consideration of long-term developments (assuming no limitations to capacity to supply and to demand) tend to break down when it comes to diversion of capacity and consideration of most profitable use of existing capacity and existing demand. Total profitability can then only be considered in terms of the most profitable combination of products.

The technique of linear programming in certain circumstances is likely to be of value in tackling this problem.

The particular application which will be illustrated is perhaps best suited to processing industries utilizing large, heavy, or expensive units of equipment, and perhaps working round the clock, where short- and medium term bottle-necks arising from changes in demand pattern are not readily removable. With increased automation this situation will grow.

It will later be noted that in the example we shall be dealing with output measured in homogeneous units of machine-hours per unit, perhaps in turn, though not necessarily, derived from other units expressed in terms of tons, lb., yards, gallons, square feet, etc., though probably differing in nature, coarse to fine, small to large, crude to refined, thick to thin, etc. Where the units flowing through the processes are not, or are not measured, in homogeneous units; where there are intermediate waste losses, products fan out apart, or are later amalgamated, it may be desirable to devise some common unit of measurement with which intermediate components can be equated, e.g. being treated as being equivalent to so many units of the end products or the main ingoing raw material. To simplify computation, a limited number of typical products may sometimes be taken as being representative samples from groups of products.

Long ago it was discovered that certain problems to which hitherto correct answers could only be found by a laborious system of experimenting by trial and error could quickly and correctly be solved by simple algebraic equations. Later someone discovered how to solve simultaneous equations and how to apply them to the solving of other problems.

Apparently, however, until very recently no one had discovered (except by trial and error) how to get the answer quickly and correctly to another group of problems —finding the maximum or minimum value for the sum of ($\sum$) certain unknown quantities which could involve a group of simultaneous equations and other equations (inequations) which were not necessarily equal, but could also be more than ($>$) or less than ($<$) a certain value. In the 1940's a mathematician working in America evolved a method of solving such problems precisely, which was apparently a major mathematical advance, but which (after discovery) is in practice a fairly straightforward routine. The method is allied to the solution of simultaneous equations, and involves making the data, which is not necessarily an equation (i.e. is equal to or less than or equal to or more than) into an equation by the use of notational numbers (slack variables), which are used in the calculation but do not form part of the result. It has been found that it has and is likely to have wide industrial application.

Most profitable product mix problems within the capacity of the existing (or the projected) equipment are an example of this type, where alternative products can be sold which can be produced on alternative machines, but which must not use more, but could use less, than the capacity at each process (including the capacity of the selling process).

In such a product mix problem the question is: Process I with such and such a capacity could produce so much of Products $A$, $B$ and $C$ in varying undetermined proportions, but could also produce $A$ and $B$ or $A$ and $C$ or $B$ and $C$ or any one of them in differing proportions, leaving some idle capacity (in which a notional Product $P$ could be produced), and similarly at Processes 2 and 3, etc. For each product the difference between sales price and variable costs per unit is known. Problem: Find the quantity of $A$, $B$, and $C$ to be produced and sold to give the maximum profit.

For example—

Processes I and II each have 420 hours capacity. At Process I Product $A$ requires 6 hours per unit and Product $B$ 2 hours per unit.

At Process II, *A* requires 5 hours per unit and *B* 5 hours per unit also.

Sales price less variable cost for Product *A* is £8 per unit and for *B* £9 per unit.

*Question* (1) What quantity of *A* and *B* will balance the plant to capacity?

*Question* (2) What contribution (*MC*) to fixed overheads and profit will this produce?

*Question* (3) Is this the best profit?

*Question* (1) can be solved by simultaneous equation thus—

Let *x* and *y* be the unknown quantities of *A* and *B*, then—

(*a*) $420 = 6x + 2y$;

(*b*) $420 = 5x + 5y$.

Multiply (*a*) by 5 and (*b*) by 6, then—

$2,100 = 30x + 10y$

$2,520 = 30x + 30y$

Subtract—

$420 = 20y$

$y = 21$

Substitute in (*a*)—

$420 = 6x + 42$

$\therefore 378 = 6x$

$x = 63$

*Proof*—

|  | Process I |  | Process II |  |
|---|---|---|---|---|
| 63*A* @ 6 hours = | 378 hours | 63*A* @ 5 hours = | 318 |
| 21*B* @ 2 hours = | 42 hours | 21*B* @ 5 hours = | 105 |
|  | 420 hours |  | 420 |

= Capacity of Process I and of Process II.

*Note.* The original equation (*a*) could also be written

$$6x = 420 - 2y$$

and both sides could be divided by the same number (say 2) without invalidating the equation, e.g.—

$$3x = 210 - 1y$$

This gives a clue to some of the subsequent procedure.

If we regard *A* and *B* as the unknown quantities of *A* and *B* and place this reference in a different heading up position for the equation, the initial equations could be rewritten—

$$\begin{array}{cc} A & B \\ 420 = 6 & + 2 \\ 420 = 5 & + 5 \end{array}$$

For *Question* (2) the answer is—

$$\begin{array}{lr} & £ \\ 63A @ £8 = & 504 \\ 21B @ £9 = & 189 \\ \hline \text{Total } MC & £693 \end{array}$$

∴ Exactly balancing the plant to capacity produces a marginal contribution (*MC*) to fixed overheads and profit of £693.

*Question* (3) asks: Does this produce the maximum profit? The answer is No.

Though in this simple example the correct answer to Question (3) can perhaps be found by inspection or at least by trial and error, where there are say about 10 processes and 10 products that is virtually impossible with any confidence.

The form of the equation to solve this problem, assuming that full capacity perhaps might not be called into use at all processes, to give the best answer and assuming that

$p_1$ and $p_2$ were the number of unknown hours of idle time would be—

| Process | Capacity | Quantity | | Idle Time |
|---------|----------|----------|---|-----------|
| I | 420 | $= 6x + 2y$ | $+$ | $1p_1$ |
| II | 420 | $= 5x + 5y$ | $+$ | $1p_2$ |

In the alternative form the preceding equations would appear—

$$
\begin{array}{cccc}
A & B & P_1 & P_2 \\
420 = 6 + 2 + 1 & & & \\
420 = 5 + 5 & & + 1 &
\end{array}
$$

($P_1$ and $P_2$ are referred to as slack variables, and can be looked on alternatively as having a rate of production of one and a profit of zero.)

These equations cannot be solved by ordinary simultaneous equations. There are too many unknowns and too few equations. (Simultaneous equations can only be solved where there are as many equations as unknowns and the profit element has not been embodied.)

The problem can, however, be solved by the linear programming procedure, the name given to the method of solution which is a development from simultaneous equations. The linear programming procedure will be illustrated by a product mix problem in a situation where demand exists, and it is capacity to supply that limits profits.

The procedure (using the so-called Simplex Method) involves forming a matrix (like a crossword puzzle) which reads both vertically and horizontally. In the product mix problem one column of the matrix starts off with containing the full capacities of each process in hours, completely unutilized except by idle time. These capacities are gradually replaced by the quantities of the products brought into the programme. (Some unused capacity may be left at the end.) These substitutions are made in further matrices (iterations). One starts with capacity unused and *nil* contribution (*MC*) and works up to the best programme. The increasing profit is revealed in a square at one corner of the matrix. The objective or base line of the matrix provides an ingenious signalling system which shows when the best answer has been reached. (This point is reached when all negative values disappear from the base line.) The problem illustrated can be tackled thus. Hereafter *MC* will be used for marginal contribution.

### 1. *Set Up the Matrix*

Set up the initial matrix which would appear

| *MC* | | o | 8 | 9 | o | o | Ratio |
|---|---|---|---|---|---|---|---|
| | | $P_0$ | *A* | *B* | $P_1$ | $P_2$ | |
| | Programme | Capacity/ Products | | | | | |
| o | $P_1$ | 420 = | 6 | 2 | I | o | |
| o | $P_2$ | 420 = | 5 | 5 | o | I | |
| Base Row | | | | | | | |

This will be recognized as the equation set out before, with the addition of the *MC* for each product set out across the top line, two additional columns at the left (the stub), a space at the right, and a space at the bottom (the base row). The heavily outlined box at the left-hand end of the base row and which forms part of the base row will contain the total marginal contribution for each programme.

The first matrix programmes nothing but idle time, for which there is no *MC*. Idle time is represented by $P_1$ and $P_2$. $P_1$ and $P_2$ can in fact be regarded as fictitious products requiring one hour per unit. (Idle time is converted to this product notation to achieve uniformity in classification.)

The sum of the multiplication of the figures in the first and third left-hand column when added together are entered at the foot of the third column to give the total *MC* for the listed programme. At the start this is *nil*.

## 2. *Insert the Base Row*

Where a nought appears on the top line a nought is inserted in the corresponding space in the initial base row. Where the product's marginal contribution appears in the top line the negative of this value is inserted in the corresponding space in the base row. The first base row will then appear—

|  | Col. $P_0$ | Col. $A$ | Col. $B$ | Col. $P_1$ | Col. $P_2$ |
|---|---|---|---|---|---|
| Base Row | 0 | − 8 | − 9 | 0 | 0 |

The initial programme of idle capacity has thus no Marginal Contribution to Fixed Overheads and profits as shown by the "0" at the foot of col. $P_0$.

## 3. *Select Key Column*

The next stage is to select the column whose product if included in the programme would add most marginal contribution at this stage. This is Column $B$ with the largest negative value $(-9)$.

This is referred to as the Key Column.

## 4. *Find Key Row*

The next stage is to find the row where there is the tightest bottle-neck if the key column Product $B$ is included in the programme. This is done by dividing the positive figures or zero already in the $P_0$ (Capacity/Product) column by the positive figures in the Key Column, producing a ratio or index number thus—

$$420 \div 2 = \frac{420}{2} = 210$$

$$420 \div 5 = \frac{420}{5} = 84$$

The smallest answer indicates the bottle-neck for the proposed product to be inserted in the programme. The row with the smallest answer is referred to as the Key Row and is the one in which substitution of a product for idle capacity is commenced. (If the ratios happen to be the same for two rows, the row which has the larger figure in the Key Column is chosen as the Key Row.)

*Note.* It may be seen that the division of the process capacities (each 420 hours) by the hours per unit of Product $B$ (2 and 5) required out of these capacities results in the number of units of Product $B$ which can be got out of the capacity available there at this initial stage, i.e.—

$$\frac{\text{Capacity Hours}}{\text{Hours per Unit}} = \text{Number of Product Units}$$

It may also be useful to note that—

$$\frac{\text{Capacity Hours}}{\text{Number of Product Units}} = \text{Hours per Unit}$$

### 5. *Select the Key Number*

The figure at the intersection of the Key Column and the Key Row is referred to as the Key Number or Pivot, and is usually then circled. (It is the processing time per unit in relation to capacity which has created the bottle-neck.) In this case it is 5.

The first matrix filled in with these details now appears thus—

| MC | | 0 | 8 | 9 | 0 | 0 | Ratio |
|---|---|---|---|---|---|---|---|
| | | $P_0$ | $A$ | $B$ | $P_1$ | $P_2$ | |
| | Programme | Capacity/ Products | | | | | |
| 0 | $P_1$ | 420 | 6 | 2 | 1 | 0 | $\dfrac{420}{2} = 210$ |
| 0 | $P_2$ | 420 | 5 | ⑤ | 0 | 1 | $\dfrac{420}{5} = 84$ |
| | | 0 | − 8 | − 9 | 0 | 0 | |

6. *Calculate and Insert the Initial Row in a New Matrix* (in place of the Key Row).

First insert the reference to the product to come in (*B*) with its *MC* as shown on the top line (9) into the two left-hand columns (the stub) thus—

9    *B*

The figures to be inserted in the other spaces in the initial row are formed by dividing each number in the Key Row (of the existing matrix) by the Key Number (5) and substituting this for the figures which appeared in the Key Row of the existing matrix. (The figure which appears in the $P_0$ column thus becomes a quantity unit instead of a capacity in hours, this quantity being the same as that for the ratio, in this case 84 units of Product *B*.) The new initial row thus appears as—

9    *B*    84    1    1    0    $\frac{1}{5}$

(At later stages in some calculations this procedure may be reversed and initially inserted products withdrawn from the programme, and idle capacity re-created or substitute products inserted.)

### 7. *Fill in Stub*

Re-copy from the previous matrix the remainder of the data in the stub (the two left-hand columns) exactly as in the preceding matrix, i.e. in this case—

o      $P_1$

### 8. *Calculate the Figures in a New Base Row*

These are best arrived at by the following procedure. All figures in the column of the new matrix corresponding to the key column in the old matrix (with the exception of the 1 in the initial row) have to be reduced to o and related adjustments made elsewhere in the rows. To do this, take the figure in the key column of the row being recalculated. Multiply the initial row of the new matrix by this figure. Subtract the multiples of the initial row from the corresponding figures in the old row being recalculated to give the new row to be inserted in the new matrix. (The initial row remains as originally inserted.) E.g. to recalculate the base row, the figure in the key column of this row is $-9$.

| | | | | | |
|---|---|---|---|---|---|
| The initial row reads | | 84 | 1 | 1 | o | $\frac{1}{6}$ |
| Initial row $\times -9$ | $= -756$ | $-9$ | $-9$ | o | $-1\frac{4}{6}$ |
| Subtract this from old base row of | o | $-8$ | $-9$ | o | o |
| To give new base row | 756 | 1 | o | o | $1\frac{4}{6}$ |

*Note.* An alternative method to get at new squares is—

$$\text{Figure in square in preceding matrix} - \frac{\text{Corresponding Key Row Number} \times \text{Corresponding Key Column Number}}{\text{Key Number}}$$

(Double minuses which equal a plus have to be watched, also such as $0 \times 5 = 0$, $0 - 5 = -5$, $2 \div 0.04 = 50$.)

All the base row figures are now in fact positive so that one is lucky enough in this case to have reached the end of the computation: but assuming for the moment they are not, the next step is—

## 9. *Scan Calculated Base Row for Negative Values*

Negative values in the Base Row indicate that further improvements in the programme for optimum marginal contribution can be effected, and that after filling in all the other squares in this matrix yet a further new matrix (referred to as an iteration) will have to be compiled.

## 10. *Complete the Matrix*

Fill in all the other vacant squares in the matrix on exactly the same formula as for the squares in the base row.

*Note.* It is useful to know that if a zero appears in the Key Column of the preceding matrix all the numbers in that *row* are the same in the following matrix. If a zero appears in the initial row in the preceding matrix all the numbers in that column are the same in the following matrix. The reasons for this become manifest when actual computations are done. Similarly, the column of numbers under an objective that also appears in the stub is always a number of zeros and a single one.

This calculation will include the vacant square in the $P_0$ column which in the preceding matrix shows a capacity figure of 420 hours. This becomes—

$$420 - (2 \times 84)$$
$$= 420 - 168 = 252 \text{ hours}$$

What one is doing here is adjusting the balance of the available capacity elsewhere to allow at all processes for the effect of the inclusion in the programme of 84 units of Product *B*.

The 252 then represents the balance of unused capacity after inclusion of this quantity of Product *B*, and can be related to the initial unused capacity of 420. The adjustment of the other figures is also a reflection of this. This matrix completed then appears thus—

| MC | | 0 | 8 | 9 | 0 | 0 | Ratio |
|---|---|---|---|---|---|---|---|
| | | $P_0$ | $A$ | $B$ | $P_1$ | $P_2$ | |
| | Programme | Capacity/Products | | | | | |
| 0 | $P_1$ | 252 | 4 | 0 | 1 | $-\frac{2}{5}$ | |
| 9 | $B$ | 84 | 1 | 1 | 0 | $\frac{1}{5}$ | |
| | | 756 | 1 | 0 | 0 | $1\frac{4}{5}$ | |

If there were any negative figures in the Base Row a further matrix would be compiled by repeating the process. Since the matrix and the Base Row are already here this follows—

3. Select Key column.
4. Find Key Row.
5. Select Key Number.
6. Calculate Initial Row new matrix.
7. Copy in Stub.
8. Calculate new Base Row.

9. Scan for all positive. Stop if yes. If no—
10. Fill up all vacant squares—repeat till all Base Row positive.

## Checking the Base Row

It should be noted that each Base Row computed by the formula indicated can also be computed by the following process (which can also be used for completing the initial matrix), and it is usually advisable to do so, though it is only a partial check.

This is done by multiplying the separate figures in a column by the figure in the extreme left-hand column (the $MC$ per unit for the programme), adding the results together for the column and deducting the figure at the top of the column (the $MC$ per unit), thus for the original base row the calculation would be—

| Col. $P_0$ | Col. $A$ | Col. $B$ | Col. $P_1$ | Col. $P_2$ |
|---|---|---|---|---|
| 0 × 420 = 0 | 0 × 6 = 0 | 0 × 2 = 0 | 0 × 1 = 0 | 0 × 0 = 0 |
| 0 × 420 = 0 | 0 × 5 = 0 | 0 × 5 = 0 | 0 × 0 = 0 | 0 × 1 = 0 |
| — | — | — | — | — |
| 0 | 0 | 0 | 0 | 0 |
| − 0 | − 8 | − 9 | − 0 | − 0 |
| — | — | — | — | — |
| 0 | − 8 | − 9 | 0 | 0 |

These results are entered in the base row thus—

| 0 | − 8 | − 9 | 0 | 0 |

## Examination of Results

One may now examine the conclusion of this exercise. A marginal contribution to fixed overheads and profits of £756 is shown (from which fixed overheads, not shown, have to be deducted to get at profit). This compares with a figure of £693 previously calculated when all capacity was used. Against $P_1$ 252 hours unused capacity appears. One can check the use of capacity thus—

At Process I:   84 units of $B$ at 2 hours = 168 hours
                Unused capacity         252 hours
                                        ————
                                        420 hours

i.e. original capacity

At Process II:  84 units of $B$ at 5 hours = 420 hours

i.e. original capacity

All the figures appearing in any matrix have some significance. Thus a negative figure appearing in the Base Row against an actual product indicates that (up to a point) *at this stage* for every additional unit of that product which can be added to the mix, a certain additional margin per unit will be added. (A similar positive figure in the Base Row indicates the reverse.) A zero in the base of the $P_1$, $P_2$, etc., columns indicates that all capacity is in use for the process to which $P_1$, etc., applies. A positive figure in the Base Row of the $P_1$, $P_2$, etc., columns indicates that within the other limits of the product programme indicated a certain additional marginal contribution will become available for every additional unit of capacity added to the capacity of the process at which the $P_1$ or $P_2$, etc., applies. (Introducing one unit of $A$ reduces $MC$ by £1 to £755, and adding 5 hours capacity at process 2 adds $5 \times 1·8 = £9$ to $MC$ by allowing another unit of $B$ to be produced.)

This same procedure applies to large programmes with numerous processes and numerous products.

*Sales Constraints*

This example has only covered the effects of processing limiting factors or constraints. So far no reference has been made to the embodiment of limitations or constraints on the amount that can be sold (e.g. not more than, or exactly, so much).

A sales restraint of "not more than a certain quantity of a certain product will be saleable" is brought into the computation in this manner. It must be brought in as a further equation in both the vertical and the horizontal pattern. The maximum number of *units* of the product which can be sold are inserted in the $P_0$ Column right at the start, and a further fictitious product is utilized. Thus if the constraint in the foregoing example was that no more than 60 units of Product $B$ could be sold, the equation would read—

$$60 = 1 \times x \text{ units of Product } B + 1 \times y \text{ units of Product } P_3$$

or in our tabular matrix—

$$\begin{array}{cccc} \text{Column} & P_0 & B & P_3 \\ \text{Figures in Column} & 60 = & 1 & + & 1 \end{array}$$

For the converse—"at least 60 units of $B$ must be sold,"— the insertions in the equations are more elaborate. (Only a few of the features are dealt with here.)

It is worth noting that the number of products which will be embodied in the most profitable product mix will be no greater than the number of constraints applied in the computation (at producing and sales capacities and any others).

## Basic Data

The basic data which is, therefore, required for this type of computation is—

1. The capacity available at each process, i.e. number of machines and working hours.

2. Rate of production—the rate at which units are produced at each machine at each process per hour or per week (or for the process as a whole), which can also be

expressed as the machine-hours required to produce one unit of product.

3. The variable cost per unit of each product.

4. The selling price of each product—4 minus 3 giving the marginal contribution to fixed overheads and profit per unit for each product.

5. The sales constraints applicable to each product.

In the following example it will be assumed that all the products listed are producible at Process I and II but at different rates of production at the latter process. Only Products *B* and *E* go through the third process. (Where the same product can be made by alternative methods at different costs, it would be treated as two or more products for purposes of computations.)

## A Complex Example

It may now be possible to illustrate a more complex example which might initially appear thus (machines can be used for alternative products)—

| Process | 1 | 2 | 3 | Maximum Saleable Quantity at Current Price | Marginal Contribution to Fixed Overheads and Profit per Unit |
|---|---|---|---|---|---|
| No. of Machines | 24 | 24 | 8 | | |
| Product | Full Capacity Rate of Production per Week at Each Process for any one Product | | | | |
| A | 120 | 360 | — | 300 | £ 12 |
| B | 120 | 180 | 96 | 200 | 17 |
| C | 120 | 120 | — | 100 | 20 |
| D | 120 | 90 | — | 200 | 21 |
| E | 120 | 72 | 96 | 500 | 25 |
| F | 120 | 60 | — | 150 | 28 |

*Notes.* There are no constraints on the supply of materials or labour.

Assume working hours per week are 75.

Assume fixed costs to be deducted from total marginal contribution are £1,896. The objective is to find the product mix which produces maximum profit.

In this case the data have made their appearance in the first instance in terms of numbers of machines and rates of production per week. It would appear that for linear programming purposes these data have to be converted to hours of capacity and hours per unit (i.e. capacity ÷ rate of production) to give homogeneous data.

(Rates of production are non-additive, hours per unit produced can be added together.)

The data converted to this basis then appear, and set up as an initial matrix are as follows, capacity being arrived at by multiplying the number of machines by running hours ($24 \times 75 = 1,800$), and hours per unit by dividing capacity by rate of production ($1,800 \div 120 = 15$).

| MC | | 0 | 12 | 17 | 20 | 21 | 25 | 28 | 0 | 0 | 0 | 0 | Ratio |
|----|----|---|----|----|----|----|----|----|---|---|---|---|------|
| | | $P_0$ | A | B | C | D | E | F | $P_1$ | $P_2$ | $P_3$ | $P_4$ | |
| | Pro-gramme | Capacity/Product | | | | | | | | | | | |
| 0 | $P_1$ | 1,800 | 15 | 15 | 15 | 15 | 15 | 15 | 1 | | | | |
| 0 | $P_2$ | 1,800 | 5 | 10 | 15 | 20 | 25 | 30 | | 1 | | | |
| 0 | $P_3$ | 600 | — | 6·25 | — | — | 6·25 | — | | | 1 | | |
| 0 | $P_4$ | 100 | — | — | 1 | — | — | — | | | | 1 | |

Reading across the matrix (excluding the stub) we have a series of equations stating that an unknown quantity of various products taking so many hours per unit plus an unknown quantity of idle time at one hour per unit will balance to the capacity at a process.

Reading vertically we see the time required for each product per unit at each process.

This and subsequent matrices appear in the table on p. 263.

The best short-term programme which emerges is 15B, 100 C, and 5 F, giving MC of—

| | | £ |
|---|---|---|
| 15 B @ £17 | . . . | 255 |
| 100 C @ £20 | . . . | 2,000 |
| 5 F @ £28 | . . . | 140 |
| | | 2,395 |

from which fixed costs of £1,896 fall to be deducted, using capacity—

| | Process 1 | Process 2 | Process 3 |
|---|---|---|---|
| 15 B | 15 × 15 = 225 | 15 × 10 = 150 | 15 × 6·25 = 93·75 |
| 100 C | 100 × 15 = 1,500 | 100 × 15 = 1,500 | 100 × 0 = 0 |
| 5 F | 5 × 15 = 75 | 5 × 30 = 150 | 5 × 0 = 0 |
| | 1,800 | 1,800 | 93·75 |
| Total Capacity | 1,800 | 1,800 | 600 |
| Unused Capacity | Nil | Nil | 506·25 |

*Note.* It would seem that for purposes of measuring capacity in order to achieve the answer it is immaterial whether Number of Machines × Weekly Running Hours at Each Process (in Process 1, 24 × 75 = 1,800) is used, or the entire process is taken as being one machine having one, seventy-five, or one thousand hours capacity. It is the establishment of the ratios between all the various data that is significant. Thus—

$$\frac{1,800 \text{ hours Capacity}}{120 \text{ Rate of Production}} = 15 \text{ hours per unit}$$

$$\frac{75 \text{ hours Capacity}}{120 \text{ Rate of Production}} = 0·625 \text{ hours per unit}$$

But 1,800 ÷ 15 gives a production programme of 120 units, and 75 ÷ 0·625 also gives a production programme of 120 units.

Machine-hours and machine-hours per Unit of Output will frequently, however, give more clearly understandable data in the matrix, though when electronic computers are used for such calculations equations may have to be modified to give units best suited to computer storage.

## A Significant Advance

The invention of the linear programming technique (of which there are some modified versions) marks a significant advance on previously available techniques. Apart from product mix problems, the technique is applicable to a wide range of other industrial problems, of which the solving of problems of lowest cost mixture of alternative raw materials with limits on impurities in mix, shortest route plant layout are others; e.g. a further modified form of the technique can be applied when the problem starts at the other end with certain exact quantities which have to be given the most economic allocation between resources, as in production planning problems in some industries.

Like other tools and data such as total costs or marginal costs, results can be wrongly interpreted and wrongly applied. One thing to guard against is that in simple and initial applications it tends to stress the advantages of alternative short-term rather than to give consideration to long-term patterns of activity.

The two are not always completely compatible. Long-term data, such as the effect of expansion of plant capacity by the installation of additional equipment (at an additional fixed cost) can, however, be catered for by using projected rather than current data.

## TABLE OF ITERATIONS

| MC | | | 12 | 17 | 20 | 21 | 25 | 28 | 0 | 0 | 0 | 0 | |
|---|---|---|---|---|---|---|---|---|---|---|---|---|---|
| | | $P_0$ | A | B | C | D | E | F | $P_1$ | $P_2$ | $P_3$ | $P_4$ | Ratio |
| | Pro-gramme | Capacity/Product | | | | | | | | | | | |
| 0 | $P_1$ | 1,800 | 15 | 15 | 15 | 15 | 15 | 15 | 1 | | | | 120 |
| 0 | $P_2$ | 1,800 | 5 | 10 | 15 | 20 | 25 | (30) | | 1 | | | 60 |
| 0 | $P_3$ | 600 | | 6·25 | | | 6·25 | | | | 1 | | |
| 0 | $P_4$ | 100 | | | 1 | | | | | | | 1 | |
| | | 0 | −12 | −17 | −20 | −21 | −25 | −28 | 0 | 0 | 0 | 0 | |
| **1st Iteration** | | | | | | | | | | | | | |
| 0 | $P_1$ | 900 | $12\frac{1}{2}$ | (10) | $7\frac{1}{2}$ | 5 | $2\frac{1}{2}$ | 0 | 1 | $-\frac{1}{2}$ | | | 90 |
| 28 | F | 60 | $\frac{1}{6}$ | $\frac{1}{3}$ | $\frac{1}{2}$ | $\frac{2}{3}$ | $\frac{5}{6}$ | 1 | | $\frac{1}{30}$ | | | 180 |
| 0 | $P_3$ | 600 | | $6\frac{1}{4}$ | | | $6\frac{1}{4}$ | | | | 1 | | 96 |
| 0 | $P_4$ | 100 | | | 1 | | | | | | | 1 | |
| | | 1,680 | $-7\frac{1}{3}$ | $-7\frac{2}{3}$ | −6 | $-2\frac{1}{3}$ | $-1\frac{2}{3}$ | 0 | 0 | $1\frac{4}{15}$ | 0 | 0 | |
| **2nd Iteration** | | | | | | | | | | | | | |
| 17 | B | 90 | $1\frac{1}{4}$ | 1 | $\frac{3}{4}$ | $\frac{1}{2}$ | $\frac{1}{4}$ | 0 | $\frac{1}{10}$ | $-\frac{1}{20}$ | | | 120 |
| 28 | F | 30 | $-\frac{1}{6}$ | 0 | $\frac{1}{4}$ | $\frac{1}{2}$ | $\frac{3}{4}$ | 1 | $-\frac{1}{30}$ | $\frac{1}{20}$ | | | 120 |
| 0 | $P_3$ | $37\frac{1}{2}$ | $-7\frac{13}{16}$ | 0 | $4\frac{11}{16}$ | $-3\frac{1}{4}$ | $4\frac{11}{16}$ | 0 | $-\frac{5}{8}$ | $\frac{5}{16}$ | 1 | | |
| 0 | $P_4$ | 100 | | | (1) | | | | | | | 1 | 100 |
| | | 2,370 | $2\frac{1}{4}$ | 0 | $-\frac{1}{4}$ | $1\frac{1}{2}$ | $\frac{1}{4}$ | 0 | $\frac{23}{30}$ | $\frac{11}{20}$ | 0 | 0 | |
| **3rd Iteration** | | | | | | | | | | | | | |
| 17 | B | 15 | | | | | | | | | | | |
| 28 | F | 5 | | | | | | | | | | | |
| 0 | $P_3$ | $506\frac{1}{4}$ | | | | | | | | | | | |
| 20 | C | 100 | 0 | 0 | 1 | 0 | 0 | 0 | 0 | 0 | 0 | 1 | |
| | | 2,395 | $2\frac{1}{4}$ | 0 | 0 | $1\frac{1}{2}$ | $\frac{1}{4}$ | 0 | $\frac{23}{30}$ | $\frac{11}{20}$ | 0 | $\frac{1}{4}$ | |

All base row positive ∴ best possible programme with marginal contribution to fixed overheads and profit of £2,395.

Similar comments might apply to product-pricing policy.

*Weaknesses in Basic Data*

Like accounting data, the technique may tend to give the impression of a spurious precision, but the results will only be as valid as the data on which they are based. (This would apply to any method of computation.)

Weaknesses in the data may, for example, lie in the assumed sales constraints or future prices.

Linear programming assumes that variable cost (and some other) data in fact are linear, i.e. follow a straight line up or down *pro rata* to activity (as in a simple break even chart). It is widely recognized that so-called fixed costs are only fixed within certain limits of change, and that variable costs vary only up to a point, and that it is difficult to make a cast-iron division between the two. If variable costs are shown as a figure higher than they would be in practice, and if in practice they will not in fact vary as they are presumed to do in the computation, the advantage of certain programme changes will be overstated. If variable costs are shown lower than they would be in practice the advantages of programme changes will be understated.

## Checking Feasible Alternatives

Linear programming techniques applied to the product mix problem follow the shortest route from *nil* profit to maximum profit. All possible alternatives and combinations do not, therefore, appear. Some of these could approach fairly near to the linear programming answer, and sometimes in fact be more suitable in the long run as against the short run, bearing in mind probable future trends in demand and the possibility of plant expansion with changes in fixed costs.

Thus in the detailed problem appended, other alternative programmes which do not make their appearance in the computation are 60*B*, 40*C*, 20*F* and 60*A*, 60*E*.

The last mentioned produces this result from which have to be deducted fixed costs of £1,896.

| Giving *MC* of | | Using Capacity at Process | | |
|---|---|---|---|---|
| | £ | 1 | 2 | 3 |
| 60*A* @ £12 | 720 | 900 | 300 | 0 |
| 60*E* @ £25 | 1,500 | 900 | 1,500 | 375 |
| | 2,220 | 1,800 | 1,800 | 375 |

Although this gives a poorer result than "the best," it uses more capacity. The "best" provides a standard of comparison.

Linear programming does not automatically link programme changes to changes in working capital employed, and the relation of profit to capital employed may have to be watched.

Means may have to be devised for squeezing out some of the other alternatives from linear programming data by imposing constraints such as "at least so much of certain products must be included in the mix." A programme embodying some such constraints may be desirable in any event to weigh up considerations of the principle of not having too many eggs in one basket.

Older alternative approximation methods can be brought into play here, such as dividing quantities of products with relevant processing capacities into various fractional combinations such as—

$$\tfrac{1}{2} \ \tfrac{1}{4} \ \tfrac{1}{4}, \quad \tfrac{1}{3} \ \tfrac{1}{3} \ \tfrac{1}{4} \ \tfrac{1}{8}$$

using combinations of fractions down to say $\tfrac{1}{10}$, and then allowing for the constraints of the bottle-neck.

*Sensitivity Testing*

Not one but several modified programmes are likely to be called for in a product mix problem to evaluate fully the position in any set of circumstances, having regard to both long-term and short-term considerations—

(a) A programme with the sales constraints included.

(b) A most profitable mix assuming no sales constraints and that all that can be produced can be sold at present prices. This would form a kind of reference target.

(c) A modified programme testing for price sensitivity by reducing the margins of products appearing in the "best" programme by say 5 per cent and increasing the margins of products excluded by 5 per cent.

(d) A programme computing the actual current production programme on the basic data identical with that used for alternative programmes, to check that data used are realistic and practical, and to compare with actual recorded results.

(e) A modified programme showing the effect of expanding capacity by overtime, night shift or subcontracting (means are available for incorporating such modifications in the calculations).

(f) A modified programme showing the effect of plant expansion on profitable programmes.

Modifications in the technique are available for computing such alternatives, and it is not always necessary to carry out complete re-computations.

Long-term sales demand trends must be kept in mind.

## The Work Involved

Whilst the major portion of the work connected with applying the technique of linear programming is likely to relate to the reliable collection of basic data, the programming computations themselves can be tiresome. Smaller programmes are manageable with a small desk calculator, and some large-scale problems can be condensed and simplified to bring out their fundamental features and make them manageable by this method without distorting the conclusions.

The computational work associated with an extensive and elaborate matrix will best be carried out by hiring computer time.

The tricky point lies in getting the initial matrix into proper form and ensuring that all data are expressed in properly related terms.

## Note on Differential Calculus

There are certain calculations in management accounting which, if graphed, result in curves which drop and then rise again or rise and then fall again. This is typical where a falling trend in one item has to be combined with a rising trend in another. Smooth curves can often be expressed as an algebraic equation in terms of $x$ and $y$, the measurements on the horizontal and vertical axes of the graph. Whilst the lowest (or highest) point on such a curve can be found by graphing in any specific case, it can also be calculated by formulas.

The basic principle lies in the fact that the slope of a curve can be roughly represented at any stage by the slope of the hypotenuse of a right-angled triangle (the size of two of the sides being measured by part of the vertical and horizontal axes of the graph). If the vertical side of this triangle is called $AB$ and the horizontal $AC$, the slope of $BC$, instead of being expressed, say, as 60° can be expressed as the ratio of $\dfrac{AB}{AC}$. When $AB$ is set to equal nothing there is no slope, and the curve is at its lowest or highest point.

(The equivalent of $\dfrac{AB}{AC}$ appears as the $\dfrac{dy}{dx}$ of calculus formulas.)

The "Cost Balance" problem is a perennial example,

typified by the judging of what is the economically justifiable thickness of steam pipe lagging where, up to a point, the saving of heat losses outweighs the (average annual) cost of extra lagging, but beyond which point the position is reversed. It ranges from this to the assessment of the justifiable scale of automation.

### REFERENCES

*Readings in Mathematical Programming*, by S. Vajda. (Sir Isaac Pitman & Sons Ltd., London.) (1958.)

*Elementary Mathematical Programming*, by R. W. Metzer. (John Wiley & Sons.) (1958.)

*Linear Programming (Fundamentals and Applications)*, by Ferguson and Sargent. (McGraw-Hill Book Co.) (1958.)

*Mathematics in Management*, by A. Battersby. (Penguin Books.) (1966.)

# Appendix I

## COSTING METHODS

THE fundamental principle of costing is to find the cost of each product, process, operation, or department.

In order to achieve this it is necessary properly to allocate the correct share of each element of cost, either directly to the product or indirectly to the producing centre and thence to the product itself.

### Direct Materials

The allocation of direct materials is relatively simple. Purchase invoices may sometimes be directly allocated to the job or process concerned.

A routine should be devised whereby the invoice is clearly marked by a responsible party as to its proper allocation. Invoices may then be sorted into groups and totalled, or entered in columnar form and posted to particular accounts. (Cards may be punched therefrom for machine sorting.)

If purchases are allocated to stores (a suitable subdivision of Stores Accounts should be in operation), the final analysis to jobs, operations, or processes will be derived from the stores requisitions.

The stores may be provided with planned bills of material for certain jobs which will authorize issue against requisition. Bin cards and/or Stores Ledgers should be kept, and regularly entered up to show the balance of the different stocks on hand.

Stores requisitions will be priced and extended from these store records. They will then be sorted according to job, process, or operation, and charged thereto.

## Direct Labour

There are various methods of recording labour costs for cost purposes. Time clocks providing a record of the total time each man works in the factory should be used. All further detailed records for cost purposes should be reconciled with the record of the total time worked.

The following possible methods are available for recording job or process costs, but if a full analysis is required, it will be best, if possible, to have the time spent on each particular job or operation by each man recorded on a separate card or slip, to facilitate sorting. There are cases, however, where the simplicity and convenience of more condensed records, and the disadvantages of voluminous stationery, may outweigh the advantages of the separate card per operation method. though, with proper routine, these disadvantages may be eliminated.

(1) Analysis from pay-roll only by check No. (Times taken from clock card.)

(2) Clock card and job card combined (suitable where few jobs per week).

(3) Clock card together with daily or weekly time sheet per man.

(4) Clock card together with card per job per man.

(5) Clock card per man, with job sheet following job through all operations. All men working in this job book time on that job on the one job sheet.

(6) Clock card per man and time sheet for machine running times on jobs.

(7) Any of methods (1)–(5) without the clock card— practically applicable where workers are on a salary basis.

Other methods and combinations are possible, e.g. group time recording, recording time on a blackboard. etc., but the above cover the principal modern methods.

It should be seen that every possible precaution is taken to ensure that the time recorded is as accurate as possible.

Time so recorded may be analysed in columnar form, or the slips or cards may be sorted into the required grouping by check number, then by job number, and machine-totalled. Rates will have to be entered and calculations extended. Where a piece-rate or a premium bonus system is in operation, the Wages Department will be responsible for seeing that rates earned on operations performed are carried to the pay-roll.

## Overheads

The first essential in ensuring proper allocation of overheads is adequate analysis. The line of demarcation between analysis and allocation is only faintly drawn, but certainly all such items as indirect labour (labourers, storekeepers, inspectors, foremen, etc.) and indirect supplies (oils, grease, loose tools, etc.) should be analysed as far as possible directly to the departments or processes to which they refer. For this to be regularly carried out a proper system of recording and analysing expenses must be in force. To facilitate matters, each class of expense and each department is usually designated by a code number. Those items which cannot be directly charged to a particular section will require to be allocated.

One object of the detailed analysis is to enable each job to be charged with its proper share of overhead expenses.

For this to be done at all accurately, it is necessary to analyse and allocate all works overhead costs, first to departments, and then to production centres (e.g. to machines where it is machine work, or to men where it is hand labour). The final allocation (or absorption) to individual jobs is best done by charging a share of the overhead cost of each production centre to the jobs being carried out at that centre, according to the time spent on each job, i.e. by machine-hour or man-hour rates. Another method is to charge a percentage on the direct labour cost on each job.

## Distribution of Overhead

Departments may be classed as Production Departments and Service Departments. The first allocation is the distribution of overheads to these departments. The total cost of the Service Departments (which will include, perhaps, heating, lighting, power, internal transport, stores, etc., and all administrative offices) will then require to be allocated to the Production Departments.[1]

### Works Overhead

The following are the principal classes of expense which will require to be allocated to processes, departments, or production centres as scientifically as possible. The most commonly accepted basis is indicated.

(1) *Depreciation.* Apportioned on capital value of plant or buildings.

(2) *Rent and Rates.* Apportioned on floor area or cubic capacity.

(3) *Fire Insurance, etc.* Per policy, capital value of machines, buildings, etc.

(4) *Heating.* Cubic capacity or floor area.

(5) *Lighting.* Number of lighting points and rating, as per meter or per floor area.

(6) *Power.* Per meter or per horse-power, or hours run.

(7) *Internal Transport.* Per usage, perhaps on basis of short-period recorded test.

---

[1] Where possible a better method of allocating service departments is to split their costs as accurately as possible into fixed and variable charges. The fixed charges are allocated to productive departments at a predetermined figure on a basis of "designed use." Variable charges are then allocated according to "ascertained consumption" by the productive departments. (See also footnote, page 241.)

(8) *Maintenance.* Per work done or per technical estimate.

(9) *Receiving and Stores.* Per usage or per material costs.

*Note.* Receiving, stores, internal transport, and other handling charges may not be allocated to departments or production centres, but charged directly to particular jobs as a percentage on materials or as a rate per unit.

(10) *Packing and Dispatch Department.* May be treated as part of the cost of manufacture, in which case it may be possible to charge a proportion to each job on the basis of time spent, or as a percentage on materials cost, or a rate per unit. Carriage should be charged direct to orders if possible, or it may be included in the above.

## ADMINISTRATION EXPENSES

Under this heading falls the cost of all administrative offices—clerical salaries and office expenses, salaries of executives, legal expenses, and bad debts, etc. Selling expenses should be excluded. Administration expenses may be allocated to particular departments and recovered in job costs as a particular percentage for that department, or the allocation may be made direct to the job, usually as a percentage on total cost.

Where centralized offices have to be allocated to departments, the basis of usage should be employed if reasonably practicable. Estimates of work done for other departments may be obtained from the heads of the central offices.

Other bases of allocation to departments might be on sales or direct labour, or on direct plus indirect labour, or direct labour plus works overhead expenses. See Fig. 26.

## SELLING EXPENSES

These should be separated from administrative expenses unless relatively insignificant, and will include salaries,

# ALLOCATION OF OVERHEADS

| Item | Administrative Departments | | | | Service Departments | | | | Production Departments | | | | Grand Total |
|---|---|---|---|---|---|---|---|---|---|---|---|---|---|
| | Design | Secretary | Accounts | Sub Total | Stores | Int. Transport | Inspection | Sub Total | A | B | C | Total | |
| | £ | £ | £ | £ | £ | £ | £ | £ | £ | £ | £ | £ | £ |
| Indirect Labour | 10 | 10 | 20 | 40 | 50 | 20 | 70 | 140 | 130 | 200 | 400 | 730 | 910 |
| Indirect Supplies | 20 | 5 | 10 | 35 | 60 | 50 | 80 | 190 | 80 | 100 | 300 | 480 | 705 |
| Repairs | — | 5 | 10 | 15 | 20 | 10 | 10 | 40 | 20 | 20 | — | 40 | 95 |
| Fixed Charges | 10 | 10 | 10 | 30 | 30 | 10 | 20 | 60 | 100 | 80 | 120 | 300 | 390 |
| Total | £40 | £30 | £50 | £120 | £160 | £90 | £180 | £430 | 330 | 400 | 820 | 1550 | 2100 |
| [1] Allocation of Stores Department | | | | | | | | | 30 | 50 | 80 | 160 | |
| [1] Allocation of Transport Department | | | | | | | | | 10 | 20 | 60 | 90 | |
| [1] Allocation of Inspection Department | | | | | | | | | 30 | 30 | 120 | 180 | |
| Total Works Overheads | | | | | | | | | 400 | 500 | 1080 | 1980 | |
| [1] Allocation of Administration | | | | | | | | | 20 | 20 | 80 | 120 | |
| Total Overheads | | | | | | | | | £420 | £520 | £1160 | £2100 | |
| Direct Labour | | | | | | | | | 250 | 250 | 500 | | 1000 |
| Direct Materials | | | | | | | | | | | | | 3000 |
| Total Cost | | | | | | | | | | | | | £6100 |

[1] Preferably split between "fixed" and "variable."

FIG. 26

expenses of sales offices and showrooms, travellers' and agents' salaries and commission, advertising, and publicity.

Work in progress values should include only manufacturing cost and should never be inflated by selling or distribution expenses. In practice, even administrative expenses may be excluded in a conservative valuation and only direct works overheads included.

Selling expense is usually allocated to jobs as a flat percentage on sales values or total cost, though a graded scale showing a lower recovery rate on higher selling values may sometimes be considered to show a truer incidence of selling costs.

### INTEREST

The question of inclusion of interest as an item of cost has caused endless argument.

Overdraft interest is often included in administration expenses, as may also be interest on other temporary loans. Where, however, there is a large amount of borrowed capital in the form of loans and debentures the question increases in importance. It is quite common to include such interest in administrative costs.

It has been argued that if it is included, costs will not be comparative with those of firms where no borrowed capital is employed. Such an argument, however, cannot carry much weight, as the true object of costing is to find the cost of running one's own business—though the excesses which may affect competitive prices should be shown up.

From the costing point of view one of the occasions when the inclusion of interest is urged is to afford true comparison between the cost of running two departments (or machines), one employing expensive and the other cheap plant.

The system of charging interest on work in progress

in each department as part of cost control has been referred to. The calculation of interest on capital locked up in stocks and in debtors can also be envisaged as having an effect on the attitude towards large balances on these accounts.

In general it is considered that fictional interest charges should only be introduced into statistical memoranda, and should be excluded from the book-keeping system. In any event such notional charges should be excluded from stock valuations.

## Overhead Absorption Rates

The final allocation of overhead costs to individual orders or jobs is carried out by means of absorption rates or percentages applied to standard or actual data.

For works overhead the following methods are available—

(1) Machine-hour rate. (This rate may include direct labour costs as well.)

(2) Rate per actual hour worked. Applicable especially to hand operations, fitting, etc.

(3) Rate per standard (allowed) hour produced.

(4) Rate per unit produced.

(5) A percentage on actual direct labour costs.

(6) A percentage on standard direct labour costs.

(7) A percentage on wages plus materials.

Administration overheads and selling expenses may be recovered as a percentage on total works costs though the latter is better based on selling values. A rate per unit may also be suitable.

For works overhead recovery, a rate per hour, or per unit, will produce the most accurate results, the other methods being liable to produce misleading figures. The hourly rate is calculated by allocating all the overhead costs as indicated as accurately as possible to departments.

The final analysis by production centres, i.e. machines or men, is carried out on the same basis as before. For a machine-hour rate, depreciation, insurance, and interest for a department will be allocated to the machine on the basis of capital value; rent, rates, light and heat, etc., on the basis of floor space; power on horse-power hours; indirect materials on estimated usage; superintendence on direct labour usage.

The total overhead cost so allocated is then divided by the total estimated number of productive hours for the future cost period (usually one year) for that production centre, to give the overhead absorption rate per hour.

If direct labour costs are to be incorporated in the rate, the total direct labour cost estimated for the same period will be divided by the estimated productive hours to give a labour rate per hour which may be added to the overhead rate per hour. The relative proportion of the constituents of this combined rate should always be known.

If the percentage on direct labour method were used, the percentage would be established by determining the ratio of works overhead to direct labour for each department for the future period and applying this percentage to each individual job.

## Under-absorbed and Over-absorbed Costs

Throughout the year the rates determined as above will be applied to the jobs passing through the works. Regularly each period the costs recovered, i.e. charged to jobs, will be set against the actual costs.

It will be found at the end of the year that there will be a balance of costs over- or under-absorbed. This will be written off to the Profit and Loss Account. The over- or under-absorbed cost may be written off each month if full monthly accounts are kept.

Under-absorption of overheads can arise from two

main factors: (a) actual expenses in excess of forecast (or standard) expenses, (b) volume of activity (hours worked or direct labour) less than forecast (or standard) activity on which it was estimated the overhead recovery rates set would absorb expenses. The converse also applies. This gives rise to what is respectively referred to in standard costing parlance as Overhead Variance and Volume Variance.

### MANUFACTURING ACCOUNT (Financial)

| OUTPUT | | £ | Per cent to Output |
|---|---|---|---|
| Sales | | 18,000 | |
| Deduct Opening Stock of Manufactured Parts and Work in Progress | | 4,000 | |
| | | 14,000 | |
| Add Closing Stock of Manufactured Parts and Work in Progress | | 6,000 | |
| Output | | £20,000 | |
| COST OF PRODUCTION | | | |
| Purchases—Direct Materials | | 12,000 | |
| Add Opening Stock, Purchased Materials | | 2,000 | |
| | | 14,000 | |
| Deduct Closing Stock, Purchased Materials | | 1,500 | |
| | | 12,500 | 62·5 |
| Direct Labour | | 2,100 | 10·5 |
| Works Overheads— | £ | | |
| Indirect Labour | 1,200 | | |
| Indirect Supplies | 800 | | |
| Fixed Charges | 1,500 | 3,510 | 17·5 |
| Factory Cost of Production | £18,100 | | 90·5 |
| Factory Profit £1,900 | | | |
| Administration Expenses | | 1,000 | 5·0 |
| Total Cost | | 19,100 | 95·5 |
| NET PROFIT | | 900 | 4·5 |
| | | £20,000 | 100·0 |

FIG. 27a

### The Manufacturing Account

For Budgetary Control purposes a modern layout of the Manufacturing Account is required (see Figs. 21*a* and 21*b*).

This Account may also be prepared in analytical form by departmental or product group.

Where Work in Progress and Finished Manufactured Stock fluctuates to any degree it is necessary to distinguish "Output" from Sales or Deliveries, and "Materials Consumed" from Purchases. Only by so doing can the factory effort be judged and the relative incidence of the various cost elements intelligently compared period by period.

When costing is carried out the Manufacturing Account can usually be produced in two distinct forms each of which ties up with the other.

MANUFACTURING ACCOUNT (Costs)

|  | | £ | Per cent to Sales |
|---|---|---:|---:|
| Sales . . . . . . | | 18,000 | 100 |
| Deduct Cost of Sales . . . . | | 16,800 | 93·4 |
| | | 1,200 | 6·6 |
| Deduct Unabsorbed Overheads | | | |
| Factory . . . | 200 | | |
| Administration . . | 100 | 300 | 1·6 |
| NET PROFIT | | £900 | 5·0 |

FIG. 27*b*

In Fig. 27*b* if, say, overhead expenses and overhead absorption had been forecast at £3,400 works, and £950 administration, by interpolating these figures, the under-absorption could be shown as—

|  | £ | £ |
|---|---:|---:|
| Volume Variance— | | |
| Forecast Absorption £3,400 + £950 . . | 4,350 | |
| Actual Absorption £3,300 + £900 . . | 4,200 | |
| | | 150 |
| Overhead Variance— | | |
| Forecast Expenses £3,400 + £950 . . . | 4,350 | |
| Actual Expenses £3,500 + £1,000 . . . | 4,500 | 150 |
| | | £300 |

The set out of the Cost Accounts relative to the Manufacturing Accounts, Fig. 27b, might be as follows—

Transfers are cross referenced alphabetically in sequence.

The Control Account in the Cost Ledger is an exact contra to the corresponding account in the Financial Books from which Manufacturing Account, Fig. 27a, can be prepared.

### COST LEDGER CONTROL ACCOUNT

| | | £ | | | £ |
|---|---|---|---|---|---|
| To Sales (i) . | . . | 18,000 | By Balance (a) | . . | 6,000 |
| „ Balance c/d | . . | 7,500 | „ Purchases (b) | . . | 12,000 |
| | | | „ Labour (c) | . | 2,100 |
| | | | „ Overheads (d) | . | 3,500 |
| | | | „ Admin. Expenses (e) | . | 1,000 |
| | | | „ Profit (m) . | . . | 900 |
| | | £25,500 | | | £25,500 |
| | | | By Balance c/d | . . | 7,500 |

### PURCHASED STOCKS ACCOUNT

| | | £ | | | £ |
|---|---|---|---|---|---|
| To Balance (c) | . . | 2,000 | By Issues (f) . | . . | 12,500 |
| „ Receipts (b) | . . | 12,000 | „ Balance c/d | . . | 1,500 |
| | | £14,000 | | | £14,000 |
| To Balance b/d | . . | 1,500 | | | |

### MANUFACTURED PARTS AND WORK IN PROGRESS ACCOUNT

| | | £ | | | £ |
|---|---|---|---|---|---|
| To Balance (a) | . . | 4,000 | By Cost of Sales (j) | . | 16,800 |
| „ Materials (f) | . . | 12,500 | „ Balance c/d | . . | 6,000 |
| „ Labour (c) | . . | 2,100 | | | |
| „ Overheads (g) | . . | 3,300 | | | |
| „ Expenses (h) | . . | 900 | | | |
| | | £22,800 | | | £22,800 |
| To Balance b/d | . . | 6,000 | | | |

### OVERHEAD ABSORPTION ACCOUNT

| | £ | | £ |
|---|---|---|---|
| To Works Overheads (d) . | 3,500 | By Absorption to Work in | |
| „ Admin. Expenses (e) . | 1,000 | Progress— | |
| | | Works Overheads (g) | 3,300 |
| | | Admin. Expenses (h) | 900 |
| | | „ Manufacturing A/c | |
| | | Under-absorption— | |
| | | Works (k) . . | 200 |
| | | Admin. (l) . | 100 |
| | £4,500 | | £4,500 |

### MANUFACTURING ACCOUNT

| | £ | | £ |
|---|---|---|---|
| To Cost of Sales (j) . | 16,800 | By Sales (i) . . . | 18,000 |
| Under-absorption | | | |
| Works Overheads (k) | 200 | | |
| Administration (l) . | 100 | | |
| Profit (m) . . | 900 | | |
| | £18,000 | | £18,000 |

Movement from one account to the other is signalled to the office by the receipt of stores requisitions, completed job or batch cards or production schedules, and finally copy despatch notes or sales invoices.

## Appendix II

## MONTHLY ACCOUNTS

PROFIT and Loss Accounts which are only presented annually are of limited practical value from a management control point of view, save as a guide to the broad general policy of the business. There is too long a time lag between the events and the presentation of the report thereon (the Profit and Loss Account). This is often further aggravated by the delay in making up the accounts.

For effective control the method of monthly or four-weekly accounts is being widely adopted.

Monthly accounts need not have the strict accuracy striven for in the annual accounts. Reasonable estimates will suffice in cases where the value of prompt figures much outweighs that of delayed though meticulously accurate ones. Any differences can be adjusted in later periods. Figures to the nearest pound may be sufficient for supporting statements, and slide-rule calculations supply quick and sufficiently accurate percentages and ratios.

The question whether a monthly or a four-weekly period is to be adopted must be settled. In a purely trading concern a monthly basis may be reasonably satisfactory, for the fact that accounts are usually rendered both to and by the firm on a monthly basis will generally simplify the procedure, though year by year similar months will not be strictly comparable owing to the varying incidence of week-ends. In a manufacturing concern employing a costing system, the four-weekly period will usually be found more suitable, owing to the fact that wages are paid by the week, and labour cost records are more easily accumulated in corresponding periods. With a four-weekly period there is no need to calculate accrued wages or labour costs. A four-weekly period ending, say, on Friday nights, does not entirely eliminate unevenness of costs owing to the interference of holidays, and further adjustment may be necessary to bring figures absolutely down to date at the financial year end. A further possible method might be envisaged of endeavouring to divide the year into even periods making allowances for holidays, or of using a 4, 4, 5 week sequence.

The use of the four-weekly period implies the necessity of taking out a total of purchases and sales to the end of each four weeks in addition to making the more usual monthly accumulation taken when making up accounts. This should not, however, present any difficulties, especially if machine posting is used.

The value of stocks and work in progress should be obtained from the cost accounts. For stocks, control accounts under the principal divisions should be kept and debited with purchases and credited with issues; the balance should represent a sufficiently accurate figure for monthly accounts, and if detailed stock accounts and/or bin cards are kept, periodic checks may be made therewith, supplemented if possible by a perpetual physical check system.

Work in progress control accounts in the Cost Ledger should provide the figure for this item, and their totals should agree with the totals on individual job accounts, taking the basis that against all sales the "cost of sales" is written off. Where there are part deliveries, a conservative estimate of cost of sales will be taken.

Even where proper cost accounts are not in force, a reasonably accurate figure of work in progress can usually be calculated by taking the cost of sales as being the sales less the ascertained previous average gross profit margin for that product group (allowing for recent trends), and deducting this from the corresponding relative debits made to work in progress. In certain circumstances a reasonably accurate physical stock-taking can sometimes be made without excessive trouble.

For monthly accounts themselves to be effective they must be presented promptly after the period end, say within one to three weeks.

On the sales side no difficulty should be found in obtaining prompt figures. Prompt notification of delivery (say duplicate advice notes) followed by prompt pricing, issue and listing of invoices is required. Purchases may cause some difficulty owing to invoices from suppliers arriving late, or to delay in checking or passing invoices. This may be partly minimized by notifying suppliers of the necessity for prompt invoices and by tightening up the internal routine, and the balance handled by making out an estimated reserve list (priced from orders and estimates) of goods received but not invoiced (made up from stores materials received notes.)

Adjusting entries will be made in the accounts therefrom each period and subsequently reversed.

Fixed charges are taken into the cost accounts from the nominal accounts at an estimated thirteenth of the year's charge, unless and until any alteration in the charge is noted. A routine list of other accrued or prepaid charges can be made up; lists of salaries and cash expenditure are easily dealt with. Indirect works expenditure can simply be accumulated by proper methods of recording.

Finally, for promptitude to be achieved, it is essential to secure active co-operation from all departments handling any records whatsoever. This is usually the weakest link in the chain, but where the business is properly organized it is possible to ensure a quick, steady flow of information to the accounting department. Effective liaison between accounting and buying, stores, inspection, time office, progress and works office, must be secured.

## Appendix III

# THE FIXING OF STANDARD TIMES
# AND RATES

The accuracy and consistency of complete standard costs depend to a large degree on accuracy and consistency in setting standard times.

## Standard Times

The standard time for a job may be said to be the time required by a workman of average ability working at normal speed and effort, having regard to the equipment available and allowing for normal relaxation.

Standard times should be based on properly carried out studies of the work, undertaken if possible by specially trained work study men. (The term "Work Study" is growing in favour and embraces method, motion, and time study, and can include first-class ratefixing.)

Unfortunately this is not always the case, nor is it always possible, and practice varies, from the foreman estimating the time to detailed micro-motion studies. Between this are standard times compiled from tables and charts prepared from previous studies or from recorded experience, standard times estimated from drawings and technical data on machine speeds, and even times literally argued out between the operator and the ratefixer.

Officially standard times are negotiated. In Engineering Agreements we find: "Piecework prices and bonus or basis times shall be fixed by mutual agreement between the employer and the worker who is to perform the work (or by such other methods as now exist or may hereafter be established by agreement in any trade or district) . . .

No piecework, bonus or basis times once established may be altered except for the following reasons.

(1) A mistake in calculation on either side or
(2) The material, means, or method of production or the quantities are changed.
(3) A mutual arrangement has been come to between the employer and the worker in the same way as a new price is arranged."

## METHOD STUDY

Method study should precede time study, but the two should never be divorced. Time spent on method study in the early stages will usually be more profitable than time spent on pure time study. Method study may start with an overall study of the entire production process and the preparation of a Process or Flow Chart setting out the various operations, and the movements of the part throughout the factory; efforts should then be made to reduce the distance travelled and the number of loadings and unloadings, and to reduce the time required for handling, transportation, inspection, and storage. Consideration will be given to revised routing and to improved layout of machines, benches and stores; the possibilities of conveyors and other handling equipment will be investigated. These questions should also be asked. "Can any of the operations be eliminated or combined?" "Is this the best material for the job?" etc.

After this follows the consideration of the methods employed at each stage. "Can the design be simplified?" "Is the best machine being used?" "Can jigs or special tools be used or can they be improved?"

## MOTION STUDY

From this stage we proceed to Motion Study, paying particular attention to the principle of motion economy and the elimination of all unnecessary or fatiguing movement.

Efforts should be made to approach as near as possible to the following conditions, having regard to the materials and equipment available and the nature, volume and duration of the work. (Materials may vary from a watch spring to a two-ton forging.)

(1) Materials, hand tools and machine controls should be placed within the area of easiest reach in an arc in front of the operator and should facilitate the best sequence of operations. (There should be one definite location for materials and tools where these will be instinctively found, bins or racks may be provided and there should be a definite place for disposal of finished parts.)

(2) Unnecessary lifting and lowering, bending and stretching should be eliminated. (Raw materials should be placed or conveyed to the level of operation as near to the operator as possible. "Drop" disposal is best where suitable chutes can be provided. Full use should be made of gravity.)

(3) Provision should be made for pre-positioning materials and tools by providing recesses, sockets, hangers, etc.

(4) The hands should be left as free as possible and foot or pedal actuation used where applicable.

(5) Both hands should be used simultaneously in symmetrical and rhythmic movement.

(6) Good illumination and suitable seating should be provided.

Before fixing standard times it is of fundamental importance that a procedure is in force, or is inaugurated, to provide a service to the productive worker to ensure that the following essentials are available at hand when the work is to be commenced: (a) The Machine,

(b) The Jigs, (c) The Tools, (d) The Drawings, (e) The Raw Materials, (f) Arrangements to remove the completed parts. This is a function of organization and management. Standard times fixed without proper attention being paid to these fundamentals may have to be accepted, but there is a danger of wide variations arising between standard and actual.

## TIME STUDY

When the basic conditions are right, the fixing of standard times may be undertaken.

Fixing a standard time is both a science and an art. Consider the factors involved—average ability—normal speed and effort—equipment and materials—relaxation.

*Average Ability.* When taking a time study it is considered best to choose a workman who is regarded as nearly of average ability as possible. This is not essential, however, for there is a technique of "making allowances" or "rating" the operator for skill.

*Normal Speed and Effort.* The observer during his study should also incorporate a rating factor or index for the speed and effort used as the work progresses. This is often a combined factor for skill and effort. The commonly accepted system is to apply a factor of 60 for what is judged as normal and to work up and down the scale from this point, e.g.

30 Very Poor
45 Poor
60 Average (Normal)
75 Good
90 Very Good.

The application of these factors to recorded times, and a reduction to the base of 60 gives a weighted average at normal skill and effort. (If an index of 100 were used for average, "Very Good" would have an index of 150.)

*Operation Analysis.* Time study is carried out on the principle of analysis. The job is broken down into its elementary motions and each motion is timed. A time study is made of repeated sequences of these motions or elements and the details recorded. A selected representative time is taken for each element (usually the average after elimination of abnormal times).

Time must be recorded for the full sequence, including operations which occur only at the start and finish, or only once in a number of cycles; e.g. "gauging," "lubricate tool," and the time for normal unavoidable delays must be incorporated.

(A separate time may be set for "Preparation.")

The conversion of a selected time for an element of 12 sec. for an operator working at "80" to the "Normal" time would be—

$$12 \times \tfrac{80}{60} = 16 \text{ sec.}$$

The total converted selected times for the job are then added together.

*Materials and Equipment.* The nature of the material may govern the speed at which an operator can work, and in the case of machine work as distinct from hand assembly the speed of the machine may control the speed of output in certain elements. This involves the rather detailed study of feeds and speeds. Tables, formulas and graphs can be built up, based on recorded times for certain elements, combined with machine speeds, to provide standard times for a range of similar operations or a range of sizes for the same part. ("Synthetic times.")

*Relaxation.* Even working at normal speed a man is not expected to keep his nose to the grindstone all the time. Certain jobs are more fatiguing than others and personal needs have to be allowed for. An additional allowance is therefore given on top of the total selected time and may normally vary from 5 to 20 per cent added to the total time.

When all these factors are taken into account the Standard Time can be fixed and the Time Observation Sheet should be completed and filed with full details incorporated as to the conditions relative to the study. The accumulation of Standard Times on work done becomes the Standard Hours produced.

Those wishing to pursue the matter further should consult an accepted text book.

Ideally the "Allowed Time" should probably be the Standard Time for an operator working at a 60 rating, plus the allowance for relaxation. This would enable a good operator working at a 75 rating to earn 25 per cent bonus in terms of time. Again using this basis, Standard Times should not be tampered with, as any adjustments to earnings should be achieved through changes in the wage rates. However, a variety of bonus schemes are operated in practice, often with the bonus element applied to only part of the wage rate; and it may not be the rate of pay which is adjusted, but the Allowed Time. The Standard Time should never be lost sight of nevertheless, and any adjustments in Allowed Time should be indicated separately in the records as an additional policy bonus margin.

To ensure that the operator gets the full bonus to which he is entitled, it is necessary for him to book to "Idle Time" all unavoidable delays not allowed for, e.g. "Waiting for Inspection."

In some continuous process industries the results of work study are applied differently in evaluating the number of machine points an operator can tend and from this, the target or standard output per operator.

When industry first grew big, piecework prices were

based mainly on practical experience and the collection of data as to machine feeds and speeds, and a vast amount of accumulated, and largely uncoordinated data on this subject exists in this country. Often these standards were remarkably accurate.

The development of stop-watch studies has, however, taken place with the growth of light engineering and complicated hand assembly work, where machine speeds are not the controlling factor. In some older established and in the heavy engineering industries operation studies based on detailed personal stop-watch analysis and measurement are regarded as distasteful by the workers and are viewed with suspicion, through the ingrained fear that any improvements in production are to be gained at their expense. This does not necessarily mean, however, that reasonably accurate standards are not in vogue.

A knowledge of standard times is exceedingly valuable even where a system of payments by results is not used. Standard times form the basis of a co-ordinated production plan.

### Standard Rates

A large section of the engineering trade still works on a system of straight piecework prices. The Rowan, Weir and Halsey schemes are not now widely used and the present method of paying a Base Rate plus a full bonus for all time saved over time allowed at Base Rate plus a flat rate National Bonus, which is in use in hundreds of engineering factories, has no accepted name, and seems to have been largely ignored in text books. (It will be noted that there is a fixed and a variable factor.)

Many firms give merit allowances on top of the official minimum, and also set bonus margins well in excess of the minimum stipulated; sometimes from policy, sometimes merely from bad ratefixing.

Other firms are, and have been, paying varying rates of bonus calculated on a consolidated Base Rate plus National Bonus.

Similar complications arise in many other industries.

## SETTING STANDARD RATES

It will be seen from the above that there can be no standard rule for setting a standard rate, and for standard cost purposes we are forced back to the compromise of determining what is "normal" or standard. (Particularly in view of the fixed and variable factors involved.)

A practical standard rate per allowed hour as suggested in the text can be arrived at by grouping the labour in each main department into sections and establishing a standard rate for each labour class. The class of labour required for each job would be noted on the Route Card or Job Card and on the Standard Cost Card.

Classification might be—

|                          | Males Class | Females Class |
|--------------------------|:-----------:|:-------------:|
| Skilled over 21          | A           | F             |
| Semi-skilled over 21     | B           | G             |
| Unskilled over 21        | C           | H             |
| Youths and Young Women   | D           | I             |
| Boys and Girls           | E           | J             |

Further analysis may be necessary.

(Investigation may reveal the need for a policy of wage rate standardization for classes within the factory.)

Using this grouping, standard rates per allowed hour, calculated on the policy bonus margin, can be arrived at for each group.

Alternatively, by suitable analysis of the payroll over a period, excluding abnormalities, the average earnings per allowed hour for each class in each main department or section can be arrived at, to get an average rate which may be treated as standard.

(Additional payments for overtime should be treated as overheads.)

Once the initial compilation of standard rates is completed, the manifest simplifications and savings from the use of predetermined standard costs will make themselves felt.

## Machine Efficiency

Complementary to the setting of standard times for manual effort consideration has to be given to the establishment of standard speeds and outputs for machine controlled production.

In this sphere the concept of "Machine Efficiency" is valuable. The theoretical output of the machine running non-stop at the scheduled speed for the normal hours is represented by 100 per cent. Theoretical non-stop output reduced by standard stoppages for cleaning, feeding and off loading give "Expected Efficiency," say 90 per cent. The "Actual Efficiency," say 88 per cent, is obtained by recording the actual output and relating this to the theoretical non-stop output. Work study would attempt to raise expected and actual efficiency, and technical improvement in speeds, etc., may cause the 100 per cent to represent yet higher production.

Periodic comprehensive sample studies of the proportion of preparation time, loading and off-loading time, running time and other time of machines planned to operate can contribute to constructive action.

# BIBLIOGRAPHY

*The Mechanism of Standard Cost Accounting and Efficiency Records*, by Thomas Downie, Jnr., C.A. (Gee & Co. (Publishers) Ltd., London.)

*Standard Costs (Installation, Operation and Use)*, by G. Charter Harrison. (Machinery Publishing Co. Ltd., London.)

*Business Budgets and Budgetary Control*, by A. W. Willsmore, F.R.Econ.S. (Sir Isaac Pitman & Sons Ltd., London.)

*Higher Control in Management*, by T. G. Rose, M.I.Mech.E., M.I.P.E., F.I.I.A. (Sir Isaac Pitman & Sons Ltd., London.)

*Standard Costs for Manufacturing*, by S. B. Henrici. (McGraw-Hill Publishing Co. Ltd., London.)

*An Introduction to Budgetary Control, Standard Costing, Material Control, and Production Control.* (The Institute of Cost and Works Accountants.)

*Productivity Report on Management Accounting.* (Anglo-American Council on Productivity.)

*Standard Costing*, The Institute of Chartered Accountants in England and Wales. (Gee & Co. (Publishers) Ltd., London.)

*Standard Costing*, by J. Batty, M.Com., A.C.W.A., M.O.M.A., (Macdonald & Evans, London.)

*(Shown in order of first editions.)*

# INDEX